# Public Education as a Business

## *Real Costs and Accountability*

Myron Lieberman
Charlene K. Haar

A SCARECROWEDUCATION BOOK

The Scarecrow Press, Inc.
Lanham, Maryland, and Oxford
2003

A SCARECROWEDUCATION BOOK

Published in the United States of America
by Scarecrow Press, Inc.
A Member of the Rowman & Littlefield Publishing Group
4501 Forbes Boulevard, Suite 200, Lanham, Maryland 20706
www.scarecrowpress.com

PO Box 317
Oxford
OX2 9RU, UK



British Library Cataloguing in Publication Information Available

**Library of Congress Cataloging-in-Publication Data**

Lieberman, Myron, 1919–
Public education as a business : real costs and accountability / Myron Lieberman, Charlene K. Haar. p. cm.
"A ScarecrowEducation book."
Includes bibliographical references and index.
ISBN 0-8108-4719-1 (pbk. : alk. paper)
1. Education—Economic aspects—United States. 2. Education and state—United States. 3. Public schools—United States. I. Haar, Charlene K. II. Title.
LC66.L47 2003
338.4'337973—dc21 2002155197

∞™ The paper used in this publication meets the minimum requirements of American National Standard for Information Sciences—Permanence of Paper for Printed Library Materials, ANSI/NISO Z39.48-1992.
Manufactured in the United States of America.

To my daughter, Elizabeth Haar Prais, and son-in-law, David Prais: wonderful family and delightful friends.

—Charlene Haar

# Contents

# *Preface*
## The Business of Education

Although many citizens of the United States recognize that education is indeed "big business," most are unaware that the field of formal education employs more people than any other industry in the United States. In the fall of 2002, about 78 million people were involved in providing or receiving formal education.[1] In the 2001–02 school year, expenditures for public and private education, from preprimary through graduate school, were estimated to be nearly $700 billion.[2] Of the $700 billion spent nationwide at all educational levels, an estimated $423 billion (about 60 percent) was spent on public and private elementary and secondary education.[3]

For constitutional and historical reasons, education is primarily a state and local fiscal responsibility, but parents of public school pupils pay fees and out-of-district tuition that accounts for 2.5 percent of public elementary and secondary school revenues. Percentages may vary slightly from year to year, but in 1998–99, local governments provided 41.7 percent of the revenues, states provided 48.7 percent, and the federal government's share was 7.1 percent of the revenues provided for public elementary and secondary schools.[4]

The federal budget for education increased from $92.8 billion in fiscal year (FY) 2001 to an estimated $147.9 billion in FY 2002.[5] The following chart shows the scope and variety of some of the major federal education programs, including the federal agency through which the programs were administered for FY 2001, and the percentage that each program represented of the federal education allocation:[6]

Major Educational Programs Funded through Federal Agencies, FY 2001, Including Department and Major Programs, Percentage of Federal Allocation, and Expenditure Amount:

*U.S. Department of Education (39.6%): $36.8 billion*

Elementary and secondary education programs:

*Title I: Grants for the disadvantaged

Title II: Dwight D. Eisenhower Professional Development Program

Title III: Technology for Education

Title IV: Safe and Drug-Free Schools and Communities

Title V: Promoting Equity

Title VI: Innovative Education Program Strategies

Title VII: Bilingual Education, Language Enhancements, Language Acquisition Programs

Title VIII: Impact Aid (see Department of Defense)

Title IX: Indian, Native Hawaiian, and Alaska Native Education

Title X: Programs of National Significance

Title XI: Coordinated Services

Title XII: School Facilities Infrastructure Improvement

* Title names were changed and/or programs combined in the 2002 Reauthorization of the Elementary and Secondary Education Act, known as *No Child Left Behind Act*, Public Law 107-110, January 8, 2002; 115 Stat. 1425; 670 pages.

Special Education and Individuals with Disabilities Education Act (IDEA)

Postsecondary education programs

Student assistance and loans

Other education programs

Rehabilitative and administration services

Research programs

Office of Educational Research and Improvement (OERI)

*U.S. Department of Health and Human Services (21.0%): $19.5 billion*

Head Start

Social Security student benefits

Payments to states for Temporary Assistance for Needy Families Program

National Institutes of Health training grants

*U.S. Department of Agriculture (11.9%): $11.0 billion*

Child nutrition programs

Extension Service and National Agricultural Library

*U.S. Department of Labor (6.1%): $5.6 billion*

Job Corps

Training programs

*U.S. Department of Defense (4.8%): $4.5 billion*

Junior and Senior Reserve Officers Training Corps (ROTC)

Overseas dependent schools (DoDDS)

Section VI (also known as Title VIII or Impact Aid) (DDESS)

Tuition assistance for military personnel

*U.S. Department of Energy (3.8%): $3.5 billion*

Energy conservation for school buildings

Pre-engineering program

*U.S Department of Veterans Affairs (2.3%): $2.1 billion*

Noncollegiate and job training programs

Dependents' education

Vocational rehabilitation for disabled veterans

Educational assistance for veterans and reservists

*U.S. Departments of Commerce, Housing and Urban Development, Interior, Justice, State, Transportation, and Treasury (4.5%): $4.2 billion*

Bureau of Indian Affairs (BIA) schools

FBI National Academy

Tuition assistance and scholarships

*NASA and other programs (6.0%): $5.6 billion*

National Science Foundation

AmeriCorps and other programs in the Corporation for National and Community Service

*Total for major federal government education programs: $92.8 billion*

Source: U.S. Department of Education, National Center for Education Statistics, figure 20 and table 364: Federal on-budget funds for education, by agency, *Digest of Education Statistics, 2001*, Washington, DC, 2002, 419, 423–428.

Of the federal program funds totaling $92.8 billion shown in the previous chart, $48.7 billion was allocated for elementary and secondary education, $15.3 billion for postsecondary education, $22.8 billion for research and related institutions, and $6.0 billion for other education programs.[7] Since passage of the Elementary and Secondary Education

Act of 1965 (ESEA) and subsequent reauthorizations, the federal government has earmarked federal funds for programs to compensate for the link between family poverty and low student achievement. More than 90 percent of all school districts provide supplemental instruction for 12.5 million students through Title 1, the largest federal program of the U.S. Department of Education to improve academic achievement for children from low-income families.[8] Under the Individuals with Disabilities Education Act (IDEA), over 6 million students from ages 3 through 21 received special education services.[9]

The $423 billion estimate for 2000–01 elementary and secondary expenditures represents an increase in total expenditures for instructional services, supplies, textbooks, personnel, capital outlay, and interest on school debt. For 2000–01, the National Center for Education Statistics (NCES) estimated that, on average, $8,830 would be spent in membership on each student enrolled in public elementary and secondary schools.[10]

In 1998–99, the latest year for which actual expenditures are available, three states—New Jersey ($10,145), New York ($9,344), and Connecticut ($9,318)—spent more than $9,000 per pupil. The District of Columbia, which comprises a single urban district, spent $9,650 per pupil. Only Utah had expenditures of less than $4,500 for each pupil in the public schools ($4,210).[11] These per-pupil expenditures did not include the costs of capital improvements or of other costs to be discussed.

According to NCES, about $187 billion was spent on instructional services, and $103 billion was spent for student services, administration, and student transportation costs in 1998–99. An additional $13 billion was spent on noninstructional services such as food service, bookstores, computer time, and interscholastic athletics. Of the $356 billion spent for public elementary and secondary programs, approximately $32 billion was spent for facilities acquisition and construction, $8 billion for replacement equipment, and another $8 billion for interest payments on school debt.[12] The remaining $5 billion was spent on other programs such as adult education, community colleges, private school programs funded by local and state education agencies, and community services that are not part of public elementary and secondary education.

The clientele served in 1998–99 included over 46.5 million public school students in kindergarten through twelfth grade. Of the more than 5.6 million staff members, 2.9 million were teachers in public elementary and secondary schools.[13] When private and higher education are included, more than one in every four Americans is involved in some aspect of education as student, administrator, teacher, or support staff.[14] This ratio remained constant in 2001 and 2002 when education was the "occupation" of more than 78 million people in the United States.[15]

## THE REVENUES FOR PUBLIC EDUCATION: AN OVERVIEW

In general, government surveys categorize public elementary and secondary education revenues as revenue from local, intermediate, state, federal, and other sources. Although property, income, and sales tax are the major sources of revenue, varying amounts of revenue are derived from other taxes, fees, charges, penalties and interest, and gifts. Sixteen states earmark some or all lottery proceeds to help fund education; in this case, school revenues are not derived from a tax on the sale of a product or service, but from the product sales per se.

From data derived from Census Bureau and NCES surveys, local and state governments and the federal government collected over $347 billion for public elementary and secondary education for school year 1998–99 in the 50 states and the District of Columbia.[16] Total revenues ranged from a high of around $40 billion in California, which serves about one out of every eight students in the nation, to a low of about $709 million in North Dakota, which served a total of 115,000 students. Despite the reported revenues of $347 billion in 1998–99, the NCES cites expenditures for the same year as approximately $366 billion. The deficit spending of over $8 billion for school year 1998–99, however, was not likely due to the usage of fund balances to cover expenses not paid from current revenues.[17]

State, intermediate, and local governments collected about $323 billion, or 92.9 percent of all revenues. The federal government contributed about $24.5 billion, or 6.8 percent, to primary and secondary education costs. For school year 1998–99, local and intermediate sources provided

44 percent of school revenues; state revenues provided 49 percent, and the remaining 7 percent came from federal sources.[18]

In most states, expenditures for public schools are the largest single item in the state's general fund budget. Since the late 1960s, school finance litigation challenging the equity and adequacy of state aid to education has emerged in 41 states. The outcome of this litigation is that the states are playing a more active role in education finance.

Although a legislative concern in this litigation has been a more equitable distribution of support for education, coping with the pressures to increase revenues for education has also been a major legislative concern. Our study suggests that the amounts that are being spent for K–12 education have been substantially underestimated. If this is the case, and we believe that it is beyond a reasonable doubt, policymakers may be forced to reconsider their approach to school finance, and ultimately to the delivery system served by it.

In our view, the absence of accountability is a more serious problem than any errors in estimating the amounts being spent for public education. After all, if the American people know how much they are spending for K–12 education (the level of instruction, not the age of the students receiving the instruction) and are satisfied that the results are commensurate with the expenditures, then the serious question becomes "What do we know about the costs and the results?" Our study is intended to clearly present helpful information about the cost side of the policy issues.

## NOTES

1. U.S. Department of Education, National Center for Education Statistics, *Digest of Education Statistics 2001*, NCES 2002-130, Washington, DC, 2002, 1.
2. Ibid., 3.
3. Ibid., 33.
4. Ibid., 179.
5. U.S. Department of Education, National Center for Education Statistics, *Federal Support for Education: Fiscal Years 1980 to 2002*, Charlene Hoffman, NCES 2003-006, Washington, DC, 2002, iii.
6. U.S. Department of Education, *Digest of Education Statistics 2001*, 423–428.

7. Ibid., 409.

8. Mary T. Moore, "Prospects for Title 1 in the Early 21st Century: Are Major Changes in Store?" in *Education Finance in the New Millennium*, Stephen Chaikind and William J. Fowler Jr., eds. (Larchmont, NY: Eye on Education, 2001), 53.

9. Stephen Chaikind, "Expanding Value Added in Serving Children with Disabilities," in *Education Finance in the New Millennium*, 67.

10. U.S. Department of Education, *Digest of Educational Statistics 2001*, 191.

11. Ibid., 195.

12. Ibid., 184–185.

13. Ibid., 92.

14. Ibid., 1.

15. Ibid.

16. U.S. Department of Education, National Center for Education Statistics, *Statistics in Brief*, NCES 2001-321, Washington, DC, March 2001, 1.

17. Ibid., table 6.

18. Ibid., table 1.

# *Acknowledgments*

We would like to thank Lawrence R. MacDonald and Sharon Meade at the U.S. Census Bureau, Governments Division, who were especially helpful in clarifying the data collection processes, and to the Census Bureau's coordination with officials at the U.S. Department of Education. We express our appreciation to William J. Fowler Jr. and Charlene Hoffman at the National Center for Education Statistics, who provided data and explanations that no one not familiar with the data collection process could have offered. We are also indebted to James R. Fountain Jr. and David Bean for their research, practical knowledge, and insights into the Governmental Accounting Standards Board and its new requirements for reporting financial data.

This study would not have been possible without the support of the Social Philosophy and Policy Foundation, Bowling Green State University, Bowling Green, Ohio. We are grateful for the foundation's interest, patience, and morale as well as financial support since the study was envisaged.

Of course, we are solely responsible for any errors or deficiencies in the study.

CHAPTER 1

# Introduction

In 1987, the educational world was stunned by a remarkable exposé. The exposé was the work of a West Virginia psychiatrist, John Jacob Cannell, who had become interested in student achievement as a result of his professional practice.[1] Cannell found that his minor patients with abysmal educational achievement had nevertheless received passing, even good grades in school, and he was puzzled by how this could be. The more he inquired, the more it became clear to him that government reporting on educational achievement was frequently misleading. Average test scores were high because poor students did not take or were not allowed to take the tests. Sometimes, inappropriate tests were used, or the testing was not monitored carefully. In some cases, teachers taught test items that pupils were supposed to answer without being prepped on the right answer. The upshot was that Cannell published a small book that showed that according to official reports of the state departments of education, the pupils of every state were achieving at above-average levels.

Cannell's exposé generated an avalanche of criticism, but his basic point withstood the criticism. To those knowledgeable about government reports, however, Cannell's study came as no surprise. Governments at all levels typically release information that puts government in a favorable light. The exception occurs mainly in the cases wherein one government agency is assigned the task of critically reviewing the performance of a different agency, product, or service. In this respect, government practice simply illustrates a general rule: The providers of information usually provide information that promotes their interests, and omit information deemed contrary to their interests.

The Cannell report was not the only or the first time that government in the United States has been identified as a source of misleading or inaccurate information; on the contrary, a plethora of books and articles have emphasized this point.[2] It is, therefore, remarkable that so little attention has been paid to the erroneous government statistics on the costs of public education. When educational test scores are the issue, the government statistics exaggerate the beneficial results. If costs are the issue, we would expect the government statistics to understate the costs; like overstatement of results, understatement of the costs also redounds to the benefit of government as the producer of education. Our analysis confirms this expectation.

## PRACTICAL IMPLICATIONS: AN OVERVIEW

In the private sector, accurate reporting of costs has become a major public policy issue; however, in the public sector, accurate reporting of costs is usually taken for granted. In public education, however, accurate cost reporting is especially urgent, due to the magnitude of the costs and their critical role in educational policy. According to estimates published by the National Center for Education Statistics (NCES), local, state, and federal governments spent approximately $392 billion in 2000–01 for public elementary and secondary schools.[3] As we shall see, this figure is an underestimate, but it illustrates the fact that even small percentage errors involve large dollar amounts.

As a practical matter, errors in the cost figures often result in erroneous policy decisions. To take a relatively simple case, suppose a school district is considering whether to contract out its transportation services. Obviously, safety, reliability, convenience, ability to respond to emergencies, and liability, among other factors, should be taken into account. The simplest way to compare costs and services is to hold the costs constant and then evaluate the differences, if any, on the services side. If, however, the cost estimates, whether for government or privately provided services, are substantially inaccurate, the policy decisions are likely to be flawed as well.

We do not contend that accurate reporting of costs would always lead to decisions to utilize the most efficient option available. School operations are funded from a combination of local, state, and federal sources of revenue. Suppose the total cost of education is greater than the cost of the same service when provided only by state and local funds. In the latter situation, the direct cost to local school boards and the states would be greater, even though the total costs of education would be less. Consequently, the states and local school boards could achieve savings in their taxes through increases in federal support for public education, the least efficient way to provide the service.

Similarly, the accuracy of the cost figures for public education is very important in charter school and voucher controversies. Obviously, if the cost figures show substantial inaccuracies, the policy decisions are more likely to be erroneous. Many educational voucher and charter school proposals set the amount of the vouchers or the amount available to charter schools as a certain percentage of the per-pupil cost of public schooling. If the government-calculated per-pupil cost of public schooling is significantly less than the actual costs, the voucher-redeeming and charter schools will be deprived of the revenues intended by the legislatures.

## DISTINGUISHING "EXPENDITURES" FROM "COSTS" OF PUBLIC EDUCATION

The distinction between "costs" and "expenditures" must be kept in mind throughout this study. Expenditures are cash outlays; "costs" is a more comprehensive concept. For example, suppose a teacher is paid $40,000 a year to teach in a public school. Suppose also that the state is obligated to contribute 5 percent of the teacher's salary to the teacher's retirement plan. Suppose also that, as often happens, the state fails to make its contribution in a given year. In that case, the expenditure for the teacher's services would be $40,000 but the cost would be $42,000, the $40,000 salary plus the $2,000 that will have to be paid to the teacher's pension plan. When the $2,000 is eventually paid, it is an expenditure that does not add to the total costs for the teacher's services.

Sometimes "costs" and "expenditures" are identical for all practical purposes. If you buy candy for one dollar, the cost of the candy and the expenditure for it appear to be the same. But suppose that you had to walk a mile to the store for the purpose of buying the candy. The value of your time in walking to and from the store would be part of the cost, but not part of the expenditure, for the candy.

In many instances, we know the expenditures but not the costs of public education. This study is an effort to narrow the information gap between the expenditures and the costs. It is inherent in such a study that the costs will exceed the expenditures. In some cases, we can only guess or provide a range in which the costs would fall. And needless to say, parties interested in alternatives to our existing system of education should also be aware of all of the costs of whatever system they are promoting.

The costs of public education cannot always be expressed in dollar figures, but they should not be ignored for that reason. Actually, some of the benefits as well as the costs are not easily converted to dollar amounts, a consideration that renders it difficult to evaluate the costs and benefits of public education. The emphasis upon test scores as the overriding measures of student achievement is partly a reaction to these problems; the more difficult it is to evaluate student achievement, the more emphasis is placed upon factors that appear to be objective yardsticks for measuring student progress.

Three ways of defining a cost of public education must be distinguished. Each is legitimate for certain purposes, but the costs identified pursuant to each do not necessarily apply to the other ways of estimating the costs.

### 1. Government "Costs" of Education

Every state requires school districts to report their income and expenditures in a certain format. The state figures are collected by the U.S. Bureau of the Census and the National Center for Education Statistics (NCES) and combined with federal figures to show the total cost of public education.

The Bureau of the Census/NCES estimates of expenditures are the cost figures most often cited in publications on school finance and in the media. As this study shows, however, these estimates omit several items that would be included under generally accepted accounting principles (GAAP). GAAP, however, was established by the Financial Accounting Standards Board (FASB) for accounting in the private sector. Because GAAP standards are not always appropriate in the public sector, a somewhat different set of standards and procedures has been established for governments by the Governmental Accounting Standards Board (GASB). We shall occasionally point out the differences between GAAP and the GASB standards, but for the most part, the estimates based on the GASB standards are much closer to "the real costs of public education." It should be noted, however, that recently approved GASB standards will not be fully operational until 2004 at the earliest, and reliable data on the impact of the GASB standards on government reporting of costs may not be available for several years thereafter.

## 2. Economists' Definition of "Cost"

Economists define cost in the following way, even though the specific language may vary.

> Cost: "The value of what is foregone because of the action selected. Cash or other asset that must be surrendered or future claim that must be given in order to achieve a specific goal."[4]
> Cost: "Resource sacrificed or foregone to achieve a specific objective."[5]

Thus to the economists, the costs of a product or service consist of the value of all the resources utilized or expended to provide it. This definition is much broader than that of the government costs. For example, it includes parent and student time. The value of student time is what students could have earned if they were not in school. In the elementary grades, the costs of student time are minimal because elementary pupils are not able to earn very much, if anything, if they are not in school. In countries that allow child labor at lower ages than the United States allows, the costs of student time would be higher (although still not very much) by U.S. standards. Obviously, as students reach secondary levels and exceed the age limits for compulsory education, the costs of their time increase.

### 3. Accountants' Definition of "Cost"

The accounting definition of "cost" is as follows:

> Cost: "The cash or cash equivalent value required to attain an objective such as acquiring the goods and services used, complying with a contract, performing a function, or producing and distributing a product."[6]

Although the accounting definition overlaps with GAAP, public policy must consider the nongovernmental costs as well. For example, suppose a developer is required to build a school in order to build and sell houses in a new subdivision under construction. The dollar equivalent of the cost of the school would be its economic cost, but it would not be a school district cost. Instead, it would be a cost to the developer, who presumably would try to recoup the costs from the people who buy houses in the subdivision.

We do not assert that all of the costs of public schools should be included in estimates of the per-pupil costs. If government statistics were clear on what is included in the per-pupil costs, and what is not, the public would not necessarily be misled. The raison d'être for our study lies partly in the fact that several substantial government costs that should be included are not, and the public has no idea of the magnitude of these costs. Nor do we assert that the costs or outcomes of public education should be considered in isolation from each other, or are the only basis for deciding whether to maintain, amend, or replace public education. Data on both costs and outcomes are necessary but not sufficient to make defensible decisions about whether to change our educational system.

## PUBLIC AND PRIVATE SCHOOL COSTS

Although some of the data in this study would be relevant to comparisons, this study is not an effort to compare public to private school costs. First, we lack the data, especially on private school costs, to make meaningful comparisons. Second, comparisons between averages that include very different schools are apt to be misleading for any policymaking purpose. Third, comparisons of existing schools do not provide data on the costs of new schools, public or private, that are structured differently from existing schools. For example, data on costs in existing private schools do not tell us very much, if anything, about what the costs would be if we had a competitive education industry. Thus, although the analysis occasionally refers to private school costs, no comprehensive comparison is attempted.

The preceding point is important to avoid exaggerating the differences between public and private school costs. Suppose public schools provide textbooks that must be purchased by parents of children enrolled in private schools. In this situation, there is no difference in the total costs of education, but there is a difference in who pays for specific costs. From an accounting standpoint, the per-pupil cost in public schools would be higher than in private schools, but this fact per se would not justify claims that the private schools are more efficient than public schools.

At the risk of belaboring the point, let us cite another example. Supporters of school choice sometimes compare the low tuition in private schools to the per-pupil cost in public schools as conclusive evidence of the private schools' greater efficiency. The fact is, however, that many private schools require parents to contribute a certain number of hours of work for admission. The value of the contributed time is a cost that is not reflected in the statistics on the costs of private schooling, but it should be if we wish to compare the efficiency of public and private schools. By the same token, some economic costs of public education are not included in government statistics but are included in the statistics on the costs of private education. For instance, when tenure decisions are made by private school officials, the time they devote to the issue is a cost that shows up, directly or indirectly, in their salary; it is one of the things they are paid to do. In contrast, when state legislatures consider tenure issues for public school employees, the costs of initiating legislation, holding hearings, and guiding the legislation through the legislature are not shown as costs of public schools. Instead, they are reflected in the figures on the costs of the legislative branch of government.

In some situations, the full costs of implementing state tenure policies are not shown as a cost of public education. For example, in California, teachers can appeal adverse tenure decisions to a three-member board that includes an impartial third party from the state's administrative agency. The costs of this board are not shown as costs of public education, which they are in fact.

Between 1983 and 1999, 17 state supreme courts held that their state systems of education finance were unconstitutional under their states' constitutions. Litigation over "adequacy" and "equity" in school finance has become widespread, and these cases are heavily dependent on data regarding expenditures for education.[7] Unless all of the government costs are included, erroneous conclusions about government expenditures for education will be pervasive.

Some states invest much more heavily than others in school facilities, and less on current operations. The states that allocate more to school construction may appear to be spending less for education but may actually be spending more for it, and vice versa. The media rarely point out the facts requiring qualification of government estimates of costs; hence public opinion often comes to erroneous conclusions on the subject. This study is partly an effort to estimate the cost of public education to government, if and when all of its costs are recognized as they would be in the private sector. We shall also comment on private school costs that are not but should be recognized in estimating the costs of public education. Of course, some private school costs, such as advertising for students, have only a minimal counterpart, or none at all, in public schools.

Even if comprehensive, accurate data on public and private school costs were available, the data would not necessarily resolve all of the policy issues on which costs are an important factor. For example, no matter how much data we have on the costs of education in noncompetitive environments, they will not be informative about the costs of education in a competitive education industry.[8] Inasmuch as a competitive education industry does not exist anywhere in the United States, we have no direct evidence on the issue and cannot derive it from private school costs in a noncompetitive environment. Several economists, such as Nobel prize winner Milton Friedman, believe that the results of competition in a variety of industries provide adequate evidence of its probable outcomes in education; others do not share this conclusion.

Readers can decide for themselves whether the understatements exist, their magnitudes and their implications, but clearly major deficiencies in government statistics are not unusual. The tendency of government statistics to misinform is not a conservative/liberal or a Republican/Democratic issue. The difference between political or ideological groups is not that some are more scrupulous than others in citing data; it is that their tendencies to do so come to the fore on different issues, or in conflicting ways on the same issue. To be sure, the errors in government statistics do not necessarily imply deliberate falsification; in some instances, significant differences can be traced back to differences in the data collection process.

At the risk of belaboring the issue, let us review the rationale for trying to ascertain the total as well as the government costs. Suppose that one of our concerns is the cost of achieving universal literacy of the American people. In that case, we would want to know the total amount spent to achieve literacy; the school district costs would be only a part of the answer. In addition to the amount spent by school districts, our armed forces, prisons, philanthropic foundations, and denominational and charitable organizations also contribute resources to foster literacy. Policymakers interested in promoting literacy should be aware of the total amount spent for this purpose, not simply the amount spent by government in schools.

In education, the neglect of cost issues is partly the result of one-sided media preoccupation with outcomes, especially on test scores. Whenever an educational reform is assessed or proposed, the evaluative questions virtually always focus on the outcome side. This is especially evident in school choice controversies; probably 95 percent of these controversies are devoted to the educational outcomes, even though the cost implications are much more important in many cases. Thus the protagonists on choice issues frequently argue strenuously over minor improvements or declines in educational achievement, while ignoring substantial differences in the costs of the alternative ways to teach what is essentially the same subject matter. The frequency of this development is a strong reason for policymakers to devote more attention to cost issues.

## DIRECT AND INDIRECT COSTS

Costs are sometimes categorized as "direct" or "indirect," or "direct" and "overhead." These categorizations are utilized in this study. A "direct" cost is a cost that applies to a single function of an enterprise; an "indirect" or "overhead" cost is a cost that is shared among two or more functions. Teacher salaries are a direct cost of instruction. The costs of a personnel office that is responsible for recruiting teachers, cafeteria workers, custodians, and secretaries are indirect or overhead costs of instruction. Textbooks are a direct cost of instruction; office supplies are indirect or overhead costs of instruction.

Direct and indirect costs come into play when we consider the noneducational costs of public education. For instance, if a state legislature devoted 20 percent of its workload to public education, we could say that 20 percent of the costs of the legislature were indirect costs of public education. Obviously, this says nothing about the costs of whatever educational system might replace or supplement public education, whether it be a voucher system, or a system in which the costs of education are not paid from public funds. Inasmuch as there will be large numbers of public schools in the foreseeable future, the overhead costs of public education will also continue indefinitely. The nature of the overhead costs and the amounts spent for them will change constantly, as is the case now.

In education, costs are often categorized as "instructional" or "noninstructional." Efforts to estimate the percentage of expenditures "going to the classroom" are a terminological variation, but we have serious reservations about these categorizations and use them only when our data are categorized this way. The effort to show the percentage of expenditures going to the classroom is usually based on the assumption that this breakdown reveals the percentage that is spent on the educational bureaucracies; the higher the percentage going to the classroom, the more efficient the school district. For reasons set forth in chapter 11, we do not accept the rationale for looking at the costs of education this way.

## THE PLAN OF THIS BOOK

Generally speaking, we shall focus on three kinds of costs that are not included in the figures cited by government agencies and the media as the current expenditures per-pupil in public elementary and secondary schools:

- The educational costs of local, state, and federal education agencies that are not included in government statistics on the average per-pupil costs of K–12 public education. Capital outlay and interest are prominent examples. Federal statistics track these costs, but they are not included in the current per-pupil expenditures for education disseminated to the media.
- The educational costs of noneducational public agencies, such as the legislative, judicial, and executive branches of government, which are not reflected in the current expenditures.
- The nongovernmental costs of K–12 public education. Parent-paid remedial education illustrates this category.

None of the omitted costs lends itself to precise estimation; indeed, in some cases, all that we can do is identify the cost and indicate in general terms how significant it may be. Hopefully, the lack of precision does not impair the usefulness of the study; the costs that can be estimated with reasonable accuracy are frequently adequate for various policy decisions.

There was no obvious way to organize this book, but it was deemed desirable to begin with the data collection process. Consequently, chapter 2 explains how the estimates of the government costs are made; hopefully this will alert readers to the vulnerabilities of the government data. Because chapter 2 will be of interest mainly to professionals in the field of education finance, other readers may prefer to skip this chapter or treat it as an appendix, which may or may not be deemed useful after reading chapters 3 to 11.

Chapter 3 discusses the current practices of omitting the costs of capital outlay, interest, and debt service in the current per-pupil cost in average daily attendance (ADA). Collectively, these are the largest costs that are not included in the government estimates of the cost per pupil. Chapter 3 also introduces the Governmental Accounting Standards Board (GASB) and the changes it has recently adopted on a number of issues discussed in this study.

The topics discussed in chapters 4, 5, and 6 will also be affected by the new GASB reporting requirements. Chapter 4 is devoted to unfunded pension and post-retirement costs. Government acceptance and failure to account for these costs are pervasive problems of government at all levels; it would be surprising if public education had somehow avoided the problem. Chapter 5 is a discussion of parent and parent organization support for public schools. When these organizations do not come under the auspices of the school governance structure, their contributions have not been considered in the cost of operating public schools. Chapter 6 takes up foundation support for public schools. Such support is of growing importance, as more and more school districts are establishing charitable foundations to generate and receive private contributions to public schools. From an economic perspective, voluntary contributions to public education are costs of it.

Chapters 7 and 8 take up the costs of public education that are carried on the budgets on noneducational public agencies. The largest item in this category is the cost of teacher education, which is the subject of chapter 7. The following chapter takes up the costs of K–12 public education in a variety of noneducational government agencies: prisons, Indian reservations, and Department of Defense and Department of State schools.

Chapter 9 is devoted to the costs of raising the funds that support public education, that is, the costs of tax assessment and collection. Chapter 10 is an effort to estimate the disincentive effects of taxation for public schools. These effects are the negative impact that our system of support for public education has on other economic activities. It must be emphasized, however, that no effort has been made to estimate the disincentive effects of other ways of funding public elementary and secondary education.

Our concluding chapter 11 is an effort to place the study in the context of educational reform, including proposals to change our system of financial support for elementary and secondary education. This is the context in which the study is most likely to be useful, as we believe it should be.

## THE GOAL OF THIS STUDY

As the following discussion suggests, more accurate estimates of the costs of public education would often be damaging to some interest groups and/or help others. After all, if the costs have been underestimated, the parties who are dissatisfied with public education will have even more reason to be dissatisfied. Likewise, parties who are satisfied or ambivalent may come over to the need-for-change position, if and when they conclude that public education costs significantly more than the government figures show.

In the nature of the case, our study was much more likely to show that the cost of public education is underestimated; governments conceal costs as well as overestimate them. Consequently, the proponents of public education will be much more inclined to challenge our assumptions, data, procedures, and conclusions than the critics of it. In principle, we have no criticism of this reaction; the important issue is whether our study or its critics have raised legitimate points and adduced valid data and analyses to support the positions taken.

In this connection, however, we must emphasize a point that will be made repeatedly in the study. Our primary objective is not precision in estimating the real costs of public education; valid, precise estimates cannot be achieved on most cost issues. Instead, our objective is to show the kinds of costs of public education, and their magnitudes, that are routinely omitted in the government statistics on the subject. For instance, we contend that the failure to include the costs of capital outlay, interest, and debt service in the cost per pupil in average daily attendance results in a 15 percent or more underestimate of the cost per pupil in public schools. The actual underestimate might be more, and it might be less. The critical issue is whether our estimates point to significant underestimates of the real costs in the figures given to the media and cited everywhere as "the average cost per pupil" in public schools. In fact, we welcome criticism that brings the discussion closer to the real costs.

Of course, if our analysis is valid, one possible outcome might be to intensify the search for more efficient ways to operate public schools. For this reason, the fact, if it be a fact, that public education costs more than is widely thought does not necessarily justify a different system of education. Instead, a study like this one may be the stimulus needed to search for more efficient ways of operating public schools. Consequently, our analysis does not resolve or even address the issue of whether our nation or any state should change to another system of education. Nonetheless, because cost issues are relevant to the larger issue, we shall comment briefly on their implications, especially in our concluding chapter 11. In any case, we believe that our analysis points to the need for a more realistic approach to the costs of public education.

## THE POINT OF VIEW

It is our view that "objectivity" requires making one's point of view as clearly as possible so that readers are better able to detect biases in the data and/or the analysis. Thus, again in our view, the critical issue is not whether we are partisan with respect to an issue; it is whether or how our partisanship affects our argument. For this reason, a brief comment on the origins of the study and the authors' position on several issues to be discussed is in order.

The origins of the study go back to the experience of one author (ML) as a labor negotiator for school boards. It sometimes happened that districts with lower salaries provided more expensive fringe benefits, such that the total amount spent for teacher welfare was higher in the districts with the lower salary schedules. In bargaining, however, the teacher unions publicized the lower salaries and asserted that all the unions wanted was "equity" on the salary issue. In citing the lower salaries, the union data was accurate, but misleading, especially if and when the union had actually sought to allocate funds to the fringe benefit package instead of salaries. Author involvement in these issues led to the discovery that the U.S. Department of Education relied upon the country's largest union of education employees, the National Education Association (NEA), for its statistics on teacher salaries. Relying on data from a party with a strong interest in the results, without making this point explicit, raised troublesome issues. For example, the NEA-provided government statistics on teacher compensation omit fringe benefits, which are a very significant component of teacher compensation. The NEA prefers to have teacher compensation appear to be less than it is; the lower the compensation, the greater the justification for increasing it. Consequently, the NEA as well as the American Federation of Teachers (AFT) avoid calling attention to the value of teacher fringe benefits.

The practice of reporting only salaries has a historical, not a conspiratorial origin; it began in the days when fringe benefits were a much smaller component of teacher compensation. Over time, however, the cost of some fringe benefits, especially health insurance, increased substantially; hence the sole emphasis on salaries has led to significant underestimates of teacher compensation in government statistics on the subject.

It so happens that fringe benefits in public education are a much larger component of compensation than fringe benefits in the private sector. For this reason, "teacher salaries" are frequently a misleading guide to teacher compensation. The fringe benefits (most of them) were picked up on district financial statements, but the example led to a skeptical attitude toward government statistics on public education. Unfunded pension and health benefits, and the fact that school district financial statements do not include depreciation, intensified our concerns and led us to undertake a more comprehensive study of the real costs of public education.

It must be emphasized that all data collection on school finance includes or is based at least in part upon subjective decisions. For instance, "average teacher salaries" appears to be an "objective" amount. The salaries of the teachers are added and then divided by the number of teachers. Unfortunately, before this is done, there are questions to be answered:

- Who is included as "a teacher"? School nurses? Principals and assistant principals? Guidance counselors? Librarians?
- Are payments for extracurricular activities to be included or excluded from "salaries"?
- How many days and hours must someone teach to be counted?
- Is the average teacher salary the average actually paid or the average of all salaries on the salary schedule?
- Sometimes teachers prefer district payment of their health insurance to a salary increase because teachers must pay taxes on their salaries but not on district payments for their health insurance.
- Should fringe benefits, which frequently amount to 25 percent or more of salary, be included in the salary figures?
- Should the salaries of principals who teach part-time be included as teachers' salaries?

Several additional issues could be added to the above list. The point is that judgments must be made, and reasonable people can disagree on the inclusions and/or exclusions, even when there is agreement on the use to be made of the data. The resolution of each issue could conceivably affect the average; for example, if principals are "teachers," the average salary will be higher.

We do not assert that there is a "right" or a "wrong" answer to the questions posed above. There may be a correct answer in terms of the specific purpose to be served by average teacher salaries, but it is not apparent from the phrase itself. Furthermore, most people who encounter the phrase are not aware of all the decisions that must be made to get to the answer.

From the outset, it was evident that the real costs might be significantly higher than the conventional estimates and that this outcome would probably be challenged by supporters of public education. Inasmuch as the authors are on record as supportive of a competitive education industry, the study is likely to be criticized as an effort to weaken public education.[9] Or the study might be ignored in order to minimize the attention paid to it. Regardless, the real cost of public education is an extremely important issue. The test of any study of the issue is not whose interests are served by it, but whether the study includes the relevant evidence bearing on the issue, and whether its conclusions are justified by such evidence. In our opinion, the extent to which this study meets these criteria is the appropriate test of its objectivity.

In this connection, it is important to distinguish objectivity from neutrality. An objective study of an issue may lead to partisanship with respect to it. Just as an objective study of a criminal investigation may support the conclusion that X was the culprit, so an objective study of the evidence of the costs of public education may lead to the conclusion that government statistics on the subject substantially underestimate its real costs.

Lastly, we emphasize that interests affect what and how data are gathered; data are not gathered willy-nilly. Thus critics of public education cite data that purportedly show low levels of achievement in public schools; supporters of public education cite data conducive to the opposite conclusion. The data cited by both parties may be correct, but the supporters assert the lower test scores of U.S. pupils are due to the fact that the U.S. cohorts of students tested include low-achieving students who are not included in the student cohorts tested in other countries. Elsewhere, students not going on to college may no longer be in school. The test scores in all countries may have been reported accurately, but differences in who takes the tests, not the quality of education, may explain the lower U.S. test scores. The same issue arises with respect to comparisons of public to private school achievement; the higher achievement levels in private schools may be due to the fact that private schools do not enroll many students who would not achieve at high levels, no matter what school they attend. Similarly, true statements about the costs of public education can be misleading in the absence of contextual data.

## SUMMARY

The main objective of this study is to present a more comprehensive analysis of the costs of public elementary and secondary education. We do not allege that government statistics deliberately falsify the costs; in some instances, the understatements are inherent in the data collection process. In other instances, omissions in reporting are a long-standing tradition, neither questioned as omissions nor encouraged as inclusions in the statistics of the costs of public education.

Determining the real cost of public education is an extremely important issue. Substantially underestimated costs deceive the taxpaying public, mislead government officials who initiate legislation, and deprive students of educational financial equity. Although local, state, and federal governments spent $392 billion for public elementary and secondary education in 2000–01, the following chapters show this is significantly less than the actual cost to government. Reasonable people can disagree about the policy implications of this conclusion, but the disagreements should be based upon more comprehensive data than has been available in the past.

Finally, we recognize that our statistical and accounting data are not an easy read. At all times, we have tried to strike a balance between the complexity of the issues and editorial simplicity. It is for readers to decide whether we have struck the right balance, but we hope that this study, despite its deficiencies, will foster more attention to the real costs of public education.

The neglect of actual costs is a pervasive problem in U.S. politics. A major causal factor is the way the polling industry operates in the United States. As Robert Weissberg point out, polls in political campaigns do not mention the costs to taxpayers in asking respondents whether they favor additional improvements or benefits. When the costs to taxpayers, individually or collectively, are explicitly included in the questions, voter support declines substantially.[10]

The 2002 election in Florida provided a telling example. Constitutional Amendment 9, an initiative to limit class size, did not mention costs but passed by a narrow vote. The James Madison Institute, a Florida think tank, estimated that it would cost $27 billion over the next eight years.[11] If taxpayers/voters had been aware of the fact that the benefit entailed such huge costs, it is extremely unlikely that Constitutional Amendment 9 would have passed. Some observers believe that the political tendency to avoid candid discussion of costs in legislating benefits has already reached the crisis stage. For example, Peter Fisher, the undersecretary of the treasury for domestic finance, stated that the federal government's promises to pay for future benefits exceed its anticipated revenues by $20,000,000,000,000—in short, 20 trillion dollars.[12] The political conflicts over which promises will be kept, and which ones will not be, will inevitably become the focal point of domestic politics for a long time to come.

Unfortunately, the failure to consider costs is characteristic of evaluation in educational research generally. Henry Levin reviewed the evaluations presented at the annual meetings of the American Educational Research Association (AERA) from 1985 to 1988; he found that fewer than 1 percent considered cost-effectiveness issues. Levin also concluded that the attention paid to cost analysis remained relatively constant during the 1990s.[13]

In another study, David J. Monk and Jennifer King Rice found that 75 percent of the evaluations in a scholarly educational journal ignored cost, whereas only 20 percent of the evaluations in a comparable public policy journal failed to include cost analysis. Another study by Rice compared the attention paid to costs in peer-reviewed journals in education, health care, and public policy and concluded that "education policy evaluation pays substantially less attention to cost considerations than do other fields of public policy."[14] We agree and hope that this study is a step in a more positive direction.

## NOTES

1. John J. Cannell, *Nationally Normed Elementary Achievement Testing in America's Public Schools: How All Fifty States Are Above the National Average* (Daniels, WV: Friends for Education, 1987).

2. For example, see Robert Higgs, "Official Economic Statistics," *Independent Review* (Summer 1998): 147–153; James T. Bennett and Thomas J. DiLorenzo, *Official Lies* (Alexandria, VA: Groom Books, 1991).

3. U.S. Department of Education, National Center for Education Statistics, *Digest of Education Statistics 2001,* NCES-2002-130, Washington, DC, 2002, 34.

4. Jerold L. Zimmerman, *Accounting for Decision Making and Control* (New York: McGraw Hill/Irwin, 1995).

5. Charlene T. Horngren, George Foster, and Srikant M. Datar, *Cost Accounting: A Managerial Emphasis*, 9th ed. (Upper Saddle River, NJ: Prentice Hall, 1997).

6. Institute of Management Accounting (formerly the National Association of Accountants), "Statement on Management Accounting," *Management Accounting Terminology*, Statement Number 2, June 1, 1983.

7. Richard A. Rossmiller, "Funding in the New Millennium," in *Education Finance in the New Millennium,* ed. Stephen Chaikind and William J. Fowler Jr. (Larchmont, NY: Eye on Education, 2001), 22.

8. A "competitive education industry" is an industry in which (1) there is ease of entry for new producers, (2) no producer or consumer controls the prices or quantities of what is produced, (3) adequate information about prices is readily available, (4) the survival of the school depends on the school's ability to attract students, and (5) government regulation is limited to health, safety, fraud, and civil rights—matters affecting all charitable and/or for-profit entities.

9. For the requirements of a competitive education industry, see http://www.educationpolicy.org.

10. Robert Weissberg, "The Problem with Polling," *Public Interest,* no. 148 (Summer 2002): 37–48.

11. *The 2002 Florida Constitutional Amendments* (Tallahassee, FL: James Madison Institute, 2002).

12. David Wessel, “U.S. Promises are $20 Trillion in the Hole,” *Wall Street Journal*, November 21, 2002.

13. Henry M. Levin and Patrick J. McEwan, “Cost-Effectiveness and Educational Policy,” in Henry M. Levin and Patrick J. McEwan, eds., *Cost-Effectiveness and Educational Policy*, 2002 Yearbook of the American Educational Finance Association (Larchmont, NY: Eye on Education, 2002), 1–17. Despite its pro-public school bias, the AEFA yearbook includes several useful analyses of cost issues and helpful references on cost issues.

14. Jennifer King Rice, “Cost Analysis in Education Policy Research,” in *Cost-Effectiveness and Educational Policy,* 21–36.

CHAPTER 2

# The Data Collection Process

Although everyone recognizes that formal schooling requires substantial resources, measuring the costs of education is not an accurate science. In gathering information about costs, federal agencies rely on the validity and accuracy of the reports submitted by local school districts and state departments of education. These reports are often inaccurate, especially when funding is involved. For example, the state controller of California audited the student attendance figures submitted by the Los Angeles Unified School District (LAUSD) and found the figures to have been "routinely inflated" in the 1996–97 sample.[1] As a result, California's largest school district owed the state $120 million in August 2001. Because of a "pattern of poor financial controls and recordkeeping," school officials had counted students not in attendance on the day the official student count was required. As a result, the state overpaid the LAUSD $30 million a year.[2] Errors such as these at the local level become errors at the state and federal levels as well.

Federal education officials require accurate fiscal and attendance data in order to allocate federal funds to state and local education agencies. Furthermore, school district statistics are widely compared and analyzed to identify issues and trends in public elementary and secondary school finance and to assess the status of school finance in each state. How are these calculations made? Who collects and analyzes the data? What is the process? At what points are errors likely to be made? This chapter is an effort to answer these questions about government data on the costs of public education.

## NCES/CENSUS BUREAU COLLABORATION

Several federal agencies collaborate to implement the federal law that authorizes and requires the collection of school district financial data.[3] For example, the United States Office of Management and Budget (OMB) approves the survey forms that are administered by the Census Bureau, an agency of the U.S. Department of Commerce. Under the auspices of the U.S. Department of Education, the National Center for Education Statistics (NCES) collects, analyzes, and distributes education statistics.

While the surveys are in progress, Congress routinely makes changes in the programs, funding levels, purposes, and even titles of federal education programs. For example, more than half of the programs in 1980 had been combined into block grants or discontinued by 1990. Similarly, new state and federal initiatives may have special instructions for reporting the appropriate classification of the revenues and expenditures. The Census Bureau and the U.S. Department of Education provide instruction booklets as well as training for the state officials (generally designated by the state's chief school officer) who are responsible for completing the surveys.

One such survey is the National Public Education Financial Survey (NPEFS), also known as ED Form 2447. This annual state-level survey collects school finance data derived from administrative and fiscal records from the 50 state educational agencies (SEAs), the District of Columbia, and the outlying areas under U.S. jurisdiction (American Samoa, Guam, Northern Marianas, Puerto Rico, and the Virgin Islands).

The U.S. Department of Education, through the NCES, partially funds the NPEFS data collection set, which is part of the Census Bureau's annual financial survey of federal, state, and local governments.[4] As local governments, each school district provides financial data that become part of the larger survey. From the financial data submitted by the local governments, the Census Bureau extrapolates the information to Form F-33, the Annual Survey of Local Government Finances: School Systems. Form F-33 is a data processing worksheet, not a data collection instrument, but the data are supposed to provide a comprehensive picture of revenues and expenditures, and debts and assets, of local education agencies (LEAs).

Census Bureau and NCES personnel work closely together to review and compare current- and prior-year data by using a computer edit procedure to check for internal and longitudinal consistency. When requested information is missing, and verification from a state agency is not forthcoming, federal government agencies use a procedure to impute an amount for education revenue or expenditures. Through an established methodology, technicians create a comparable subset, calculate the missing data, and include it in the national data set that covers the fiscal year beginning July 1 and ending June 30. Footnotes that accompany the tables in NCES publications indicate if imputations are included and the value of the imputation. Census Bureau officials report that these imputations usually do not affect state totals and rarely affect the per-pupil expenditure calculations.[5]

The process of gathering the data for the current fiscal year (FY) begins after the audit of public school revenues and expenditures for the just completed fiscal year. For example, in FY 2001–02, federal officials are working on FY 2000–01 data. Although the collected data can be submitted as early as mid-March to the Census Bureau, the mandatory deadline for submitting the school districts' fiscal data for the previous year is the first Tuesday in September after Labor Day. The data set file is then sent to NCES in November after all information has been collected and edited for accuracy by the Census Bureau. In December, the Census Bureau releases the information on the Internet and prepares and distributes various Census Bureau publications, such as *Public Education Finances*, an annual publication.

NCES also analyzes the data from the National Public Education Financial Survey and disseminates it in many different types of publications. NCES publications include the *Statistics in Brief* series, the annual *Digest of Education Statistics*, the *State Profiles of Public Elementary and Secondary Education*, and the *Common Core of Data*.

Data from the Census Bureau's fiscal survey are used in determining the states' allocations for federal education programs that target low-income students, programs for migrant, handicapped, neglected, and delinquent children, Indian education, and the Individuals with Disabilities Education Act (IDEA), to cite some of the most common federal allocations. Inasmuch as states and local school districts cannot tax federal installations, such as military bases, that employ the parents of school-age children, the federal government appropriates "impact aid" to compensate states and local school districts for their inability to tax federal installations that add significantly to their student populations.

Because the data are used in determining state and federal grant allocations, state fiscal records may be audited. Auditors include the Office of the Inspector General of the U.S. Department of Education, authorized representatives of the Comptroller General of the United States and the U.S. General Accounting Office, auditors conducting audits required by the Single Audit Act of 1984, and certain nonfederal auditors. If auditors discover inaccuracies in state fiscal data, the U.S. Department of Education may seek to recover overpayments for the applicable programs.[6]

## ESTIMATES OF PER-PUPIL EXPENDITURES

In its directives, NCES cautions state authorities completing the survey to "report the amounts for State Per-Pupil Expenditure (SPPE) correctly."[7] NCES uses state per-pupil expenditures in order to compare per-pupil expenditures among states or when calculating *state* allocations for certain federal programs.

Second, state per-pupil expenditures are calculated for allocation purposes for *federal* grant purposes. From the state's net current expenditures, NCES subtracts community services expenditures, Title I expenditures, Title VI expenditures, revenue from pupils for food services, textbooks, and student body activities, tuition paid by nonresident students educated by another school district, transportation fees paid by students, and student tuition for summer school. The result of this calculation is the net current expenditures for the state, which must then be divided by the average daily attendance (ADA) to arrive at the state per-pupil expenditure.

Twenty-nine states and the District of Columbia define ADA by state law or regulation. Absent such a state requirement, states and territories use the definition provided by NCES: "An SEA [state education agency] must collect attendance figures from each school or school district in the state on a daily basis and then divide that figure by the actual number of days the school or district is in session. The resulting figures are then added for the entire state."[8] Regardless of which method is used, states are required to report an ADA figure that includes every school district, or local education agency—including students attending charter schools and special schools (such as schools for the deaf)—for which expenditures are reported. To do otherwise would result in an incorrect amount for the state per-pupil expenditure.

Because figures for the state per-pupil expenditure involve current expenditures, it is important to understand the items that are included in this category. The current expenditures category *includes* all expenditures that the local education agency (LEA) used during the current year to educate elementary and secondary students. The critical point here is that the category of current expenditures *excludes* expenditures for: (1) property acquisition, (2) debt retirement, (3) programs for non–public school programs, (4) adult/continuing education, (5) community college education, and (6) community services programs.[9] As will be evident, the current expenditures category also excludes several other costs that can fairly be considered government costs of elementary and secondary education.

In an effort to relate the costs of a service to the amount of benefit received by each program and student population, NCES distributes the current expenditures among those pupils in average daily membership (ADM) in each program. Average daily membership is calculated by using the aggregate membership of a given school during a reporting period (normally a school year) divided by the number of days school is in session during this period. Only days on which the pupils are under the guidance and direction of teachers are considered as days in session. The more direct the relationship between an allocation basis and the cost of support services received by the benefiting program, the more closely the resulting estimated program costs will approximate the real program costs. However, it must be recognized that ascertaining the actual program costs can only be a goal, which will never be reached without a margin of error.

Still another calculation is average daily enrollment (ADE). Realizing that all students enrolled in a school, whether in attendance or not, would be provided educational and support services if they were in attendance, NCES also calculates per-pupil expenditures by distributing current expenditures among all students enrolled. Calculations using ADM and ADE are likely to lower the per-pupil cost, since the costs of current expenditures are allocated among more students than if average daily attendance (ADA) is used.

To avoid confusion, it is necessary to review the data along with the definitions used in the presentation of the data. What is especially confusing is the fact that a number of items, included in one survey as separate items, either do not show up on other forms, or the data are combined with other categories on the survey. For example, Form F-33 reflects only the actual receipts and expenditures of the local school systems; hence no contributions from foundations or organizations, or in-kind contributions—such as the value of computers or software or other contributed items—are counted in the costs of public education as calculated by either the Census Bureau or the Department of Education. As pointed out in chapters 5 and 6, these items can become a significant factor in determining the expenditures or the costs of public education.

It should be emphasized that some data are collected, but not used, in the calculations that estimate the per-pupil costs. For example, school districts report their expenditures for capital outlay, including construction, improvements to land and existing structures, instructional equipment, and other major equipment. Similarly, the districts report both the long-term and short-term debt of the school district, as well as debt retired during the fiscal year. NCES included the total expenditures in table 167 in its *Digest of Education Statistics 2001*. However, in publications intended for a broad public audience, NCES usually omits these items. For example, when NCES released its 12-page "Statistics in Brief, March 2002" to the media, NCES included calculations for the per-pupil costs based only on current expenditures, rather than on total expenditures. To further cloud the picture, the NCES summary included only the cost "per pupil in membership" without any indication of the omissions or their magnitude. Consequently, the reported per-pupil cost was significantly less than if the per-pupil cost had included total expenditures and had been based on average daily attendance. As a result, the public is easily misled by NCES's per-pupil cost figures. As table 2.1 shows, the differences in per-pupil costs vary by more than $1,000 per pupil, depending upon whether the average is of total expenditures or current expenditures.

The NCES rationale for the exclusions is that because capital outlay

**Table 2.1. Variations in Per-Pupil Costs in Public Schools, 1997–2000, in Constant 2000–01 Dollars**

| | *Expenditure Per Pupil in Average Daily Attendance*** | | *Expenditure Per Pupil in Fall Enrollment*** | |
|---|---|---|---|---|
| *School Year* | *Total Expenditures* | *Current Expenditures* | *Total Expenditures* | *Current Expenditures* |
| 1997–98 | $8,339 | $7,227 | $7,731 | $6,700 |
| 1998–99 | 8,639 | 7,463 | 8,016 | 6,925 |
| 1999–00* | 8,787 | 7,591 | 8,155 | 7,045 |
| 2000–01* | 8,830 | 7,628 | 8,194 | 7,079 |

*Estimates

**NCES reported the fall enrollment in 1998 in public elementary and secondary schools was 46,539,000 while the average daily attendance for the 1998–99 school year was 43,187,202, indicating that on average, approximately 3.4 million students were absent each day of the school year.

Source: U.S. Department of Education, National Center for Education Statistics, *Digest of Education Statistics 2001* (Washington, DC, 2002), 56–57, 191.

costs vary substantially from year to year and district to district, inclusion of these expenditures in its estimates of the per-pupil costs would mislead users of the data. Apparently, the possibility that the exclusions would also be misleading was not persuasive. Again, it must be emphasized that NCES has useful data on the exclusions; it simply does not factor them into the most widely used estimates of the average per-pupil cost. NCES could just as easily include the total expenditures in per-pupil cost, so that anyone who wanted the less comprehensive figure need only subtract the total cost of facilities from the total per-pupil cost, but NCES has chosen not to present the data this way. Because the media and many professionals are not aware of the exclusions, we believe that the more comprehensive estimate would be preferable, especially when appropriations for charter schools, contracts to provide services for school districts, and/or vouchers are under consideration.

The data collected for NCES include education programs that are not part of school district operations. These include programs such as schools for the deaf or other special-needs students that are financed and run by a state department of education, or the schools in juvenile custodial institutions, or in the state prison system.[10] Since the *local* school systems are not making these expenditures, they are not included in the Census Bureau survey of local education agencies. This is legitimate, but the additional information is required if we wish to know the total amount spent for K–12 public education.

The Census Bureau survey instruments do not require that information pertaining to public charter schools be carved out of data totals. In contrast, NCES data collection forms request that public charter school data be reported separately from the regular school district data. NCES classifies and presents charter school expenditures as "direct program support for public school students." Attendance calculations are the same for charter school students as for other public school students; however, because public revenues for charter schools flow directly to charter schools in some states, and pass through LEAs in other states, some double counting of revenues is possible.

## DATA COLLECTION ACCURACY PROBLEMS

Accurate collection of data through national surveys is complicated in significant ways, such as the need to reconcile dozens of diverse formats used by local school districts and state education offices, some with different fiscal year designations. In addition, not all applicable data are readily available. For example, about half the school districts make teacher pension payments directly to the state's retirement or pension systems. When the school district makes these payments, the government surveys capture the payment amounts on its survey instrument. However, when the state or intermediate government (city or county) pays the employer's contribution by transferring a lump sum to the state retirement fund for public employees, it is impossible to isolate payments for individual school districts. Because local school districts never actually receive these funds, LEAs do not include them in year-end financial audit reports to the SEA. Under these circumstances, it may be impossible to determine the amount attributable to the employer's contribution for eligible instructional employees, administrators, or support personnel. In such cases, the Census Bureau "produces" the retirement payment made on behalf of the school district by using the current salary data, number of eligible employees, and percentage contributed. Precise accuracy is impossible, but we have no reason to challenge the Census Bureau procedure.

## NONFISCAL SURVEY DATA

Because NCES's goal is to provide a comprehensive and timely national statistical database of all public elementary and secondary schools, education agencies, and programs, it collects nonfiscal data as well. Nonfiscal information includes names, addresses, and administrative information, numbers of students and staff, demographic information on students and staff, high school completion rates, and student dropout data. NCES collects this data through annual surveys administered by the Census Bureau. As they do for the fiscal surveys, the government agencies provide training for the nonfiscal coordinators responsible for providing the nonfiscal data.

In 2001, for the first time, NCES cross-checked the fiscal calculations of average daily attendance with student population numbers submitted on the nonfiscal survey for the 1999–00 fiscal year. Even though exact calculations are impossible, NCES was anticipating that the data would be comparable. Auditors in the field prompted this change because they had concluded that the federal and state data are irreconcilable. Even though NCES officials as well as auditors recognize that some states, such as California, have large migrations of students that flow in and out of the schools, the number of students and average daily attendance must be more closely aligned. Comparability is especially significant because of the federal and state allocations for programs such as Title I.

As part of the change, NCES revised the reporting procedure for nonfiscal data so that it matches the federal chart of accounts for fiscal data more closely. To encourage compliance, NCES will review the data submitted from three or four states each year to assess comparability.[11]

## DEPENDENT AND INDEPENDENT SCHOOL DISTRICTS

The distinction between dependent and independent public school systems complicates the task of assessing the cost of public education. "Independent school districts" are districts that have the authority to raise school district revenues; "dependent school districts" lack such authority. In 1997, the U.S. Bureau of the Census identified 15,178 public school systems in the 50 states and the District of Columbia. Of these, 1,452 were dependent school districts and 13,726 were independent school districts.

Property taxes are the main source of school district revenues, but there are differences from state to state on the taxing authority of independent school boards. Even when the same kind of tax is available, there may be differences in the tax limits, whether a simple or supermajority is required to pass a levy, and in several other aspects of the tax. In states that have both dependent and independent school districts, the large urban districts are the most likely to be dependent.

Table 2.2 shows the breakdown of dependent and independent public school systems by states.

When a school district is dependent, some of its overhead costs, such as auditing, insurance, and negotiating labor contracts, are often absorbed by another unit of government. For instance, because the municipality may levy the taxes required for school district operations, it may insist upon conducting the negotiations with school district employee unions. The problem of identifying the costs is further complicated if, as is sometimes the case, the city government negotiates with all of the municipal unions. In such instances, how much of its bargaining costs should be allocated to public education? There are several allocation problems of this nature, and only district-by-district studies, which would require substantial funding, could resolve the issues.

In Maryland, for example, there are no independent school districts because the school systems are part of a countywide and/or citywide system of government. Maryland has 23 counties; hence its public school system comprises 23 districts. However, its public school system in Baltimore is part of Baltimore's citywide government. Certain expenditures, particularly for capital outlay, are often included in the lump sums of the city or county expenditures. Although reporting officials attempt to isolate the expenditures that relate to the school system, it is often difficult if not impossible to do so accurately. If the expenditures for public education are not allocated properly, the result will be inaccurate statistics on the costs of public education.

In addition to reporting complications arising from school district designations, some programs pose reporting problems as well. For example, Medicaid is a program with high potential for erroneous finan-

**Table 2.2. Dependent and Independent School Districts by State**

| *12 States with All Dependent Districts* | *30 States with All Independent Districts* | *8 States with Mix of Dep. and Ind. Districts* |
|---|---|---|
| Alabama | Arkansas | Arizona |
| Alaska | Colorado | Georgia |
| California | Delaware | Maine |
| Connecticut | Florida | New Hampshire |
| Hawaii | Idaho | New York |
| Maryland | Illinois | North Carolina |
| Massachusetts | Indiana | Pennsylvania |
| Mississippi | Iowa | South Carolina |
| Nevada | Kansas | |
| Rhode Island | Kentucky | |
| Tennessee | Louisiana | |
| Virginia | Michigan | |
| | Minnesota | |
| | Missouri | |
| | Montana | |
| | Nebraska | |
| | New Jersey | |
| | New Mexico | |
| | North Dakota | |
| | Ohio | |
| | Oklahoma | |
| | Oregon | |
| | South Dakota | |
| | Texas | |
| | Utah | |
| | Vermont | |
| | Washington | |
| | West Virginia | |
| | Wisconsin | |
| | Wyoming | |

Source: Education Commission of the States, *ECS State Notes, Finance: Fiscally Dependent/ Independent School Districts* (Denver: Education Commission of the States, 1997).

cial statistics. Medicaid is a jointly funded federal/state health insurance program for low-income and needy persons. Through school-based programs or through a linked health clinic, schools can provide health services to students under the Individuals with Disabilities Education Act (IDEA) for routine preventive care, or for ongoing treatment. Complications arise in determining whether the state education agency, the local education agency, or an outside vendor who provides the services must account for the allocation of federal funds under this program. The state plan and changes in Medicaid policies also affect the accounting for federal funds, or even if these funds are accounted for at all.

Accounting for the expenditures and revenues in the E-Rate program also provides some challenges. On May 7, 1997, the Federal Communications Commission (FCC) adopted a Universal Service Fund for Schools and Libraries, implementing the Telecommunications Act of 1996. As part of Public Law 104-104, the Telecommunications Act was designed to ensure that all eligible schools and libraries have affordable access to modern telecommunications and information services through discounted rates. To fund the Universal Service Fund, telephone companies charge their customers a "universal service" fee on their phone bills. Since January 30, 1998, eligible schools and libraries have been awarded E-Rate discounts of $7.95 billion;[12] however, none of this $7.95 billion, nor the subsequent E-Rate discounts, are included in the government statistics of the per-pupil cost of public education.

Because the education-rate, or E-Rate, funding formula favors urban and rural applicants, the neediest schools have received the most. The program provides discounts (ranging from 20 to 90 percent) that can be used for internal connections, telecommunications services, and Internet access. The per-student funding ranges from $109 per student in the poorest districts (75 percent or more eligible for free and reduced lunch) to $12 in the wealthiest districts (1–20 percent eligible for free and reduced lunch).[13] Similarly, the national average for internal connections was $45 compared to $80 in the highest-poverty districts, and the national average for telecommunications and dedicated services was $14 compared to $32 in the highest-poverty districts.[14]

The not-for-profit Universal Service Administrative Company (USAC) is responsible for administering the fund under the direction of the FCC. The Schools and Libraries Division of the USAC administers the schools and libraries program. Public and private schools are eligible. Libraries use the discount percentage of the school district in which they are located.[15]

Although NCES provides instructions on how to report these discounts and expenditures to implement the E-Rate program, the questions raised by reporting officials at an NCES conference in 2001 suggested significant potential problems even in the reporting. For example, in September 2001, the San Francisco school district turned over personnel and financial records to a federal grand jury investigating possible fraud and kickbacks connected to the district's $48 million federal education-rate telecommunications grant.[16] The inquiry stems from investigations by the FBI and the U.S. attorney for San Francisco into how hundreds of millions of dollars in voter-approved bond funds for new facilities and renovations were used and whether criminal wrongdoing occurred.

In January 2001, federal money was cut off in the second year of a three-year $28.8 million commitment of federal money for the largest E-Rate project in Georgia.[17] In addition to an audit of the finances, the project to provide teleconferencing and digital videos to hundreds of public schools in Georgia is the subject of a possible FBI investigation as well. Despite its having received nearly $18 million in federal E-Rate discounts and hundreds of thousands of dollars from school districts, the project may never get off the ground. The 34,000-student Savannah-Chatham County school district invested about $400,000 of its own money in the project. Other participants included the school districts of Atlanta, DeKalb County, Decatur, and Glynn County.

Despite such problems, in May 2001, NCES issued a progress report indicating that 98 percent of all public schools were connected to the Internet as a result of the E-Rate discount program.[18] Criticisms of the E-Rate program continue, including an FCC report based upon its investigations of fraud and financial malfeasance by program officials and contractors. Nevertheless, the billions spent for the E-Rate discounts never show up in the per-pupil costs. These are only a few of the problems facing local and state levels of government in preparing data utilized by federal agencies to determine per-pupil cost calculations.[19]

## SUMMARY

The preprimary through graduate school education industry spent nearly $700 billion in the 2000–01 school year, according to statistical data compiled by state and local governments and combined and analyzed by several federal agencies. Because state and local reports contain inaccuracies such as inflated student attendance, the data available to the public are inaccurate, and the inaccuracies have significant consequences. Per-pupil expenditure comparisons between states will be erroneous. Inaccurate data for federal grant purposes result in misallocations of federal funds. Furthermore, the costs used in the government calculations *exclude* several significant expenditures, because the excluded costs are not considered current expenditures. Other costs are not included because the city or county governments, or individual taxpayers, pay the costs on behalf of the school district without the allocation of the cost to the cost of operating the school. In 1999, the Governmental Accounting Standards Board (GASB) adopted several reporting procedures to achieve more realistic statements of the costs of public education. The implications of the GASB Statement No. 34, especially as they affect infrastructure costs, are discussed in chapter 3

## NOTES

1. Beth Barrett, "LAUSD Says State Audit Flawed," *Daily News Los Angeles,* August 7, 2001. At http://www.dailynewslosangeles.com/news/articles/0701/31/new01.asp [accessed August 7, 2001].

2. Ibid.

3. Section 406(b) of the General Provisions Act, as amended (20 U.S.C. 1221e-1); the purpose of the National Center for Education Statistics is to collect and report "statistics and information showing the condition and progress of education in the United States and other nations in order to promote and accelerate the improvement of American education"—Section 402(b) of the National Education Statistics Act of 1994 (20 U.S.C. 9001).

4. U.S. Department of Education, National Center for Education Statistics, *The National Public Education Financial Survey, ED Form 2447, Fiscal Year 2000,* Washington, DC, 2001, 13 pp.

5. Frank Johnson, NPEFS, survey director, remarks made during a workshop session at the Stats DC Summer NCES Data Conference, July 25, 2001.

6. U.S. Department of Education, National Center for Education Statistics, *The National Public Education Financial Survey Instruction Booklet,* Washington, DC, 2001, 2.

7. Ibid., 7.

8. Ibid., 8.

9. U.S. Department of Education, National Center for Education Statistics, *Digest of Education Statistics 2001*, NCES 2002-130, Washington, D.C., 2002, 185.

10. Ibid., 7.

11. U.S. Department of Education, National Center for Education Statistics, *Instructions for Completing the Nonfiscal Surveys of the Common Core of Data: School Universe Survey, Agency Universe Survey, State Nonfiscal Survey,* 2000–2001, Washington, DC, 2001.

12. Julie Blair et al., "Technology Counts 2002: E-Defining Education," *Education Week* 21, no. 35 (May 9, 2002): 69.

13. The Urban Institute, *E-Rate and the Digital Divide: A Preliminary Analysis from the Integrated Studies of Educational Technology*, DOC #00-17 (Washington, DC: U.S. Department of Education, 2000), 50.

14. Ibid., 61.

15. Ibid., 99.

16. Chuck Finnie and Julian Guthrie, "Grand Jury Investigating S.F. Schools," *San Francisco Chronicle,* September 23, 2001.

17. Andrew Trotter, "Federal Scrutiny Stalls Troubled E-Rate Project in Georgia," *Education Week* 20, no. 18 (January 17, 2001): 9.

18. U.S. Department of Education, Office of Educational Research and Improvement, *Statistics in Brief: Internet Access in U.S. Public Schools and Classrooms: 1994–2000,* NCES 2001-071, Washington, DC, May 2001, 1.

19. John Schwartz, "Schools' Internet Subsidies Are Called Fraud-Riddled," *New York Times*, January 10, 2003.

CHAPTER 3

# Infrastructure Costs and GASB Statement No. 34

The most important fact about public school infrastructure costs is that the accounting treatment of them is in the process of basic change. Instead of first discussing the accounting treatment of these costs prior to September 1, 2002, we have elected to contrast the changes that are taking place with the soon-to-be-outmoded treatment of infrastructure costs.

Throughout this study, we identify some costs of public education that are not reported at all and some that are reported but not included in government statistics on the per-pupil costs of public education. After the initiation of this study, the Governmental Accounting Standards Board (GASB) confirmed the existence of both kinds of omissions, some still ongoing in 2003. Because the GASB actions also provide the most promising way to remedy the omissions, careful attention must be paid to the GASB's role in estimating the costs of public education.

## THE ROLE OF THE GASB

We begin with the GASB history and operations. In 1984 the Financial Accounting Foundation (FAF) organized the GASB to establish standards of financial accounting and reporting for state and local governments, including school boards. The GASB standards guide the preparation of financial reports of state and local governments; when an accounting firm states that its report has been conducted in accordance with generally accepted accounting principles, the reference is to the GASB standards.

The FAF exercises general oversight over the GASB and its counterpart, the Financial Accounting Standards Board (FASB), which establishes standards of financial accounting and reporting in the private sector. FASB is considered by many to be the best private-sector standard-setting structure in the world, and its standards are frequently the basis for recommended changes in government financial statements. The FAF selects the seven members of the GASB and its Advisory Council, funds their activities, and exercises general oversight. The GASB is independent of all other government and professional associations.

The goals of government entities are to provide goods and services efficiently and effectively rather than to generate profit. Unless financial reports of governmental entities provide accurate information, users are not able to fully assess a local government's performance or hold it accountable for the management of taxpayer resources. The GASB standards are intended to meet these objectives. Consequently, government financial reporting must help users (1) determine whether current-year revenues were sufficient to pay for current-year services; (2) ascertain whether resources were obtained and used in accordance with the entity's legally adopted budget; and (3) assess the service efforts, accomplishments, and related costs of the government entity.[1]

## HOW GASB STANDARDS ARE ESTABLISHED

Accurate financial reporting demonstrates financial accountability to the public and is the basis for investment, credit, and many legislative and regulatory decisions. By July 2002, 15 states reported that the GASB requirements necessitated changes in their statewide finance reporting.[2] School district management typically relies on an auditor's statement of compliance with the Board's standards in order to secure bond financing for building renovations or new construction. Without compliance with generally accepted accounting principles (GAAP) and GASB requirements, school district financial statements would ordinarily not be acceptable to the bonding and financial institutions from which school districts seek funding. Federal and state agencies, such as the U.S. Department of Education and the Environmental Protection

Agency, that provide competitive grants to school districts may also require school district financial reporting to be GAAP/GASB compliant as a condition of making the grant. State legislators are increasingly requiring compliance with GASB standards on such important issues as government obligations for pension funds and reports of school foundations.

Despite the fact that the American Institute of Certified Public Accountants (AICPA) recommends compliance with the GASB, seven states and other individual school districts continue to use a cash or other inadequate accounting system. For example, California requires only that school districts comply with the policies and procedures of the California School Accounting Manual, which allows several deficiencies that are remedied by the GASB standards. Compliance with the GASB standards is voluntary, and some California school districts have selected this option. Similar statutes in other states result in continuing difficulties in comparing school district financial reports. Adding to the inconsistencies, conscientious individuals among more than 87,000 local governments may simply be unaware of the GASB requirements and financial accounting standards. Occasionally, political changes affect implementation of suggested financial standards. For some governments, the additional cost of more financial details, reconstructing some accounts, and inclusion of the cost of previously unreported items may be an expense that their leaders determine they cannot afford.

The GASB establishes standards by adopting Statements of Governmental Accounting Standards. Before issuing a Statement, the Board publishes an Exposure Draft of the proposed Statement and "solicits and considers the views of its various constituencies on all accounting and financial reporting issues."[3] The Board maintains a record of its public hearings, allowing comments and discussion on the Exposure Drafts. Since 2000, the Board has also posted Exposure Drafts on its website.[4]

The GASB Statements are numbered chronologically; Statement No. 1 was issued in July 1984, and by mid-2002, 39 statements had been approved. Titles reflect the content, such as "Accounting for Compensated Absences," or "Accounting for Escheat Property." The Statement "sets forth the actual standards, the effective date and method of transition, background information, a brief summary of research done on the project, and the basis for the Board's conclusions."[5]

Early in 1997, after years of review, the GASB issued an Exposure Draft on its proposed changes to state and local government financial reporting requirements. Its approval in 1999 of Statement No. 34 will result in significant changes in school district financial reports—especially with regard to school infrastructure and facilities. Like other businesses, school districts will be required to account for all assets, not just capital assets used for business-type activities.

## THE GASB STATEMENT NO. 34

"Are you prepared for the biggest governmental financial reporting change in history?" read the headline of a brochure at the summer 2000 session of the American Institute of Certified Public Accountants (AICPA), National Governmental Accounting and Auditing Update conference. Under review for more than a decade, Statement No. 34 was issued by the GASB in June 1999. Statement No. 34 consists of 173 pages (476 numbered paragraphs); with accompanying appendixes, the document is over 400 pages in length, and preparers, auditors, and users faced its implementation with many concerns.

The sweeping changes required by GASB Statement No. 34 are being phased in over a three-year period. Implementation was required 1) after June 15, 2001, for governments with total annual revenues (excluding extraordinary items) of $100 million or more, 2) after June 15, 2002, for governments with total annual revenues of at least $10 million but less than $100 million, and 3) after June 15, 2003, for governments with less than $10 million in revenues.

Although the reporting changes are not yet incorporated into the federal surveys, the new requirements will provide significantly more information for citizens, taxpayers, customers, public interest groups, media, investors, and creditors. The following requirements and definitions from Statement No. 34 are likely to have a material effect on the per-pupil cost.

**Management's Discussion and Analysis (MD&A):** MD&A should provide an objective and easily readable analysis of the primary government's financial activities based on currently known facts, decisions, or conditions, and should include a comparison between current- and past-year performances; as appropriate, component unit significance (such as foundation or PTO/PTA support) should be presented, or separately issued financial statements be included for the component unit(s).

**Fund Financial Statements:** Governments should report governmental, proprietary, and fiduciary funds to the extent that they have activities that met the criteria for using those funds. Governmental funds include general funds, special revenue funds, capital projects funds, debt service funds, and permanent funds. Proprietary funds include enterprise funds (activities for which a fee is charged to external users for goods or services) and internal service funds. Fiduciary funds and similar component units include pension (and other employee benefit) trust funds, investment trust funds, private-purpose trust funds, and agency funds.

**Capital assets** are tangible physical assets, including rights to those assets that have useful lives extending beyond a single reporting period. Capital assets include, but are not limited to, land, easements, buildings, improvements to land and buildings, vehicles, machinery, equipment, and infrastructure assets. The historical cost is the basis for capital assets which should then be depreciated over their useful lives.

**Infrastructure assets** are long-lived capital assets that are stationary in nature and normally can be preserved for a significantly greater number of years than most capital assets. Such assets include roads, bridges, tunnels, drainage systems, water and sewer systems, dams, and lighting systems.

**Donated capital assets** should be reported at their estimated fair value at the time the assets are received.

**Depreciation expense** is defined as the process of allocating (in a systematic and rational manner) the net cost (historical cost less estimated salvage value) of capital and infrastructure assets (except land and land improvements) over their useful lives.

**Long-term liabilities**, which include both long-term debt (bonds, notes, loans, and leases payable) and other long-term liabilities (such as compensated absences, claims, and judgments), would include current- and prior-year balances and increases and decreases.[6]

GASB Statement No. 34 also requires governments to report expenditures for all capital projects. Currently, only capital assets used for business-type activities are presented on fund balance sheets for governments; most capital assets, if recorded, are considered general fixed assets.[7] When referring to capital costs and expenditures, exact definitions are problematic, because school district definitions of capital costs vary significantly, and sometimes the district definitions are applied inconsistently. Generally, capital outlay includes land purchases, building repair and construction, and major expenditures on equipment, as distinguished from "current" expenditures. The distinction is an important one. Current expenditures are those for the day-to-day operation of schools, and include expenditures *except* those associated with repaying debts and capital outlays.

GASB Statement No. 34 provides that when expenditures for capital outlays are completed, the increased value of the property owned is recorded on the school district balance sheet, and it becomes an asset of the school district. Reporting requirements also include sales or dispositions of capital assets.

One of the problematic requirements of GASB Statement No. 34 is that it requires the school districts to put a value on infrastructure assets. Because school districts have not capitalized infrastructure assets in the past, the arbitrary date of June 30, 1980, was selected for consistency among reporting entities.

Unlike supplies, which are consumed within a very short time after the school district starts to use them, the useful life of facilities extends over many accounting periods. As the useful life expires over these periods, their initial cost must be allocated among the periods through depreciation. In accounting, depreciation describes the process of allocating and charging the cost of an asset over the accounting periods that benefit from the asset's use. In the private sector, tax and depreciation rules have provided guidance in this area, but no such requirements have been applied to school districts. Because land has an unlimited life and is not consumed when it is used, it is not subject to depreciation. However, land improvements, such as parking lot surfaces, fences, and lighting systems, have limited useful lives and are, therefore, to be depreciated pursuant to GASB Statement No. 34.

In the past, school districts, like governments in the United States generally, have not accounted for the resources that depreciate with use. Unless governments systematically account for depreciation—unless they explicitly recognize that capital is being consumed—they will tend to underinvest in physical plants and allow physical facilities to deteriorate. Consequently, governments must recognize the cost of capital in order to ensure accountability for all the resources they use in producing public services.

The practical effect of accounting for depreciation will be especially evident to those who use school financial data. Governments that appeared to be operating very efficiently under the old reporting system may begin to show deficits that will have to be explained to taxpayers and the next generation of elected officials. Although listing the facilities and infrastructure as assets on the balance sheet might give the impression that the school district has received a sudden windfall, the district's financial condition will not be so favorable when it does not report an operating surplus to offset the depreciation charges. To plan for maintenance of capital assets, the depreciation charges should be funded for future capital improvements. The tax-supported sector has always focused on financial resources—"cash on hand"—because that is what the politicians in office have to spend.[8]

Large urban school districts often own schools that are empty due to declining neighborhoods. In this situation, there is a cost that is not shown on district financial statements. For example, on March 29, 2000, the mayor's Office of Property Management in the District of Columbia took control of 38 vacant school buildings previously owned by the D.C. Board of Education. Soon thereafter, the city permitted ten of the buildings to be used as homeless shelters, or as offices of the D.C. Department of Human Services, the D.C. Department of Mental Health, or of other agencies or nonprofit organizations.[9] However, these school building occupants paid no rent to the city or to the D.C. Public Schools. The cost to taxpayers is the amount the district would have received by selling or leasing its empty school buildings or available space in school buildings. The management of a private company would rightly be considered derelict if it owned 38 buildings that were neither used, rented, or sold.

In 2002, of 217 public school buildings in the District of Columbia, nine had no students enrolled.[10] Also in the District of Columbia, 20 schools operated at less than capacity; one school with a capacity of more than 2,000 had just over 1,200 students, leaving 35 vacant rooms. This underutilized space also represents an uncounted cost of public schooling. We do not know how much the district could have received by selling or leasing these facilities, but several charter schools in the district would have paid a significant amount in a purchase or rental agreement.[11] In some cases, real-estate developers were willing to pay premium prices for the real estate. The revenue loss must be considered a cost of education in the District of Columbia, as it should be in any school district in similar circumstances.

## ASSESSMENT OF CAPITAL OUTLAY NEEDS FOR SCHOOL FACILITIES

A 1989 study estimated that the replacement cost of the nation's 88,021 public school buildings at the time was $422 billion. At that time, states estimated that $84 billion was needed to meet the immediate needs for new education facilities and retrofitting of older buildings. In addition, school districts needed another $41 billion for maintenance and repairs.[12] A more recent survey of U.S. school districts concluded that public school districts spent a record $15 billion on construction in 1998.[13] Just over half, $7.9 billion, was spent on new schools to accommodate an influx of new students. A little over 25 percent went to additions to existing buildings, and about 24 percent was spent for renovation of schools.[14] More money was spent on high schools than on either middle or elementary schools.

The data provided by the federal government show even higher expenditures for facilities. For the school year 1998–99, public elementary and secondary school districts spent $39,526,645,000 for facilities acquisition and construction and another $8 billion on replacement equipment.[15] The K–12 population is now at its highest level ever, and full-day kindergarten and pre-kindergarten programs and smaller classes require additional space as well. In addition, the number of special-needs students is growing, as are the accommodations for these students. The demand for more space for computers, laboratories, additional services, and other instructional aids will increase the need for additional classroom space for several years at least. In 2000, more than 92 percent of all new elementary schools installed fiber optics and cable, and the installation percentage is even higher for new middle and high schools.

Although new school construction is taking place throughout the nation, most of the expenditures in 2001 were in the southern and western states, where the school population is increasing rapidly.[16] When amortized over 30 years, the national median cost for a 650-student elementary school was $419 per year, per student; for a 650-student middle school the median cost was $556 per student; and it was $593 per student for a high school of 1,500 students.[17]

Some questions arise in trying to allocate the cost of capital outlay to the per-pupil costs. Suppose the cost of new construction ($15,000,000) is amortized through depreciation over 30 years, and the annual cost of $500,000 is allocated to the 700 students attending the school annually. This way of estimating would increase the per-pupil cost by $714 per year.

In Michigan, where the public schools owed $9.8 billion in long-term bonded indebtedness in 2000, the capital cost (without interest) amounted to $986 for each Michigan resident.[18] If that cost were spread only among its 1.7 million students, instead of Michigan's 10 million residents, the capital cost would add $5,765 to the per-pupil cost without considering a depreciation allowance. When spread out over ten years, the amount would add $576 per year to the per-pupil cost.

The Buckeye Institute in Ohio used generally accepted accounting principles (GAAP) to calculate the per-pupil expense in the state's 611 public schools for fiscal year 1997. The Institute did this by including expenses that are traditionally *excluded* when calculating the per-pupil costs. After including capital outlay, depreciation, debt service, and miscellaneous expenses, the annual public school spending per pupil had a median cost of $5,515 in Ohio's 611 school districts. By using the new GASB standards along with generally accepted accounting principles, the total cost per pupil in the Cleveland public schools rose from $7,183 to $10,569.[19] The largest increase was in the Perry School District, where the capital outlay and debt service exceeded the annual current expenditures, resulting in a total cost of $20,808 for each pupil in the school district.[20] The Ohio School Facilities Commission utilizes a 23-year time frame in which to stagger construction costs, but we were unable to ascertain the time frame, if any, utilized in the Ohio study.[21]

As substantial as they are, increases in per-pupil costs, based on our recent experience, are probably much lower now than they will be in the next five to ten years. The reason is that the United States is at the beginning of a major expansion of school facilities. This likelihood should be kept in mind as we consider some of the additional costs associated with such an expansion.

## DEBT SERVICE AND INTEREST

When a district envisions an infrastructure project or capital outlay or facilities acquisition and the costs are known, the district must decide if it can afford the project. This step is critical because every state places debt limits on public agencies, including school districts. Generally, the debt limitation is expressed as a percentage of the assessed valuation of the school district. For example, if a district were to have an assessed valuation of $500 million with a 10 percent debt ceiling, total debt in terms of principal could not exceed $50 million.

School districts often resort to bonded indebtedness to finance school construction. Bonding is a device by which districts are statutorily permitted to incur debt for the purpose of acquiring long-term fixed assets. Procedures by which districts may incur bond debt depend entirely on the laws of each state. Bonding is a form of borrowing money, but it is different from traditional borrowing in critical ways. Although bonds create a legal debt, the mortgage (an instrument used when individuals and businesses borrow money) is replaced by the bond mechanism, which has two key features. The first is that bonds are sold at open market and purchased by many investors instead of a mortgage lender. The second feature is that public properties purchased through bond sales cannot be foreclosed. Thus a bond sale for a school facility creates neither a mortgage nor collateral. In effect, the collateral is the full faith and credit of the government, that is, the school district and/or state pledged to repay the debt.

Bonding has many benefits. Although collateral does not exist, investors see bonds as attractive investments because the chance of default is very low. Furthermore, the interest rate paid by school districts on bonds is likely to be much lower than the return on other investments due to low risk of default and because school district bonds are generally tax-exempt. The tax-exempt status of income from school bonds is attractive to investors because lower untaxed earnings may net more income than higher-yield investments after taxes.

The process of bonding follows similar steps in all states. Most states require a referendum (bond election) whenever a school district wants to develop facilities that cannot be financed from current revenues or cash reserves. A referendum is a request for approval of facility debt by placing the question on the ballot so that voters in the district can approve or reject the proposed project. The purpose of a referendum is to ensure that voters are willing to pay the extra taxes needed to retire the debt. Again, data are not comprehensive, but a General Accounting Office (GAO) survey indicated that "54 percent of both the number and the dollar amount of the local school construction bond referendums that were voted on" in 19 states in 1998 passed, representing more than $9 billion and 455 measures.[22]

When voters approve a bond issue, they are agreeing to pay taxes over time to repay the buyers of the bonds. Bonds are like promissory notes in that an investor buys one or more bonds at open sale, often in denominations of $1,000 or $5,000. The investor then expects to be repaid in the form of principal and interest over a set period of time. To amortize the bond schedule, the district levies taxes that are deposited into a special fund from which it makes semiannual or annual bond payments. Principal and interest payments are often amortized over 10, 20, or 30 years.

In addition to interest, debt service also includes the fees associated with a bond sale. Specialized legal counsel is required due to the complexity of bond laws, and financial counsel is required because the bond market is also highly complex and competitive. Advertisements and a bond prospectus must be prepared for potential investors. The discharge of the debt must be monitored closely, and sometimes it becomes necessary to refinance the debt or combine several outstanding school district debts. These costs of servicing the debt, as well as interest payments on the debt, are among the data collected by the federal government through its surveys of state and local governments.

## DEFERRED MAINTENANCE

Because most states limit the maximum permissible tax rate for capital outlay, school districts frequently cannot generate enough annual revenue to pay for large projects. As a result, current revenue is mostly confined to small projects and to current maintenance and operations budgets.[23] As a general rule, districts should spend at least 4–6 percent of the general operating budget for maintenance.[24] Unfortunately, much of the facility shortfall results from a failure to follow a program of preventive maintenance, and from the lack of sufficient funds to maintain the existing facilities and grounds. As a result, deferred maintenance problems are widespread in school districts.[25]

Furthermore, no public school district can avoid some regulations that may turn out to be very costly. For instance, schools must be in compliance with the standards of the Environmental Protection Agency (EPA) regarding protection from asbestos, radon, and lead. Standards of the Occupational Safety and Health Administration (OSHA) may require facility upgrades and safety measures. Accessibility standards under the Americans with Disabilities Act (ADA) may require expensive features that affect very few students.[26]

Despite school district investments of hundreds of billions of dollars in school infrastructure and capital improvements, many school buildings are in poor condition. Because 50 percent of all schools being used in 2000 were built between 1955 and 1967, a large number of schools are nearing the end of their life expectancy. In 1995, the U.S. General Accounting Office (GAO) estimated that $112 billion would be required "to repair or upgrade America's multibillion dollar investment in facilities to good overall condition."[27]

More recent research, however, shows that this deficit is still unfunded. The GAO severely underestimated school district costs for new construction, retrofitting, and maintenance needs because the GAO's 18-state survey sample inquired only about deferred maintenance, safety, and accessibility. Some idea of the costs involved may be gleaned from an NEA study in 2000 that estimated that $321.9 billion would be required to "modernize U.S. public schools."[28] This would be the amount required to fund deferred maintenance, new construction, renovation, retrofitting, additions to existing facilities, and major improvements to grounds, such as landscaping and paving. The NEA figure is nearly triple the 1995 GAO estimate, which was based on a sampling and did not cover all the infrastructure needs included in the NEA study. More recent data from a study in 2001 indicated that the amounts needed for funding new schools, remodeling existing facilities, and maintenance vary widely among states, from $220 million in Vermont to nearly $48 billion in New York (see Appendix A). In per-pupil terms, $1,100 can be added per student each year over a five-year period, an increase of 100 percent above current actual spending rates, to meet these needs, and the required amount will probably increase again in the near future.[29]

Capital outlay, including deferred maintenance, is the area of expenditure found to be the most sensitive to variations in total district spending. Districts with less to spend tend to focus on direct instruction and administration at the expense of capital expenditures.[30] Federal and state mandates can also add to the pressures on school districts, leading them to neglect routine maintenance as well as long-term physical plant needs. Lead and asbestos removal abatement programs caused major expenditures, as most schools built between 1920 and 1979 contain asbestos, and all schools were painted with lead paint before 1980.[31]

Although total amounts are reported, neither the Census Bureau survey nor the NCES differentiates between capital outlay for new construction and expenditures for major capital improvements such as roof replacement. Undoubtedly, some states characterize long-term maintenance costs as "facilities acquisition and construction" costs, while others categorize long-term maintenance costs as "replacement equipment."

## IMPACT FEES

In addition to financing new construction through bonding, school districts may encourage land developers to include new school construction to serve the families that will be moving into the development. Some school districts now require that purchasers of homes in newly developed areas be assessed an impact fee—that is, a fee to cover costs of a new school in the impacted area. The rationale for assessing an impact fee is that it would reduce the financial burden of current residents, who would otherwise bear the cost of additional facilities through higher taxes. Current residents in the school district are likely to support impact fees; however, new buyers might resist paying impact fees along with property taxes levied to retire public debt for existing schools.

In some instances, land developers may donate or be requested to provide enough acreage in a subdivision to accommodate a new school. Although having a school within a neighborhood is a plus in selling homes, the cost for donated property—or even a new school—may be a cost included in the price of the new homes in the development. In this situation, there is a real economic cost of public education that is not included in NCES statistics on the cost of capital outlay. If a district raises taxes to pay the costs of a new school, the costs are included in NCES statistics; if the district shifts the cost to developers or home buyers, the costs are not included. However, if and when GASB Statement No. 34 goes into effect, school districts will be required to show facilities acquired from developers at no cost to the district as capital assets that must be depreciated.[32]

As more and more states absorb the costs of financing school construction and other capital outlays, school district records are more likely to omit the costs. Although these costs will be recorded at the state, county, or city government levels, the result will be even less accurate reporting of the total cost per pupil if the reported costs include only the expenditures at the local level.

## STATE INVOLVEMENT AND LEGISLATION

Backlogs of deferred maintenance, increasing student enrollments, class-size reductions, and litigation exert pressure on legislatures to enact funding measures to repair, renovate, and build new facilities.[33] Historically, most school districts have financed their own capital outlay expenditures without assistance from the state legislature. However, what began in the early 1900s as state appropriations of emergency funds in a few southern states incapable of funding school construction with only local tax funds has now become routine state assistance for school construction and other capital outlay. The financial assistance from the states in the first part of the twentieth century, however, was small and limited, and school districts continued to rely upon school district taxes to pay for school construction. For the most part, school funding relied on the wealth of the school districts in which students resided, and the kind, number, and quality of school facilities reflected this fact.

Changes were gradual, and by 1965, about 80 percent of the states had used some method of assisting local districts in financing capital outlays and debt service.[34] Legislative grants and appropriations, including a part of the state's foundation program, state loans, state guarantees of local indebtedness, and state purchases of local district bonds were and are the most important devices used by the states to help local districts finance capital outlays. Even though the litigation in the 1970s forced states to provide a larger share of the costs of public education, little or no modification was initially made in the system to finance capital outlay.[35]

Most of the 50 states have continued to change the ways that their capital outlays are financed. Appropriations for elementary and secondary education remained relatively constant during the 1990s, at about one-third of the states' general fund budgets.[36] Nevertheless, the number of school infrastructure funding bills increased substantially throughout the 1990s. In 1994, 39 states reported spending approximately $4.1 billion on school infrastructure funding and associated debt service, but of those 39 states, 14 reported no state aid for school infrastructure. During 1998, the states passed 60 bills; in the 1999 session, 35 states passed 93 infrastructure bills, most of which provide for a larger state role in school infrastructure funding.[37] Also in 1999, 45 states reported spending approximately $10.9 billion for infrastructure funding, but of those 45 states, 15 reported no state assistance for capital outlay.[38] In 1999, the Delaware legislature enacted complete state assumption of the funding of existing and future school construction projects, the most sweeping measure to date.[39] As of 2001, 12 states still provide no support for school infrastructure.[40]

## IMPACT OF THE GASB STATEMENT NO. 34 ON PER-PUPIL COSTS

Although the new GASB standards would provide more information on infrastructure costs broadly defined, NCES figures on expenditures, which are the figures cited by the media, will not necessarily change in the next few years. Currently, expenditure data are collected, analyzed, and disseminated by the U.S. Census Bureau and the National Center on Education Statistics in the U.S. Department of Education. These agencies rely on the school districts and the state departments of education to provide accurate data. Even so, when major expenditures, such as capital outlay, debt service, and interest, are omitted from estimates of the cost per pupil, the public is being misled about the real cost to government. This trend is likely to continue in the absence of federal legislation mandating complete reporting of expenditures as a condition of federal aid to education.

Although the GASB Statement No. 34 will require the inclusion of infrastructure and facilities costs in school district financial statements, its implementation is far from assured. Cost per pupil in average daily attendance is an NCES, not a GASB, construct. Consequently, there is no assurance that NCES will include the infrastructure costs in its estimates of the cost per pupil, rather than include the infrastructure costs as only one among hundreds of tables in U.S. Department of Education publications. Furthermore, the process of reaching consensus on changes to the U.S. Department of Education survey instruments is long and tedious. However, by the summer of 2002, a representative from GASB was working with NCES staff on how to incorporate the new GASB reporting requirements for school district governments in survey instruments.

## SUMMARY

Funding for public school infrastructure and facilities has improved substantially during the 1990s, but many years of neglected and deferred maintenance have taken their toll. In addition, litigation has exerted pressure on legislatures to enact equitable funding measures to supplement local financing.

The new reporting regulations approved by the Governmental Accounting Standards Board should be in place by 2005. By then, governments must report expenditures for all capital projects, compute the present value of all capital assets and infrastructure assets, report the fair value of all donated assets, and depreciate capital and infrastructure assets, except land and land improvements. Long-term debt—bonds, notes, loans, and leases payable—and other long-term liabilities must be reported also. Recognizing the cost of capital will be a major step toward more accurate estimates of the costs of public schooling. If the costs of building, remodeling, and renovating schools and the costs of obtaining the financing and paying the interest are included in the per-pupil costs of public education utilized by the media, the government costs as reported by NCES will increase substantially.

## NOTES

1. The Governmental Accounting Standards Board, *Concepts Statement No. 1, Objectives of Financial Reporting,* Norwalk, CT, 1987.

2. Handout, "NPEFS Fiscal Data Plan," Stats DC Summer NCES Data Conference, July 25, 2001.

3. The Governmental Accounting Standards Board, *Facts About GASB*, Stamford, CT, 1997.

4. See Governmental Accounting Standards Board at http://www.gasb.org [accessed November 17, 2002].

5. Ibid.

6. Governmental Accounting Standards Board, *Basic Financial Statements—and Management's Discussion and Analysis—for State and Local Governments,* GS34, Norwalk, CT, June 1999, 2–58.

7. Nicholas C. A. Alito and Dennis W. Hanson, "GASB's Proposed Changes: A Balance of Plus and Minus," *School Business Affairs* 63, no. 8 (August 1997): 36.

8. John L. Petersen, "The Not-So-Great GASB," *Governing* 13, no. 5 (February 2000): 104.

9. In a telephone discussion with the author (CKH) on May 16, 2002, the D.C. project manager, Kit Read, stated that several school buildings had been sold "for a profit," several had been sold to charter schools, and that some sales and leases were pending.

10. Information from John B. Kern, an employee of Friends Of Choice in Urban Schools (FOCUS), Washington, DC, to the author (CKH) on March 18, 2002.

11. For a method of estimating the annual costs of school facilities, see Henry M. Levin and Patrick J. McEwan, *Cost-Effectiveness Analysis,* 2nd ed.

(Thousand Oaks, CA: Sage Publications, 2001), 64–70. The NEA Resolution (and the AFT) opposes leasing or selling unused facilities to private schools, charter schools, or other organizations in direct competition with public schools. *NEA 2001–2002 Handbook*, Washington, DC, 2002, 273.

12. Education Writers Association, *Wolves at the Schoolhouse Door: An Investigation of the Condition of Public School Buildings,* Washington, DC, 1989, 4–5.

13. Bess Keller, " School Construction in U.S. Tops $15 Billion," *Education Week* 18, no. 23 (February 17, 1999): 6. At http://www.edweek.org/ew/vol-18/23build.h18 [accessed October 12, 2002].

14. Ibid.

15. U.S. Department of Education, National Center for Education Statistics, *Digest of Education Statistics 2001,* NCES 2002-130, Washington, DC, 2002, 185.

16. Paul Abramson, *2001 Construction Report* (Larchmont, NY: School Planning & Management, 2001): 7. At http://www.spmmag.com/ConstRpts/2001/2001ConstRpt.htm [accessed July 23, 2001].

17. Ibid., 6.

18. The Associated Press, "School Districts across the State Run Up Debt," *Detroit Free Press*, July 30, 2001. At http://www.freep.com/news/education/debt30_20010730.htm [accessed July 31, 2001].

19. The Buckeye Institute for Public Policy Solutions, *Public Choices, Private Costs: An Analysis of Spending and Achievement in Ohio Public Schools,* and James A. Damask, *Corrections of Appendix 1 in Public Choices, Private Costs: An Analysis of Spending and Achievement in Ohio Public Schools* (Columbus, OH, September 1998), 3, 4.

20. Ibid., 7.

21. The author of the study had left the Buckeye Institute, which did not have a forwarding address.

22. U.S. General Accounting Office, *School Facilities: Construction Expenditures Have Grown Significantly in Recent Years,* GAO/HEHS-00-41, Washington, DC, March 2000, 18.

23. David C. Thompson and R. Craig Wood, *Money and Schools,* 2nd ed. (Larchmont, NY: Eye on Education, 2001), 272.

24. Ibid., 284.

25. U.S. General Accounting Office and Health, Education, and Human Services Division, *School Facilities: Condition of America's Schools,* GAO/HEHS-95-61, Washington, DC, 1995.

26. Ibid., 256–257.

27. Ibid., 2.

28. NEA Research Division, *Modernizing Our Schools: What Will It Cost?* Washington, DC, 2000.

29. Thompson and Wood, *Money and Schools,* 259.

30. Thomas B. Parrish, Christine S. Matsumoto, and William J. Fowler Jr., *Disparities in Public School District Spending 1989–90*, NCES 95-300, Washington, DC, February 1995, xix.

31. U.S. General Accounting Office and Health, Education, and Human Services Division, *School Facilities: America's Schools Report Differing Conditions,* GAO/HEHS 96-103, Washington, DC, June 1996: 27.

32. Alito and Hanson, "GASB's Proposed Changes," 36.

33. Faith E. Crampton, "Financing Education in the Twenty-First Century: What State Legislative Trends of the 1990s Portend," *Journal of Education Finance* 27, no. 1 (Summer 2001): 487.

34. Ibid., 258.

35. Percy E. Burrup, Vern Brimley Jr., and Rulon R. Garfield, *Financing Education in a Climate of Change* (Needham Heights, MA: Allyn and Bacon, 1999), 256.

36. Ibid., 482.

37. Ibid., 487.

38. U.S. General Accounting Office, *School Facilities,* 2000, 17.

39. Crampton, "Financing Education," 489.

40. Thompson and Wood, *Money and Schools,* 271. In addition, figure 9.3 in Thompson and Wood provides a state-by-state breakdown of methods of aiding capital outlay and debt service, 264–266.

CHAPTER 4

# Unfunded Pension Obligations

When this study was first suggested in the early 1990s, many state retirement systems had pension obligations that exceeded their assets. Where this was the case, it appeared that higher taxes would be needed to fulfill the states' obligations to their retired teachers.[1] Unfunded pension obligations materialize when benefits promised are not funded by immediate appropriations to cover the costs. When the additional funds required to meet system obligations are appropriated, they are counted as a current cost of education and thus included in the cost of public education. Under sound accounting principles, however, the states with unfunded pension obligations should have shown the amounts required to meet the future obligations of the retirement system as these obligations materialized. When this does not happen, the pension plan has unfunded obligations that accumulate and are carried forward year after year.

For example, after it was established in 1913, the California State Teachers Retirement System (CalSTRS) granted retirement service credit to California public school teachers for the service they performed prior to that date. Because neither the teachers nor their employers had made contributions into a retirement system prior to that time, the CalSTRS began with unfunded obligations.[2] To cover the retirement payouts in 1913, active members of CalSTRS were required to contribute $12 per year, and the state of California made a contribution as well. However, the amounts contributed then and now would not be sufficient to pay retirement benefits if all California public school teachers suddenly retired and applied for retirement benefits, even though the market value of the fund was $88 billion in 1998.[3] By

2002, CalSTRS had become "the nation's largest public school teachers' pension organization" with more than 605,125 active and retired members.[4]

Estimating unfunded teacher pension obligations is often complicated by the fact that the teachers are included in state retirement systems that cover other state and local public employees. However, the fundamentals are the same regardless of whether nonteacher employees are included in the system that covers teachers.

## IMPACT OF UNDERFUNDING ON PER-PUPIL EXPENDITURES

Although difficult to calculate precisely, unfunded liabilities add significantly to the per-pupil costs in some school districts. National averages are not very helpful on this issue because some teacher pension funds have small or no unfunded liabilities, whereas others have moderate or large liabilities. Obviously, since the extent of underfunding is closely related to the performance of the stock market, there was much more underfunding in 2002 than in 1999.

Unfortunately, underfunding is not considered in estimating the costs of public education; hence, it is extremely difficult to calculate its impact on per-pupil costs. However, a 2001 study of the Oregon Public Employment Retirement System (PERS) is instructive. To eliminate Oregon's projected $7 billion PERS deficit in 40 years, Oregon's taxpayers would have to pay $651 million annually.[5] If this were spread among Oregon's 215 school districts to its 541,000 students, the cost per student for the next 40 years would increase by $1,207 each. Of course, if the shortfall were to be eliminated in less than 40 years, the per-pupil cost to Oregon students would be more than $1,207.

The shortfall is not likely to be eliminated in the near future. Since the abovementioned study, the pension shortfall in Oregon increased to $9.72 billion as of November 2002.[6] As a result, "rate increases for state government, as well as each school district and local government, . . . will increase from 11.2 percent of payroll to 15.56 percent," not including the state employee contribution of 6 percent.[7] Even then, the rate increase is not expected to make up for deficiencies in the system. According to auditors who assessed the Oregon PERS, worker pension accounts are not lasting long enough to cover actual life spans. The shortfall in Oregon is not unique; the stock market decline starting in 2000 had disastrous effects on the state teacher retirement systems.

An earlier study of state and local public employee pensions suggested that their unfunded pension liabilities nationwide in 1980 could have been as high as $154 billion, depending on the reports available and the calculations used.[8] In the mid-1990s, however, there was a tremendous increase in the returns of pension fund investments. According to the Federal Reserve Board, state and local pension funds held $3.12 trillion at the end of 2000, up from $2.96 trillion at the end of 1999.[9] These increases eliminated most of the underfunding of the state teacher retirement systems; however, the decline in the stock market since 2000 has undoubtedly exacerbated the underfunding in several states.

As late as 1995, a report on the finances of the California State Teachers Retirement System concluded that 18 years would be required to pay off or amortize the system's current unfunded liability. In March 1998, an actuarial evaluation showed the fund to be 97.3 percent funded; however, instead of reducing the debt, legislation was enacted increasing retirement benefits as of January 1, 1999.[10] This action illustrates the legislative practice of requiring future taxpayers to absorb the costs of current benefits.

The explanation for the uncounted costs is simple enough. Teachers are paid partly in cash and partly in future payments from the state teacher retirement systems. With the notable exception of college professors in 48 states, most public school teachers (and other public-sector employees) are members of a defined benefit plan—that is, a plan that pays retirees a fixed pension for the rest of their lives. In 1998, more than 90 percent of all public employees were enrolled in defined benefit retirement plans.[11]

## HOW THE STATE TEACHER RETIREMENT SYSTEMS OPERATE

Public employee retirement funds are big business. The U.S. Census Bureau reported that in 1999 "there were 2,212 public employee retirement systems in the United States."[12] These pension plans had annual receipts of more than $297 billion a year, made payments of $91 billion, and held $2.1 trillion in assets.[13] The plans were a major source of future income for more than 5.5 million state and local workers and their dependents, of whom over 1.2 million are retired elementary and secondary teachers.[14]

As major financial contributors to these retirement systems, the states must keep their retirement plans viable, establish policies that are fair to retirees, and manage the retirement process. Both the teacher-employee and the school district and/or the state contribute to the state's public employee retirement system. Interest earned on these funds earns interest for both the teachers and the state.[15]

For a retiring teacher, a state pension typically pays about two-thirds of the teacher's average salary for the last few years of service. In 1999–2000, the average national salary for public elementary and secondary teachers was $43,153;[16] however, some school districts, such as those in Alaska, Connecticut, New York, and Michigan, pay teachers at the top of the salary schedule more than $70,000 per year. Because millions of teachers are nearing retirement, state legislators will come under strong pressure to borrow, instead of raising taxes, to fund the shortfalls in pension payouts.[17] Another option is to encourage teachers to take early retirement. Because the new teachers are employed at lower salaries than the retiring teachers, the districts save on both salary and pension contributions. Furthermore, when teachers retire before the requisite years of service and age for higher benefit levels, their pension payments are reduced. For most teachers, the retirement age with full benefits fluctuates around age 60.

A few states and school boards have adopted incentive plans to induce teachers to leave early. The incentives include, but are not limited to, flat grants, additional credit years toward retirement, and payment for unused sick leave.[18] Although most retirement matters are resolved at the state level, many school districts bargain collectively on retirement issues. Older teachers are more willing to sacrifice some salary increments immediately in exchange for better pensions later, whereas younger teachers usually prefer as much up-front money as possible.

On average, teachers contribute about 6.5 percent of their pay to the state's retirement fund.[19] Contributions vary, however, from no teacher contribution in states that have adopted defined contribution plans

(Florida, Hawaii, Nevada, Tennessee, Utah, and recently New York), to 10.5 percent of salary in Missouri.[20] Understandably, highly paid teachers enjoy higher pensions than teachers who are paid less and whose contributions are also less.

Each state guarantees employees that a retiree's pension will be there when the employee retires. In most states, the school district, county, or state government is required to make a regular contribution to the retirement system based on a percentage of the salary of every employee. Although contributions vary from year to year depending on funding requirements, in 1998–99, the employer (school districts, municipalities, and/or states) contributions ranged from 0.0 percent to 18.75 percent of salaries in Nevada; in most states, they were 12 to 13 percent of salaries. With the exception of Kansas and New Hampshire, employer contributions exceeded employee contributions. When combined, the employee and the employer contributions averaged 15.6 percent of salary.[21]

Ideally, the states would appropriate amounts annually to cover their retirement obligations in the future. Nevertheless, because the full present value of future benefits for the entire workforce need not be paid in the current year, the states contribute only part of the cost, resulting in a less than fully funded state obligation. For this reason, the teacher retirement systems depend partly upon contributions by current teachers to pay the pensions of retired teachers. When this happens, the decreasing ratio of contributing members to retired members may affect the viability of the system. In 1990, the average national ratio was 3.16 contributors for each teacher retiree, and it has continued to drop since then.[22]

Employees eligible for retirement payments from state retirement systems include teachers, other school district employees, firemen, police, and state, county, and local government employees. Sometimes teacher retirement funds are separate from the retirement funds of other government employees, and, therefore, some distinctive rules and regulations apply. States usually establish a minimum age for retiring teachers in combination with a specified number of years of service for eligibility for retirement benefits. To qualify for full retirement benefits, some states use the Rule of 85 (full retirement benefits whenever years of age plus years of service total 85) or some variation thereof.

In addition to years of age and service, all defined benefit states base their pension payments on the employee's annual salary during the last few years of a teacher's career. Most states have no upper limit on retirement benefits, although some specify that the retirement payment cannot exceed a specified percentage (for example, 90 percent) of the teacher's average salary for the final few years. Most of the 37 states that also participate in the national Social Security System do not consider the value of the Social Security benefit when determining the state retirement benefit.[23]

## COMPONENTS OF A RETIREMENT SYSTEM ASSET

For every year after the first one, the retirement system asset has three components: (a) contributions of previous years, (b) earnings from the investment of those contributions, and (c) forfeitures from withdrawing employees.[24] Future contributions of employers and employees and future earnings on assets, as well as the assets themselves, are funding sources to pay for benefits. One key issue in deciding upon a funding method is what percentage of future benefit costs should be allocated to future contributions and what percentage should be provided by assets that are supposed to be on hand.

The total annual contribution to a pension system is a combination of the contributions for current service and contributions to defray the supplemental costs of paying for the unfunded liability of the system. The supplemental cost method starts from the premise that the unfunded liability is like a debt that must be paid off over some stipulated period. The ways for dealing with this debt are comparable to the current contribution methods that treat the future benefit payment as a debt. The future debt may be paid off, like a mortgage, in equal annual installments. The problem with this approach is that in an inflationary world, the payments are too high in the early years and not high enough in the late years. The solution to this problem is to lighten the payments in the early years and increase them in the later years.

Alternatively, the debt can be paid off by payments projected to be an equal percentage of payroll throughout the amortization period. If the debt is dealt with in some sort of nonactuarial procedure for determining the employer contribution, it may be calculated as a simple percentage rate, such as 8 percent of payroll. Such rates often have a basis in past actuarial recommendations and may be checked against actuarial studies, but they are not changed as often as the other plans for dealing with the debt. Some plans use nonactuarial methods other than the fixed rate, such as having the employer contribution be a multiple of the employee contribution. Other plans may be pay-as-you-go, or methods very close to it. The majority of teacher retirement plans use actuarial methods to determine an employer contribution rate.[25] Regardless of the funding method used, it must be sufficient to accumulate an amount necessary to fund the future cost.

Despite variations of these plans, changes in funding may have substantial effects on current service costs and on unfunded liabilities. Accurate reporting of changes in funding methods, plan benefits, and actuarial assumptions is essential to understand public employee retirement plans and comparisons among plans. Not surprisingly, the Governmental Accounting Standards Board (GASB) requires that public employee retirement plans report on the ratio of unfunded actuarial accrued liability (UAAL) to annual covered payroll. Any funding excess is to be reported in the same manner as an unfunded actuarial liability. GASB requires that other long-term liabilities be reported also.

## HOW UNDERFUNDING OCCURS

State and local teacher retirement systems show unfunded liabilities when actual events do not conform to assumptions or because changes occur in assumptions about future events. For instance, underfunding may occur when the return on investments is less than anticipated, or when assets are invested in poorly performing or risky funds. In December 2001, when Enron Corporation, a worldwide provider of electricity and natural gas, declared bankruptcy, Ohio's two pension funds for government employees lost $114 million, California's pension fund for teachers lost $49 million, and New York City's municipal workers and teachers retirement fund lost $109 million.[26] Similarly, retirement funds lost millions invested in Global Crossing, an undersea fiber-optic cable network that filed for bankruptcy protection in January 2002.

Other than mandated contributions by employees, neither current teachers nor beneficiaries ordinarily have any day-to-day investment control or responsibility in how their defined benefit retirement fund is managed. The pension fund board of directors makes the investment decisions, or chooses an individual or a firm to do so. In 32 states, all board members are elected officials, or appointees of elected officials. In highly politicized pension fund boards, board members often make investment decisions that do not maximize the returns to the public employee beneficiaries of the plans. In fact, the political independence of the retirement board has a significantly positive relationship to the returns of the fund; conversely, the higher the percentage of elected board members, the lower the returns.[27]

Unfortunately, some retirement boards make investments on the basis of political considerations, such as investing in ventures located in their own states. This practice is referred to as "economically targeted investments" (ETIs). Such investments are frequently made in projects that would have difficulty obtaining private funding. One study estimated that ETIs cost public pension funds more than $28 billion in losses from 1985 to 1989.[28] Just as some states have laws that prohibit public retirement systems from investing in risky assets, other states have laws that permit risky ETIs.

Nevertheless, if pension fund assets are inadequate, governments must make up the deficiency. Funding levels have been an issue since the 1920s, when pension plans began using actuarial estimates in setting contribution or funding rates. The annual contribution made by a government is the sum of the administrative costs and the contribution level necessary to finance the benefit level, minus the return on investments. When the rate of return lags behind the rate of inflation, as in the 1970s, the adequacy of funding becomes an issue. When the rate of return skyrockets, as in the late 1990s, governments tend to reduce their contributions and/or increase the benefits, thereby endangering fund viability when the stock market drops.

## DEMOGRAPHIC CHANGES

Demographic changes also affect pension fund viability. Since life expectancy is rising, and women, who comprise the majority of the teacher workforce, have traditionally lived longer than men, the cost of maintaining the retirement system may be greater than the amounts contributed under different demographic patterns. For practical purposes, the benefits in a defined benefit system really accrue only to workers who stay in the system until their benefits have vested. Vesting guarantees that a teacher who leaves state employment before attaining the number of years of service required for retirement will still be eligible for a modest pension. Full vesting of teacher retirement benefits varies from state to state as shown in table 4.1.

Of the states that require fewer than five years of employment for full vesting, Iowa, Mississippi, Utah and Wyoming require four years; Minnesota, South Dakota, and North Dakota require three years to be vested; and Arizona and Wisconsin have immediate vesting of pension benefits.[29] Private pension plans, often defined contribution plans, are more flexible: employees can add to them, move them, determine what kinds of investments should be made with their money, and decide how they want to use or invest the money after retirement.

As teachers retire earlier (down from fully funded pensions at age 65 to 60 and even 55 in some states) and live longer, the underfunding of pension liabilities is likely to increase. It is not unusual now for teachers to work 30 years and then receive retirement benefits for another 30 years. If actuarial assumptions underestimate retiree longevity, underfunding can result.[30]

With millions of teachers approaching retirement age, some states risk overdrawing their retirement funds or having to take dramatic steps

**Table 4.1. Years of Service Required to Fully Vest Teacher Pensions**

| *Years required* | *Number of states* |
|---|---|
| 10 | 14 |
| 12 | 1 |
| 8 | 1 |
| 6 | 1 |
| 5 | 24 |
| 4 | 4 |
| 3 | 3 |
| 0 | 2 |

Source: National Education Association, *Characteristics of 100 Large Public Pension Plans*, Washington, DC, September 2000, 6–11.

to support them. Examples of such steps include raising the retirement age from 60 to 62, borrowing to avoid overdrawing the retirement funds, or raising taxes.[31] Cash-starved states frequently try to borrow from pension funds as a way to bail out bankrupt cities or fund new projects. Such efforts invariably incur strong opposition from the unions of public employees. In New Jersey, the New Jersey Education Association played a decisive role in the re-election defeat of Governor James Florio in 1993, because Florio supported borrowing from the teacher retirement fund.

## SOCIAL INVESTING

"Social investments" are investments made in whole or in part on the basis of noneconomic criteria, such as objectionable environmental or child labor concerns. NEA resolutions on the subject include "requirements that the investments be socially desirable." New Business Items adopted at the 2000 convention provide the following:

> **Educator Pension Funds**
> NEA will urge all state affiliates to ensure that state educator pension funds carry out any or all of the following graduated measures with respect to companies that invest in fund propositions or legislation aimed at weakening education associations or public education by:
>
> 1. Using their power as major shareholders in these companies to proactively communicate, through letters of warning to top corporate management, their intention to no longer tolerate such anti-beneficiary practices, and if these warnings fail;
> 2. Initiating or joining with other pension funds in proxy votes and shareholder actions to stop such practices, and if this measure fails;
> 3. In a prudent manner consistent with their fiduciary responsibilities, ERISA, and state statutes, exploring divestiture from and replacements of these companies with comparable investments. . . . (2000-37)
>
> **Pension Fund Divestiture of Tobacco Companies**
> NEA will urge state pension funds for school employees to explore divesting in a prudent manner, consistent with their fiduciary responsibili-

ties, ERISA, and state statutes, from companies that produce tobacco products. NEA will provide assistance for states wishing to urge divestiture. (2000-50)[32]

The American Federation of Teachers' (AFT's) investment policies follow AFL-CIO policies on the subject. In 1997, to assist union members of state retirement boards and other investment advisors, AFL-CIO president John J. Sweeney launched the AFL-CIO's Capital Stewardship Program to ensure that union stewards have a meaningful voice in the management of pension plan assets of union members.[33] The AFT, along with 24 other union representatives, comprised the working group that established the criteria and ratings "that can be used by trustees and other fiduciaries to judge the claims of 'worker-friendly' products."

Using these criteria, the Capital Stewardship Program reviewed almost 50 companies in real estate and mortgages, public equity, private capital, and international funds that claim to provide collateral benefits to workers, their unions, and the communities. Investment fund practices were classified as excellent, good, satisfactory, or failing. Criteria to judge the practices were based on corporate claims to create or support union jobs, inclusion of labor representation on the board, shareholder participation opportunities, and/or compliance with international labor rights and standards.

Social investing has negative effects on the rate of return. One reason is that investment policies are often driven by the cause of the moment instead of a long-term investment strategy. For example, social investing has targeted the tobacco industry, companies that sell "gangsta rap" music, and companies that trade with Burma. In its April 2000 newsletter to investors, the Teachers Insurance and Annuity Association-College Retirement Equities Fund (TIAA-CREF) announced that its "income from the Social Choice Account will rise 7.02 percent."[34] In contrast to the income generated from social investing, the TIAA-CREF Growth Account had increased by 33.82 percent.[35] Although we do not assert that social or political considerations should never take precedence over economic criteria, board members making investment decisions should not violate their fiduciary responsibilities for the sake of causes that are best promoted in other forums.[36]

In 1999, the California state treasurer "seized upon socially responsible investing as a way to make his mark," by selling off $800 million in Philip Morris Companies stock from California's two pension funds. In 2000, Philip Morris was the best performing Dow Jones Industrial Average stock. In June 2001, *Business Week* estimated that the California State Teachers' Retirement System (CalSTRS) and the California Public Employees' Retirement System (CalPERS) "could be as much as $447 million out of pocket due to the lost appreciation of their tobacco shares."[37]

Along with social investing, a significant number of shareholders of companies in which public pension funds have a high proportion of stock often target specific corporate practices. Unions frequently hire a proxy voting service, which provides reports and an executive summary of corporate board positions and votes on each issue that comes before the board meetings. Union-friendly proxy voting service companies rely on AFL-CIO criteria to judge publicly held corporations by their workplace practices, compliance with labor and environmental laws and regulations, executive compensation, corporate restructuring, and worker rights. Unions are using these tactics and litigation, allegedly to protect the retirement benefits of union members.

Social investing is an especially serious problem in teacher retirement because the boards of directors of teacher retirement funds are largely drawn from the two groups that are the most likely to support social investing for one reason or another. One is elected public officials, who comprised 42 percent of teacher retirement board membership in 2000. Elected officials are often subject to pressure from important voting blocs; for example, anti-apartheid activists exerted pressure to disinvest in any company doing business in South Africa before the dismantling of apartheid. In one study of 91 large public pension plans, 44 percent of the teacher pension fund directors were elected by active members in 2000.[38] In effect, this means that the state teacher unions exercise veto-proof power to elect these directors; the teacher unions are the only organizations that have the mailing lists and regular communications with the teachers who vote for these members of the board of directors. The same point can be made regarding the 14 percent of the board members elected by the retirees.

As we have seen, social investing has a negative impact on fund assets and income. Interestingly enough, so does increasing the number of retirement governing board directors elected by the active members. A study of 168 public employee retirement systems found that increasing the number of retirement board members chosen by active members by 10 percent resulted in a 2 percent drop in investment yields.[39]

## EXCESSIVE BENEFITS

Although there is some union oversight over pension funds, elections among the voters at large determine who will exercise state government oversight. Regrettably, some public officials utilize defined benefit retirement systems to reward their political supporters. One frequent practice is to allow substantially higher salaries during the final few years of employment that are utilized to calculate pension benefits. This practice often doubles or triples the retirement benefits for beneficiaries of this form of favoritism. For sheer audacity, however, perhaps nothing comes close to an assault on the Rhode Island state retirement fund by the leaders of the state's teacher unions.

On July 3, 1987, Rhode Island enacted Rhode Island General Law (RIGL) 36-9-33. This legislation extended the benefits of the state's retirement system to "full-time employees of organizations representing employees of the state and/or any political subdivision thereof for the purposes of collective bargaining." RIGL 36-9-33 also provided that any person who had been a full-time employee of such an organization could purchase prior service credit for such employment. The cost was set at 10 percent of the employee's earnings in the first year of full-time employment, multiplied by the number of years and any fraction thereof of full-time employment. Inasmuch as the costs for prior service credit remained at 10 percent of the first year of service, the eligible union officials were able to buy prior service credit for extremely low amounts. The statute also provided that the employees could purchase credit for any time on official leave of absence.

According to the testimony of Rhode Island General Treasurer Nancy J. Mayer, the 1987 statute had been placed on the unanimous consent calendar and enacted without debate by or even the knowledge of many General Assembly members "in a way which ensured that few people knew the details."[40] Mayer's testimony on this point is not disputed; in fact, not a single member of the Rhode Island legislature that enacted RIGL 36-9-33 was subsequently willing to assert an understanding of its implication when it was enacted.

After the *Providence Journal Bulletin* exposed the excessive benefits provided by 36-9-33 in September 1987, the statute was repealed in 1988. Subsequently, however, 24 of the 25 union officials who joined the retirement system before the repeal initiated litigation to preserve their benefits under the 1987 bill. These 24 union officials would have received $24 million in retirement benefits. Eight never worked for the state, and ten others would not have been eligible for state retirement benefits if the 1987 legislation had not been enacted. In December 1989, a Rhode Island court held that the 1988 repeal was only prospective in nature; as a result, eligible union officials who had applied for retirement before repeal were allowed to remain in the system. In 1994, however, Mayer introduced legislation to evict these union officials from the retirement system and to return their payments into it plus interest. The employee contributions plus interest were to be offset by any benefits already received. By that time, however, the nine union officials in table 4.2 had already begun to receive pensions under the 1988 court decision; for example, 54-year-old Ronald L. DiOrio, former president of NEA-RI, had already received about $162,836 when the legislature tried to turn off the spigot.

At any rate, the teacher union officials who joined the retirement system before the 1988 repeal filed suit in federal court to overturn their 1994 eviction. The crux of their legal argument was that their eviction from the retirement system was an unconstitutional impairment of the obligation of contract. In addition, the union officials contended that their eviction constituted an illegal taking without due process of law and that the eviction was a taking of private property without just compensation.

Table 4.2 shows the cost/benefit situation at the time Mayer introduced the eviction legislation. The table lists only the union officials who had already retired and were receiving state pensions when the eviction was enacted. It does not include the pension costs and projected lifetime benefits for the 15 union officials who had not retired but had purchased prior service credit under RIGL 36-9-33. Of the nine retired union officials, five were associated with the NEA, three with the AFT.

**Table 4.2. Union Employees in the Rhode Island State Retirement System Who Retired before the 1994 Eviction Bill**

| *Name* | *A Time Purchased under the 1987 Bill* | *B Individual Cost for 1987 Purchase* | *C Total Contrib. by or on Behalf of Retiree* | *D Annual Pension before 1994 Eviction* | *E Projected Lifetime Benefits from 1987 Bill* | *F Effective Rate of Return in Percent* |
|---|---|---|---|---|---|---|
| Jennie Blanchet, NEA | 23Y-10M-0D | $ 9,069 | $ 9,069 | $ 1,009 | $117,575 | 1,196 |
| Edward Casey, AFT | 30Y-0M-23D | 28,352 | 63,549 | 61,430 | 716,173 | 1,027 |
| Bernard Connerton, NEA | 20Y-8M-27D | 27,073 | 27,073 | 56,883 | 673,106 | 2,386 |
| Richard DeOrsey, IAE | 16Y-6M-0D | 14,441 | 30,026 | 24,462 | 269,204 | 797 |
| Ronald DiOrio, NEA | 21Y-10M-7D | 23,452 | 23,452 | 43,346 | 530,730 | 2,163 |
| Joseph Grande, Prov AFT | 22Y-10M-0D | 33,827 | 75,994 | 49,275 | 704,844 | 827 |
| Gloria Heisler, NEA | 14Y-9M-0D | 2,242 | 2,242 | 35,988 | 224,444 | 9,911 |
| Edward McElroy, AFT | 28Y-0M-0D | 34,386 | 64,344 | 41,958 | 618,806 | 862 |
| Bernard Singleton, NEA | 29Y-4M-28D | 25,411 | 25,411 | 62,250 | 770,849 | 2,934 |

NEA: National Education Association
AFT: American Federation of Teachers
IAE: Independent Association of Employees

Source: Affidavit of Arthur W. Anderson dated September 13, 1994, in *National Education Association-Rhode Island, Rhode Island Federation of Teachers, et al., versus Retirement Board of the Rhode Island Employee's Retirement System, et al.*, U.S. District Court for the District of Rhode Island, C.A. No. 94-0389L.
Also see: Myron Lieberman and Charlene K. Haar, "The Great Rhode Island Ripoff: A Commentary," *Government Union Review* 16, no. 2 (Vienna, VA: Public Service Research Foundation, Spring 1995), 27–41.

Column B, the "Cost for 1987," refers only to the cost of prior service credit to the individuals. In four cases (Casey, DeOrio, Grande, and McElroy), additional funds were paid by or on behalf of the retirees. The Rhode Island retirement system was not able to identify the source of these additional contributions, but they may have been rollovers from union retirement plans controlled by the individual retirees.

The critical column in table 4.2 is F, the effective rate of return on the employee's contribution. This rate is based on the present value of the benefits to be received by the retirees. The rate was calculated by subtracting the total contributions made by or on behalf of the individuals from the present value of the projected lifetime pension benefits, dividing the remainder by the retiree's total contributions, and multiplying the result by 100. Thus Bernard Singleton paid $25,411 for a lifetime annual pension of $62,250, for an effective rate of return of 2,934 percent. Of course, nothing tops the 9,911 percent rate of return for Gloria Heisler, who invested $2,242 for an annual pension of $35,988. According to the state treasurer's office, the average pension benefit purchased by the 21 teacher union officials was then $50,000 a year, whereas the average for teachers was $24,870 and for state employees only $11,004.

The NEA/AFT rationale for opposing the eviction was that to allow it would endanger the retirement benefits for all teacher members of the state retirement system. Allegedly, if the legislature were allowed to reduce contractual benefits, no teacher's pension would be safe. One of the plaintiffs suing for a resumption of pension payments for service as a union official was Edward J. McElroy Jr., who became the secretary-treasurer of the AFT while the Rhode Island legislation was pending. In this capacity, McElroy was paid $129,150 in salary and $76,745 in expenses in 1993–94; this amount does not include what the AFT paid for his fringe benefits.[41] As table 4.2 shows, McElroy, who instigated the legislation and had tried to get it enacted in the prior two years, paid $34,386 to the Rhode Island State Retirement System for an annual pension of $41,958, with projected lifetime benefits of $618,806. In other words, McElroy received more in cash in the first year of his "retirement" than the total amount he paid for 28 years of retirement credit. Interestingly enough, one of the arguments made by union officials being evicted from the retirement system was that there were hundreds of cases in which the legislature had bestowed comparable retirement benefits on favored individuals.

## THE EXTENT OF UNDERFUNDING

Despite abuses like those in Rhode Island, no state plan has ever defaulted in pension payments, although legislative and executive oversight, as well as judicial decisions, have "dramatically changed the legal landscape for funding issues."[42] Scrutiny of the Oregon Public Employees Retirement System (PERS) resulted in a warning that the rising costs of supporting the state-controlled system were proving to be unaffordable to many local governments in Oregon and unfair to the interests of taxpayers.[43] Regardless of how underfunding occurs, the responsibility falls on the legislature and state officials to make the contribution required to fund the retirement system adequately, especially when local governments, such as those in Oregon, suffer from the shortage in required contributions. Under such circumstances, state appropriations will be larger than if sufficient amounts had been set aside year by year to meet the state's obligations. In addition to state statutes on the issue, six state constitutions contain explicit constitutional provisions guaranteeing pension rights, fifteen include express guarantees in their statutes, eighteen provide pensioners with common-law contractual rights, and eleven approach the issue in other ways.[44]

## ALTERNATIVES: DEFINED CONTRIBUTION SYSTEMS

In view of the dangers of underfunded pension funds, some states have enacted statutes to strengthen their teacher retirement funds. For example, the Indiana legislature voted to pay $55 million into a special fund to pay for current and future benefits of teachers hired before July 1, 1995. The state lottery provides $30 million and the state's general fund contributes the remainder. In 1996, the legislature paid an additional $200 million out of the state's budget surplus toward reducing the underfunded pension fund.[45] Similarly, the Illinois legislature, faced with a large unfunded teacher obligation, enacted a 50-year schedule to reach 90 percent actuarial funding through a continuing appropriation for its teacher retirement system and other state-funded retirement systems. Obviously, a plan that delays full funding for such a long time raises difficult issues of intergenerational equity.

For retirement systems that have an unfunded liability, actuaries use the present value of future benefits to estimate contribution rates and suggestions for funding methods. The present value of a retirement fund consists of benefits that have already been earned and benefits yet to be earned; fund assets are a major factor in setting the contribution rate required to avoid underfunding. An asset target is a statement of the assets that *should* be on hand in a fully funded pension plan. The assets that *are* on hand are subtracted from the asset target to show the unfunded liability, sometimes referred to as the "unfunded actuarial liability," "unfunded supplemental present value," or "underfunded pension liability."[46]

The unfunded liability of a particular pension plan depends upon the method of calculating the valuation of the asset. For example, an unusually high return on investment might be averaged over a term of five years. Valuing an asset at book value or cost might result in a considerably lower asset value than if the asset were valued at its present market value. Of course, no method can remedy the problem if the unfunded pension costs are not fully reported.

As has been the case with social security, some analysts have expressed concern about the future viability of defined benefit state pension systems. By 2001, approximately three workers were contributing for each retiree; by 2020, the ratio will be two to one. Despite increased productivity, state governments will have to support their pension systems even more than they have in the past. The grim outlook for defined benefit plans has stimulated widespread interest in defined contribution plans. In defined contribution plans, retirees are entitled only to actual contributions plus investment performance.

In 1999, in response to concerns about the costs of their defined benefit retirement plans, Arizona, Montana, and North Dakota enacted defined contribution plans. Also in 1999, seven states conducted studies of defined contribution plans covering various groups of public employees.[47] By 2002, twenty-seven states offered retirement plan options to teachers and administrators.[48] The Nebraska State Employees' Retirement System and the West Virginia Teachers' Defined Contribution

Plan are defined contribution plans with specified employee and employer contributions.

In West Virginia, all new K–12 teachers since 1991 have been required to join the defined contribution plan, although veteran teachers have the option of continuing in the defined benefit plan—a plan nearly bankrupt from its unfunded liabilities in 1991.[49] In 2001, a report of the defined benefit plan of the West Virginia Teachers' Retirement System (TRS) indicated that the unfunded liability had increased and was $4.098 billion as of July 2001.[50] If the state increases its payments into the TRS, the debt is scheduled to be paid by 2034.

Because defined contribution plans are not based on a predetermined benefit, there is no underfunded or unfunded government pension liability under such plans. This important consideration is frequently overlooked in discussions of school reform. When states contribute, their contribution goes directly into individual employee accounts; hence states cannot transfer the funds to state accounts. Other advantages are the portability of defined contribution plans and individual choice in how to invest their retirement accounts. Defined contribution plans also avoid the problems associated with social investing: each participant in the plan resolves this issue to his or her own satisfaction.

Dealing with gains resulting from changes in actuarial assumptions and gains is complicated by controversies over the extent to which public plans are defined benefit or defined contribution plans. Employee organizations and teacher unions sometimes take the position that the retirement plans are defined benefit plans when actuarial losses occur, but defined contribution plans when actuarial gains are present. When teachers realize that the benefit package requires a higher contribution rate, they argue that the employer is liable for the higher rate because it was the employer who promised the benefits. When the contribution rate can be lowered, a balanced approach suggests that if the employer takes the downside risk, the employer is entitled to the upside gain. However, teachers and teacher unions sometimes contend that teachers are entitled to whatever contributions will buy as benefits; any gains resulting from plan experience should be utilized for benefit improvements.

A retirement system that distributes all gains as improvements while funding all losses will inevitably increase pension benefits and costs, regardless of the justification for increased benefits. This will happen because there will inevitably be gains and losses over time. When there are losses, the employer contribution rate will increase, never to be reduced, because gains result in benefit increases. Consequently, the employer contribution will ratchet upward. For this reason, some believe that the use of actuarial gains to "fund" benefit increases should be discouraged.[51] At the same time, new liabilities created by benefit increases should be funded promptly so that current decision makers bear the political cost of benefit improvements for current employees.[52]

## IMPACT OF GASB NO. 34

GASB's new standards identify two future benefits that require an estimate of present value. One is unfunded retirement obligations. The other is the present value of post-retirement health benefits. The funds required to pay for these benefits are so large, and the data from experience so plentiful, that it makes sense to require the current cost of this future benefit be shown. Obviously, school districts that provide post-retirement health benefits have provided a future benefit whose costs can easily become prohibitive if their present value is not shown in current district financial statements. Fortunately, the GASB standards consider the problem of how to show the present cost of future benefits. GASB Statement No. 34 strengthens GASB Statement Nos. 25 and 27, which require that districts show the current accumulated cost of the benefits. For example, a district financial statement is supposed to show the amount required to pay the benefit in full (actuarial accrued liability and unfunded accrued liability) if the benefit were terminated.

The costs of accumulated sick leave illustrate the problems of estimating future costs of benefits to be cashed out several years in the future. Before the benefit was granted, teachers used most of their sick leave. When the benefit was granted, its costs thereafter were minimal for a few years, even though teachers were allowed to cash out their accumulated sick leave at their daily rate of pay when they retired. Anyone who looked at the funds required to pay the obligation in full would have erroneously assumed that the benefit would not cost very much. Once the districts agreed to cash out accumulated sick leave, teachers did not utilize sick leave. Instead, they retired with large accumulations, and the costs escalated rapidly, far exceeding the costs in the early years. The fact that some New Jersey school districts have capped the payout for unused sick leave at $25,000 illustrates the danger of assuming that present experience is a reliable guide to the future costs of unused sick leave. In New York City, payment to retiring teachers for accumulated sick leave cost almost $100,000,000 in 2001–02.[53]

Obviously, school districts cannot afford to allow many longtime teachers to be paid for accumulated sick leave at their daily rate of pay on retirement. Of course, the districts cannot know when teachers will retire, but unless they can forecast their obligations in the future with reasonable accuracy, they should not agree to the benefit.

In practice, payment for accumulated sick leave often happened when school boards were unable to provide very much in immediate benefits. Inasmuch as payment for accumulated sick leave did not cost school districts very much when the district agreed to provide the benefit, school boards agreed to it without much concern about the cost. Before the school boards agreed to pay for accumulated sick leave, teachers had no incentive to accumulate it; instead they tended to utilize it. Over time, the cash value of the benefit increased dramatically, and school districts sought to cap the benefit by limits on the number of days the districts would pay for, and/or payment at less than the daily rate of pay upon retirement. Unfortunately, from a school board perspective, the more districts that agreed to the benefit, the more difficult it was for others to refuse to pay for it.

In most school districts, school administrators receive at least the benefits accorded teachers. Actually, payment for administrators' unused sick leave sometimes preceded its availability for teachers, and it often led to extremely generous payments to retiring administrators. New Jersey had tenure for administrators, so many of them stayed in the state for long periods of time; nevertheless, payments to administrators, especially superintendents, for accumulated sick leave are less likely to be capped than payments to teachers. Because there are fewer administrators than teachers, the total impact on district spending is less in the case of administrators, but the outcome is often an excessive benefit package. Bear in mind that administrative salaries are often much higher than teacher salaries; hence their daily rate of pay is also much higher than the daily rate for teachers.

Suppose a principal who has served as a teacher and principal in a district for 20 years was entitled to 12 sick leave days a year but used only two per year. If paid $100,000 a year for 200 workdays a year, his rate of pay would be $500 per day. This would entitle him to $100,000 for accumulated sick leave—perhaps not a golden parachute but surely a soft landing.

## SUMMARY

More stringent reporting requirements—not just suggested guidelines, but mandated reporting of unfunded liabilities, including the assumptions and data underlying the estimates—may be the only feasible way to avoid increases in unfunded pension costs. We can also surmise that if the public becomes more aware of these unfunded costs, it will become more difficult for elected officials or pension boards to increase pension benefits without increasing current taxes.

The basic problem in all of the cases discussed in this chapter is how to ensure that state and school district fiscal statements reveal the real cost of funding the enterprise. With millions of teachers approaching retirement, some states risk overdrawing their retirement funds or having to take dramatic steps to support their defined benefit plans. In contrast, because defined contribution plans eliminate the danger of any future unfunded pension liability, more states are considering plans to stabilize their defined benefit plans and to establish defined contribution plans for newly hired workers.

To maximize awareness of unfunded pension obligations, the Governmental Accounting Standards Board's new reporting criteria address the problem. Because the new criteria are being phased in, the full extent of the problem may not be evident until 2004–05, but the forthcoming publicity about underfunding may generate some momentum for reducing the unfunded pension obligations affecting school district personnel.

## NOTES

1. In 22 state retirement systems, school administrators and school district support personnel are included in the teacher retirement system; hence the

term "teacher" in this chapter includes all school district employees in these 22 states.

2. "History of CalSTRS Funding and Benefits," 1. At http://www.strs.ca.gov/aboutstrs/funding.html [accessed March 20, 2002].

3. Ibid.

4. Ibid.

5. Peter J. Ferrara, *Pension Liberation for Oregon: A Proposal to Reform PERS* (Portland, OR: Cascade Policy Institute, 2001), 4, 8.

6. James Mayer, "PERS Gap Grows to $9.7 Billion," *The Oregonian*, November 14, 2002. At http://www.OregonLive.com [accessed November 14, 2002].

7. Ibid.

8. The Urban Institute, Winklevoss & Associates, Government Finance Research Center, and Dr. Bernard Jump Jr., *The Future of State and Local Pensions* (Washington, DC: Department of Housing and Urban Development, 1981), 8–16.

9. National Council on Teacher Retirement. At http://www.nctr.org/content/indexpg/washup/fastfact1.htm [accessed October 13, 2001].

10. Emma Y. Zink, "1998 Report of the Chair," CalSTRS (Sacramento: CalSTRS, 1999).

11. Matthew Lathrop, "Defined Contribution Plans," *ALEC Issue Analysis* (Washington, DC: American Legislative Exchange Council, March 1999), 1.

12. U.S. Bureau of the Census, Public Information Office Press Release, "Retirement Assets of State and Local Government Employees at Record High, Census Bureau Reports," October 25, 2000.

13. U.S. Bureau of the Census, Federal, State, and Local Governments, 2000 State and Local Government Public Employee Retirement Systems, table 1. At http://www.census.gov/govs/www/retire00.html [accessed November 19, 2002].

14. The National Retired Teachers Association, a division of AARP, reported 1.2 million retired educator members; not all retired educators are members of NRTA. At http://www.aarp/nrta [accessed June 10, 2002].

15. Frank V. Auriemma, Bruce S. Cooper, and Stuart C. Smith, *Graying Teachers: A Report on State Pension Systems and School District Early Retirement Incentives* (Eugene, OR: Clearinghouse on Educational Management, 1992), 5.

16. U.S. Department of Education, National Center for Education Statistics, *Digest of Education Statistics 2001,* NCES 2002-130, Washington, DC, 2002, 87. The source of the data presented by NCES is the National Education Association. The American Federation of Teachers compiles its own teacher

salary statistics and reported the average national salary for teachers was $41,820 for 1999–2000.

17. Auriemma, Cooper, and Smith, *Graying Teachers* 7.

18. Ibid., 17.

19. Ibid., 14.

20. Ibid., 25–33.

21. National Education Association, Research Division, "Employee and Employer Contribution Rates," *Characteristics of 100 Large Public Pension Plans*, Washington, DC, 2000, 29–37.

22. Auriemma, Cooper, and Smith, *Graying Teachers*, 31.

23. NEA, *Characteristics of 100 Large Public Pension Plans,* 42.

24. The Urban Institute et al., *The Future of State and Local Pensions,* 8-4.

25. Ibid., 8–18, 19.

26. Steven Greenhouse, "Public Funds Say Losses Top $1.5 Billion," *The New York Times*, January 29, 2002.

27. Roberta Romano, "Public Pension Fund Activism in Corporate Governance Reconsidered," *Columbia Law Review* 93, no. 4 (May 1993): 823.

28. Edwin T. Burton, III and Matthew Lathrop, "Modernizing Public Pension Systems," *The State Factor* 25, no. 4 (Washington, D.C.: American Legislative Exchange Council, July 1999): 4.

29. NEA, *Characteristics of 100 Large Public Pension Plans*, 7–11.

30. Cynthia L. Moore, *Public Pension Plans: The State Regulatory Framework,* 3rd ed. (Austin, TX: National Council on Teacher Retirement, February 1998), ix.

31. Auriemma, Cooper, and Smith, *Graying Teachers,* 7.

32. See list of Resolutions in the *NEA Handbook*, 2000–2001, 398. In the past, the NEA has threatened to boycott companies that employed talk show hosts critical of the NEA. In some cases, the NEA has threatened retaliation against companies solely because a prominent company official has actively supported educational vouchers as an individual, not as a company official.

33. AFL-CIO, *Investment Product Review,* Washington, DC, 1999, Foreword.

34. Ibid., 1.

35. TIAA-CREF, *Outreach*, New York, NY, April 2000, 1.

36. Roberta Romano, "The Politics of Public Pension Funds," *Public Interest* (Washington, DC: National Affairs, Spring 1995), 42–53.

37. Christopher Palmeri, "Politicians Should Butt Out of Pension Funds," *Business Week*, June 11, 2001, 150.

38. NEA, *Characteristics of 100 Large Public Pension Plans,* 61.

39. Stephen Glass, "A Pension Deficit Disorder," *Policy Review* (Washington, DC: The Heritage Foundation, Winter 1995), 71–74.

40. "Testimony of General Treasurer Nancy J. Mayer on Bill No. S-2921. March 8, 1994," in *National Education Association—Rhode Island, et al., vs. Retirement Board of the Rhode Island Employees Retirement System, et al.,* Appendix in Support of Defendant's Motion for Summary Judgement, Vol. III, p. D20274. Mayer pointed out that one person had purchased thirty years in the retirement system for $28,352 and "almost immediately retired with a $61,430-a-year state pension. If this 56-year-old man had purchased an annuity from a private insurance company, it would have cost him $788,929."

41. Ibid.

42. Moore, *Public Pension Plans,* ix.

43. Ferrara, *Pension Liberation for Oregon,* 22–23.

44. Moore, *Public Pension Plans*, viii.

45. Ibid., ix.

46. The Urban Institute et al., *The Future of State and Local Pensions,* 9-1.

47. American Legislative Exchange Council, *Task Force News* 1, no. 2, Washington, DC, June 1999, 1.

48. Julie Blair, "New Pension Plans Provide Educators with Options, Risks," *Education Week* 21, no. 29 (April 3, 2002): 22–23.

49. Telephone conversation between the author (CKH) and David A. Haney, executive director of the West Virginia Education Association, a member of the committee that recommended that a defined contribution plan be included in the state's retirement system.

50. Buck Consultants, Inc., *West Virginia Teachers' Retirement System: Actuarial Valuation as of July 1, 2001,* for the West Virginia Consolidated Public Retirement Board, 2–3.

51. The Urban Institute et al., *The Future of State and Local Pensions*, 9–23.

52. Ibid., 9–26.

53. Joe Williams, "Healthy Dose of Sick Pay," *New York Daily News,* March 5, 2002.

CHAPTER 5

# Parental Support for Public Education

In this chapter, we consider the costs of public education absorbed by parents. Our focus will be on parent expenditures made to a public school or school district. The parental expenditures that we do not discuss are often more important educationally than the ones we do discuss; for instance, parent expenditures for educational books and games (which we do not discuss) are often more important educationally than parent contributions to the PTA (which we do discuss). For that matter, parental time devoted to their children's education is a cost, but we assign a dollar value to it only as an example of how this might be done.

More than 80 percent of the nation's 118,402 public and private elementary and secondary schools have a parent/teacher organization (PTO) that is not affiliated with the National PTA or any other state or national parent organization. These parent/teacher organizations raise significant funds in a variety of ways: product sales, auctions, competitions, galas, and other fundraising drives. Traditional product fundraising generates an average of $13,000 per school.[1] Nationwide, almost $2 billion is raised each school year by parent and student organizations.[2] According to the National Association of Elementary School Principals, "91 percent of schools in America raise funds to supplement government funding."[3] Along with school principals, parent organizations as well as teachers accept fundraising responsibilities. The contributions are often significant: "Nearly 40 percent of schools earn between $10,000 and $25,000 through fundraising each year; 29 percent earn between $5,000 and $10,000; while 23 percent earn less than $5,000. The remaining 8 percent of schools earn $25,000 and up."[4] A local school is typically the beneficiary of the revenue, which pays for such things as classroom equipment and supplies, field trips, library books, computers, and playground equipment.

Volunteer time is another important parent contribution. Volunteers in Public Schools (VIPS) is an organization in many schools that serves as a liaison between the school district and the community, while providing volunteer opportunities in the schools. On its website, the Little Rock Arkansas School District stated that "during the 1999–2000 school year, over 15,000 volunteers contributed 283,625.75 hours with an estimated worth of $4,055,848.23."[5] School districts elsewhere frequently make similar claims in print or on their websites.[6]

## THE NATIONAL PTA AND ITS AFFILIATES

Unlike PTOs, which have no state or national affiliations, over 24,000 local parent/teacher organizations are affiliates of the National Congress of Parents and Teachers. Better known as the PTA, the hierarchy includes state PTA affiliates as well. These local PTAs impact the programs and budgets of local schools in a variety of ways, including payment of the salaries of teachers who cannot be paid from regular school budgets. Usually this happens when a PTA is particularly interested in retaining teachers of art, music, foreign languages, or some other subject that the regular budget cannot accommodate.

In some instances, the line between schoolwork and PTA work is obliterated. This happens when school grades are based on participation in what is supposed to be a voluntary PTA-sponsored fundraiser. It is difficult to assess the frequency of such practices, but anecdotal evidence indicates that they are not unusual. It should also be noted that PTA fundraising often generates unwarranted pressure to participate. For example, if a PTA or a teacher urges "100 percent" participation in a PTA fundraiser, those students or parents who prefer not to raise funds for the PTA's agenda may feel pressured into doing so.[7]

In schools that enroll mainly affluent students, PTA fundraisers raise impressive amounts. "The Owl," a school newsletter sponsored by the Phoebe Hearst Elementary School in Washington, D.C., includes updates on the PTA's fundraising activities. To raise the $227,000 budgeted for its 1997–98 fiscal year, the school's PTA leadership anticipated that dues, fees, and seven fundraising events (nearly one per month of the school year) would bring in just over $200,000. This local affiliate also expected to raise 20 percent of its budget from one of its seven fundraising events, an evening gala and auction at a nearby embassy. Parents had made all the arrangements and, along with other attendees, bid on and bought over 300 donated items. Some of the more expensive items included a trip for two to Rio de Janeiro, a Persian rug, and a week at a beach hotel. The final event in its fundraising schedule of seven events was a grocery scrip program, in which parents purchased discounted coupons redeemable at local grocery stores.

The membership form for the Hearst PTA requests the annual $10 membership fee and an additional enrichment and assessment fee of $180. The form explains that: "The enrichment program includes payment for an art teacher, classroom aide, Spanish teacher, science/art materials, repairs to the building, and special programs." About 135 children attend the Hearst school, a public school that serves pre-kindergarten to third-grade pupils. When fully funded, the assessment fee plus the per-pupil share of the $227,000 budget amounted to $1,376 per pupil—a sizable amount in any school district. The membership form also suggests that members should check with their employers, many of whom match or exceed their employee contributions to 501(c)(3) tax-exempt organizations.[8] There are no comprehensive data on employer matching contributions to public school organizations or activities, but the total amount may not be very large in the total picture.

The Hearst PTA program is not unique, even in the District of Columbia. The PTA at the district's Horace Mann Elementary School asked parents to donate $950 per child for the 1999–00 school year. Although not all families contributed the requested amount, the PTA hired seven teaching assistants and a part-time vocal instructor from its fundraising activities.[9] Subsequently, Arlene Ackerman, the District of Columbia superintendent of schools, criticized the practice, but did not stop it. When Ms. Ackerman resigned her position in 2000, Paul L. Vance, her successor, also expressed concerns but did not try to prohibit the practice.

Like PTOs, many PTAs keep track of the hours contributed by volunteers and recognize their most active members. The Buena Vista Elementary School PTA of Greer, South Carolina, recognized 500 volunteers, who provided 100,000 hours of service to school projects.

Probably no state comes close to the hours logged by California PTA members. According to the California PTA, its "volunteers reported a total of 21,314,317 hours of service from July 1, 1993, to June 30, 1994."[10] The California PTA claimed that at $6 an hour, the volunteers provided $127,885,902 in services for which higher wages would have been paid in the marketplace. Interestingly enough, a great deal of this volunteer time was devoted to defeating Proposition 174, the November 1993 California school voucher initiative. Nationally, one survey estimates that almost 3.4 million public school volunteers logged approximately 109 million hours of work in 2000. This was reported to be roughly equivalent to 52,000 full-time staff in 2000.[11]

The cost of volunteers illustrates the distinction between total costs and government cost. Asked about the cost of parent volunteers, the vast majority of teachers and administrators would say there is no cost—the volunteers work for nothing, are "free" in other words. Pointing out that staff time might be necessary to coordinate volunteer activities might be perceived as quibbling, so let us ignore all such costs. Nevertheless, volunteer time raises equity issues.

We must distinguish costs from who pays for the costs. The time of parent volunteers is worth something, but the parents absorb the costs, or the business that allows its employees time off for school affairs pays the costs of employee time.[12] From an economic standpoint, if we compare two schools with identical government costs, but one utilizes parent volunteers and the other does not, the former costs more than the latter. How much more would be the amount required to provide services equivalent to the services provided by the volunteers.

Schools in socioeconomically middle- and upper-class neighborhoods thus receive more resources than schools in disadvantaged neighborhoods; the latter typically lack volunteers or as many volunteers as the former. This could be regarded as exacerbating equity problems, which would not necessarily be resolved by the presence of parent volunteers in the schools without them. After all, differences in the quality of the volunteer help might still leave us with an inequity.[13]

Most emphatically, we are not advocating the abolition of volunteers because their utilization might lead to inequities. Our point is that the idea that utilization of volunteers does not involve costs is simplistic. The fact that parents, not the school district, absorb the costs is important, but it does not resolve all of the policy issues relating to the practice. Some educational policy analysts would prohibit differentials in support due to differentials in parent financial contributions, but this position is not widely accepted.[14]

## THE ACCOUNTING STATUS OF AFFILIATED ORGANIZATIONS

In order to estimate unreported funds contributed by organizations not controlled by the schools, the Governmental Accounting Standards Board (GASB) conducted a survey of school districts in 34 states and the District of Columbia in 1996. One hundred eleven school districts out of 851 selected for the sample responded to the inquiry. Many of the large school districts reported that they were unaware of how many affiliated organizations operate in the schools in their district. An "affiliated organization" is one over which the school district exercises some formal authority. Table 5.1 shows the number and nature of affiliated organizations in the school districts responding to the survey.

**Table 5.1. Nature of Affiliated Organizations in 111 School Districts**

| *Types of Organizations* | *Number of Organizations* | *Percent of Affiliated Organizations** | *Percent of School Districts*** |
|---|---|---|---|
| Booster clubs | 48 | 28.1 | 43.2 |
| Parent-Teacher Organization*** | 36 | 21.3 | 32.4 |
| Parent-Teacher Association*** | 28 | 16.3 | 25.2 |
| Education foundation | 21 | 12.2 | 18.9 |
| Fundraising foundation | 12 | 7.1 | 10.8 |
| School district foundation | 9 | 5.2 | 8.1 |
| Faculty-student cooperative | 4 | 2.3 | 3.6 |
| Athletics foundation | 2 | 1.2 | 1.8 |
| Endowment foundation | 2 | 1.2 | 1.8 |
| Alumni foundation or association | 2 | 1.2 | 1.8 |
| Development foundation | 1 | .5 | .9 |
| Other | 7 | 4.1 | 6.3 |
| Total | 172**** | 100.0 | 154.8**** |

* Percent of affiliated organizations responding to the survey.
** Percent of all school districts in the sample.
*** The distinction is not clarified, but presumably PTOs are not affiliated with a national parent/teacher organization, whereas PTAs are affilates of the National PTA.
**** Some districts reported two or more affiliated organizations.

Source: Rita Hartung Cheng and Carol M. Lawrence, *School Districts and Their Affiliated Organizations: A Report to the GASB*, August 6, 1997, 2.

**Table 5.2. Methods by Which Affiliated Organizations Provided Financial Support in 111 School Districts**

| *Nature of the Transfer* | *Number of Reporting School Districts* |
|---|---|
| Reimbursement of specific expenditures | 29 |
| Pays specific bills | 7 |
| Performs supporting services | 23 |
| Discretionary transfer of financial services | 17 |
| Periodic lump sum transfers (discretionary) | 14 |
| Lump sum transfers at request of school district | 12 |
| Routinely pays salaries | 9 |
| Other | 2 |

Source: Rita Hartung Cheng and Carol M. Lawrence, *School Districts and Their Affiliated Organizations: A Report to the GASB*, August 6, 1997, 5.

The authors concluded that "an analysis of the financial condition of the AOs [Affiliated Organizations] and related school districts indicates that as a practical matter some school districts face severe financial stress and the affiliated organizations' substantial assets and contributions have a major impact." Most affiliated organizations receive services from the school districts in the form of office space, staff, or accounting and financial services. Table 5.2 shows the methods by which affiliated organizations transfer financial resources to school districts or provide support on behalf of school districts.

Annual revenues of the affiliated organizations surveyed averaged just over $643,000, and the average annual financial contribution to school districts was $179,401. Table 5.3 shows the revenues of affiliated organizations that provided detailed financial information.

**Table 5.3. Revenues (from Sample Survey) of Affiliated Organizations**

| | *Number* | *Percent* | *$ Level* |
|---|---|---|---|
| | 6 | 25.0 | <100,000 |
| | 7 | 29.1 | 100,001–200,000 |
| | 4 | 16.7 | 200,001–500,000 |
| | 1 | 4.2 | 500,001–1,000,000 |
| | 5 | 20.8 | 1,000,001–5,000,000 |
| | 1 | 4.2 | >5,000,000 |
| Totals | 24 | 100.0 | |

Source: Rita Hartung Cheng and Carol M. Lawrence, *School Districts and Their Affiliated Organizations: A Report to the GASB*, August 6, 1997, 7-8.

## PARENT-PAID REMEDIAL AND ENRICHMENT EDUCATION: LEARNING COMPANIES

Although parent-funded remedial education is not a new development, it experienced remarkable growth in the 1990s, especially as the ineffectiveness of federally funded remedial programs could no longer be plausibly denied. These federal programs originated in Title I (originally Chapter 1) of the Elementary and Secondary Education Act of 1965. Their objective was improved academic skills among low-achieving students in low income areas. The test of "low income" was the percentage of students receiving free or reduced-price lunches at school. Funding for Title I increased from just over $5 billion in 1980 to $9.1 billion in 2000 and an authorization of $13.5 billion in 2002.[15]

Private as well as public school students are beneficiaries of Title I programs. According to the Congressional Research Service, in 1999–2000, 52 percent of Catholic schools, 9 percent of other religious schools, and 9 percent of secular private schools were receiving Title I grants. By 1997, the federal government had spent $118 billion on Title I, but research on its effectiveness still failed to reveal any lasting effects of Title I programs.[16] Studies that had purported to show improvement were subsequently discredited because the districts involved had excluded low-achieving, special education, and immigrant students from the tests that allegedly demonstrated the beneficent effects of Title I.[17] As it has been since its inception in 1965, Title I was the largest single item in federally funded education programs, amounting to over 32 percent of the FY 2002 U.S. Department of Education appropriation of $56 billion.[18]

The point of interest here is the emergence of private-sector participation in remedial programs, especially by for-profit learning companies. Until the 1990s, these remedial education programs were funded only by parents. In a typical remedial program provided by the largest companies, three students are seated at a table with one teacher. The parents pay for a set number of hours of instruction over a series of sessions. The instruction is provided by former teachers or retired teachers who are employed under contract at hourly rates that vary by region and school district characteristics.

Sylvan Learning Systems, Inc., the largest for-profit company of this kind, operated more than 700 centers in 2000 and was adding 50 centers a year. Starting in 1993, when it signed a contract to provide remedial education to six Baltimore elementary schools, Sylvan at School programs were operative in 850 public and nonpublic schools with an enrollment of almost 80,000 students in 2000.[19] Of course, when school districts employ Sylvan Learning Systems to provide instruction, the company is paid from school district funds; the funds are not an add-on to district expenditures.

School district contracts with learning companies are not likely to discourage parent payments for remedial services. The reason is that the school district remediation market is very different from the individual parent-supported market; hence an increase in one is unlikely to affect the other. The individual parent market materializes in middle-class school districts that do not enroll large numbers of students who are reading poorly. In these districts, parents concerned about the low educational achievement of their children usually have no alternative to paying for remedial education from their own resources. Eligibility for Title I funds requires a concentration of low-achieving pupils; parents elsewhere must pay for remedial help from their own resources. In contrast, the learning company contracts with school districts provide remedial help for concentrations of low-achieving students in low-income neighborhoods in which few parents would pay for remedial assistance from their personal resources.

For-profit learning centers will probably expand their public school services substantially in the future. The No Child Left Behind Act (NCLBA) includes a provision, accompanied by an annual allocation of $100,000,000 for each of five years, that permits parents to leave a "low-performing public school" and exercise their choice of alternative educational services for their children.[20] Regardless, parent-paid instruction may also increase due to the continuing ineffectiveness of school district remedial instruction, and growth in the number of students needing remedial instruction and the number of parents able and willing to pay for it.

This conclusion receives some support from the fact that students in many advanced nations appear to devote more time than U.S. students to out-of-school instruction, and that remediation, not enhancement, is the dominant motive. A study based on 1994–95 data showed that U.S. students ranked twentieth out of 41 countries in the extent of out-of-school instruction in eighth-grade mathematics. Some countries in which eighth-grade students were more proficient in mathematics than U.S. eighth graders showed more participation while a substantially equal number showed less participation in out-of-school instruction.[21]

Learning company expansion to include enrichment as well as remediation is also under way. Huntington Learning Centers and Sylvan, along with Kaplan Learning Centers, the leaders in this market niche, offer instruction to help students achieve higher scores on the Scholastic Assessment Test. Physics, chemistry, biology, and foreign languages are examples of subjects routinely offered in schools that are also offered by learning centers. Potentially, the enrichment market may be much larger than the parent-paid remediation market.

Of course, there have always been families who paid for tutoring in subjects taught in the public schools. Such instruction was normally provided by individuals, who might or might not be full-time teachers of the subject. In contrast, the learning companies involve entrepreneurs, equity financing, franchising, substantial research and development, national advertising, and other characteristics of large companies providing consumer services. Obviously, much higher expenditure levels are required to support this approach to parent-paid instruction; however, the learning companies' advantages of scale frequently more than compensate for their higher entrepreneurial costs.

It is impossible to estimate with confidence the amounts spent by parents for remedial instruction. There are too many companies offering too many subjects at too many different prices at different facilities to come up with a defensible estimate. In relation to the total amount spent by public schools, parent-paid expenditures for education may be miniscule, but the tens of thousands of parents who are paying from their own resources for instruction in school subjects may have a different view of the matter.

## SUMMER CAMPS AS EDUCATIONAL INSTITUTIONS

Parent-paid summer camps are another important dimension of the private costs of elementary and secondary education. Because the camping industry has experienced substantial growth in recent years, it is much larger than most people realize. In 1999, a highly diverse group of more than 8,500 camps was located in all regions of the country. About 6,200 camps are operated by nonprofit groups and organizations, and 2,300, or 27 percent, by independent for-profit owners.[22] More than 500,000 adults work in these camps, with total employment about 900,000.[23] Almost 9 million children and adults attend summer camps. Many camps cater to adults, and many that cater to school-age children do not offer instruction in subjects in the school curriculum. The camps that do offer such instruction do not necessarily offer it as the primary feature of the camp. Nevertheless, many camps provide instruction that is intended to reinforce or supplement school instruction. For example, almost half of the camps serve campers with physical or mental disabilities. Many camps feature education in subjects like computer science that are not always included in regular school curricula.

The direct cost of attending summer camps in 1998 varied from $15 to $120 a day; to know the actual cost, it would be necessary to include the costs of transportation to and from camp, long-distance telephone charges, special clothing and equipment, and various other items deemed essential or desirable to profit from the camp experience. We have assumed conservatively that these costs are $100 per camper.

The camp experience varies in duration, but let us assume that the average duration was 42 days and the average daily cost was $67.50, the midpoint between the high and the low daily costs reported by the American Camping Association. On this basis, the direct cost of the summer camps to campers would be 9,000,000 × $67.50 × 42 ($25,515,000,000), plus 9,000,000 × $100 ($900,000,000) for travel, for a total of $26.4 billion.

All things considered, we estimate that about 10 to 20 percent of the expenditures for summer camps ($2.7 to $5.3 billion) are utilized to purchase instruction that duplicates or extends instruction or services received in public schools. A more precise estimate of the amounts spent for instruction on school subjects in summer camps would require data that are not available, but summer camps clearly provide a significant amount of instruction in regular school subjects.

Parenthetically, several other aspects of summer camps deserve more attention from educational policymakers. To teach a subject in public schools, teachers must be certified by the state as having adequate training to serve as a classroom teacher. In contrast, teachers need not be certified to teach the same subject to the same pupils in a summer camp. In fact, the instructors in summer camps are often college students years away from earning a bachelor's degree or a teaching certificate. Another significant feature of summer camps is their range of specialization, which often covers subjects that are not available in public schools. In view of the wide range of subjects offered by summer camps, it appears that there is a substantial latent demand for specialized schools unlike any that exist today.

## CORPORATE CONTRACTS

Financial disclosure of school district revenues and expenditures is required on the Census Bureau's Annual Survey of Local Government Finances. The survey requires disclosures of "Other Sales and Service Revenue," which presumably include school district revenues from contracts with soft-drink vendors and advertisers. However, these contracts may be crafted in such a way that school districts are not required to report the revenues.

Perhaps the best known example of private funding of public education is Channel One, a television program. Launched in 1989, Channel One received access to students for a twelve-minute news and advertising television program in exchange for installation and loan of a free satellite dish, internal wiring at the school, two videocassette recorders, and a 19-inch television set for each classroom. In 2000, 12,000 schools, or about 38 percent of all middle and high schools in the United States, were connected to the Channel One system. The Channel One contract requires that schools show the ten-minute programming and two minutes of commercials, on 90 percent of all school days in 80 percent of all classrooms.[24] The market value of the products and services that are contributed by Channel One varies with the number of schools and classrooms to be served, but it is significant collectively and individually.

Contracts for exclusive advertising and/or vending machine deals with soft-drink companies are often very lucrative sources of income for schools, especially if the district is represented by an experienced negotiator who is familiar with the value of such a contract. In 1993, the Texas Grapevine-Colleyville School District, an affluent community in the Dallas-Ft. Worth area, became the first school system in the nation to allow advertising and an exclusive vending machine deal. In exchange for an advertisement in the gymnasium, Schroeder Orthodontics paid Grapevine $10,000 a year. And to generate more revenue, the school negotiated a contract that allowed Dr Pepper to become the exclusive soft drink for the Grapevine-Colleyville school system. Part of the deal included permission to have the Dr Pepper logo installed on the roofs of Canon Elementary School and Grapeville Middle School so that airplane passengers could see the roof advertisements. Of course, not all schools have the same opportunities to negotiate lucrative contracts.[25]

The trend toward exclusive arrangements often applies to extracurricular events as well as regular school operations.[26] In 1997, a St. Charles (Illinois) soft-drink distributor gave the Naperville Central High School $9,000 to buy athletic equipment in exchange for the right to sell Coca-Cola products exclusively at its sports events for five years. Coca-Cola Enterprises, Inc., has been a leader in marketing so-called pouring rights contracts, but Pepsi and other bottling companies also try to convince schools and school districts to put vending machines in hallways and cafeterias in exchange for a share of the profits. Schools receive a larger share of the profits if they agree to an exclusive arrangement with a single company. The winner-take-all exclusive contract is the creation of the soft-drink companies; for example, "a beverage contract in one district has the potential to generate up to $1.5 million per year to help fund projects and activities."[27] As of March 2001, some 240 schools in 31 states had such exclusive contracts.[28] However, conflicts can arise when a PTO or PTA contracts with a different soft-drink company to provide its products at organization-sponsored events in the schools.[29]

Company demands have increased over the years. For example, in 1998, when product sales dropped in the Colorado Springs District, a district administrator sent out a list of ways that principals and teachers could increase soft-drink and juice sales.[30] Under the exclusive $11.1 million contract arrangement, if students bought 70,000 cases of Coca-Cola products per school, the district would receive revenue equal to $32.59 per student. If sales were less, the district's share would decline proportionately. The elementary schools also have contracts with Coca-Cola that stipulate they must sell a certain number of "juice" products, such as Minute Maid beverages and Fruitopia (which contains only 5 percent real juice);[31] however, many school districts that have been solicited to participate in such programs have declined to do so. For example, school officials in Philadelphia rejected exclusive vendor contracts, even though an exclusive soft-drink contract would have provided the district an estimated $43 million over 10 years.[32]

Not surprisingly, corporate and product logos appear on vending machines, product displays, message boards, and scoreboards. Frequently, these product advertisements are displayed in exchange for free equipment, such as football uniforms or musical instruments. Some schools are the beneficiaries of $3-a-year leased cars for their driver education program; the schools are required to return the cars after 3,000 miles.[33]

According to the U.S. Government Accounting Office, "no central data source tracks the value of corporate contributions to precollege education."[34] Even so, in its analysis of soft-drink agreements with six high schools in its study, the revenue or in-kind benefits ranged from $3 per student in Cibola High School in Albuquerque to $30 per student at the Ottawa Hills High School in Grand Rapids, Michigan. As previously noted, however, the corporate contributions are frequently not included in the NCES statistics on the per-pupil costs of education.

## UNCOMPENSATED OVERTIME AND SUPPLIES

The amounts paid for services by teachers, administrators, bus drivers, secretaries, cafeteria workers, and other school district employees are included in the cost of public education. However, employee services are not always compensated; hence they are economic costs that are not included in the government costs. They are economic costs despite the fact that they are voluntary and not paid for by school districts; the school district employees absorb the costs.

We can only speculate about the extent of uncompensated teacher time. The teacher unions sometimes distribute questionnaires asking teachers to indicate the hours devoted to students or school affairs that are outside the regular school day. The time outside the school day is not necessarily voluntary, uncompensated time per se; for example, football coaches are paid for workouts and games held after school is dismissed for most teachers. It is very possible if not likely, however, that teachers' estimates of their uncompensated time on a questionnaire, with a strong incentive to overestimate the time, do so by a substantial amount. This is especially the case when the data are generated by teacher unions that plan to cite the data in collective bargaining as a reason why teachers should be paid more or work fewer hours. Nevertheless, studies by independent parties would not necessarily be more accurate. Knowing that they are being observed on the issue, some teachers are likely to work more or report more uncompensated work than they would otherwise. The same considerations apply to supplies purchased by teachers for classroom use. Some unions have conducted studies on the issue, but the dynamics of uncompensated extra work also apply to uncompensated teacher expenditures for pupil benefits.

We have not made an estimate of either the value of donated time or the supplies; reliable, comprehensive data on these matters are not available. Nevertheless, the absence of data does not mean the absence of uncompensated time or purchases. Parenthetically, we do not take any position on whether teachers should be paid for either their uncompensated time or purchases for classroom use. Some employees in virtually every field do more than is required by their employer; it would be a sad day in education if this were not the case. The problem of quantification in education is exacerbated by the fact that teachers and administrators often disagree over how much time outside the regular school day, if any, can be required of teachers. The creeping school day is a legitimate teacher concern, but teachers should not simply stop helping students in the middle of a sentence at the end of the regular school day.

School board time provides additional examples of work that is not compensated or not compensated adequately. In most school districts school board compensation bears little relationship to the responsibilities, but most school administrators like it this way; the feeling is that school board members would "meddle" more in administration if they were paid more. For decades, educational policymakers have been divided over the issue of school board member compensation. One school of thought is that there should be no financial remuneration for school board service, which should be regarded as a civic obligation of qualified citizens. The contrary view is that low or no compensation limits the pool of citizens who can assume school board responsibilities, whereas the need is for a more inclusive standard. A third school of thought that is receiving considerable attention in large cities is to eliminate school boards altogether. New York City did not abolish its school board in 2002, but the legislature transferred its important responsibilities to the mayor and a school board dominated by mayoral appointees.

## IMPACT OF THE GASB STATEMENT NO. 14

The GASB Statement No. 39 might also have a major impact on school district financial statements. The gist of Statement No. 39, an amendment to the GASB Statement No. 14, is that school districts must include in their financial statements the assistance and resources of "component organizations." The GASB definition of component organizations and the rationale for their inclusion in school district financial statements are as follows:

> Certain organizations warrant inclusion as part of the financial reporting entity because of the nature and significance of their relationship with the primary government, including their ongoing financial support of the primary government or its other component units. A legally separate, tax-exempt organization should be reported as a component unit of a reporting entity if all of the following criteria are met:
>
> 1. The economic resources received or held by the separate organization are entirely or almost entirely for the direct benefit of the primary government, its component units, or its constituents.
> 2. The primary government, or its component units, is entitled to, or has the ability to otherwise access a majority of the economic resources received or held by the separate organization.
> 3. The economic resources received or held by an individual organization that the specific primary government, or its component units, is entitled to, or has the ability to otherwise access, are significant to that primary government.[35]

It should be obvious that the impact of GASB Statement No. 39 will depend in large part on how it is interpreted and applied. For instance, will the following entities be regarded as "component organizations": Independent parent/teacher organizations (PTOs), affiliates of the National PTA, booster clubs, school district foundations, local affiliates of the Public Education Network? These issues are discussed in the following chapter, but it can be noted here that the National PTA's legal position is that PTAs should not be regarded as component organizations. Instead, the PTA regards itself as a child welfare organization, despite the fact that most its local affiliates are named after schools. Needless to say, many parents and teacher PTA members will be surprised to learn that providing assistance to students in their schools is not the primary purpose of their PTA. This is much less likely to be a problem with parent/teacher organizations not affiliated with the National PTA.[36]

## SUMMARY

This chapter emphasizes the distinction between economic costs (all the resources utilized to achieve an object) and government costs. The voluntary contributions (cash, time, supplies) from parents are just a few of the economic costs that are not included in estimating the government per-pupil costs. Even in the absence of extensive research, anecdotal evidence indicates that such uncounted parental costs render equality of educational opportunity an unattainable ideal unless government restricts parental support for the education of their children in public schools. This course of action is and, in our opinion, should be politically impossible. Limits on private contributions to public education do not help poor children; they do not learn less because others learn more. It hardly makes sense to allow unlimited purchase of liquor and tobacco products while restricting private spending for more education.[37]

The inequities brought about by voluntary contributions for the benefit of some students and some schools are likely to exacerbate the controversies over implementation of GASB Statements Nos. 34 and 14. These statements require full disclosure of the private contributions that were not reported under the requirements in place in 2001. As previously noted, the requirements will be phased in over three years, so that by 2004, all school districts will be expected to comply with GASB's new reporting requirements. Until then, state legislators, parents, and taxpayers will not know how much voluntary contributions and contractual payments increase the per-pupil cost in their school and/or school district. And, unfortunately, the cash accounting procedures in seven states allow noncompliance with GASB standards, thus rendering it likely that the problems of inadequate reporting will be with us for many years to come.

## NOTES

1. Vickie Mabry, "Product Fundraising: It's a Love-Hate Thing," *Principal,* November 2000, 6.

2. Association of Fund Raisers and Direct Sellers, *The Fundraising Edge* (Atlanta, GA: Association of Fund-Raising Distributors & Suppliers, Spring, 2001), 3.

3. Ibid., Fall 2000, 4.

4. Ibid., p. 5.

5. At http://www.lrsd.org/VIPS/VIPS.asp [accessed July 15, 2001].

6. The Virginia Beach school system reported that in 1996–97, volunteers gave 344,000 hours of time, for a estimated value of more than $2,583,000. At http://www.vbcps.k12.va.us/press/122w.html [accessed July 15, 2001]. According to the Katy, Texas, district website, in 1996–97, "more than 7,000 volunteers provided Katy schools with 171,000 hours of service; if volunteers were paid for their services, the cost to the school district would have been around $2 million." At http://www.katy.isd.tenet.edu/kisd/community/vips.htm [accessed July 15, 2001].

7. Charlene K. Haar, *The Politics of the PTA* (New Brunswick, NJ: Social Philosophy and Policy Center and Transaction, 2002), 111–123.

8. PTA Membership Form, distributed at Phoebe Hearst Elementary School PTA meeting, Washington, DC, 1997–98.

9. Justin Blum, "PTAs Give Some D.C. Schools an Edge," *The Washington Post,* April 17, 2000.

10. Letter from Ann Desmond, vice president for communication, California State PTA, to Charlene K. Haar, August 17, 1994.

11. National Association of Partners in Education, "Partnerships 2000: A Decade of Growth and Change," 2001, 6.

12. Henry Levin and Patrick J. McEwan, *Cost-Effectiveness Analysis,* 2nd ed. (Thousand Oaks, CA: Sage, 2001), 77–82.

13. Ron Zimmer, Cathy Krop, et al., *Private Giving to Public Schools and Districts in Los Angeles County* (Washington, DC: Rand, 2001), 44–48.

14. John E. Chubb and Terry M. Moe, *Politics, Markets and America's Schools* (Washington, DC: Brookings Institution, 1990), 220.

15. Public Law 107-110, 107th Cong., 2d sess. (8 January 2002), *No Child Left Behind Act of 2001*, 18.

16. Lisa Snell with Lindsay Anderson, *Remedial Education Reform: Private Alternatives to Traditional Title 1* (Los Angeles, CA: Reason Public Policy Institute, January 2000), 107.

17. Amy Argetsinger, "U.S. Defeats MD Gains in Reading Test in '98," *Washington Post,* May 15, 1999; Pascal D. Forgione Jr., "Issues Surrounding the Release of the 1998 NAEP Reading Report Card," Testimony, Committee on Education and the Workforce, U.S. House of Representatives, May 27, 1999.

18. U.S. Government Printing Office, *Budget of the United States Government, Analytical Perspectives: Fiscal Year 2002,* Washington, DC, 2001, 510.

19. Snell, *Remedial Education Reform*, Executive Summary.

20. No Child Left Behind Act of 2001, Section 5247, 388.

21. David P. Baker, Motoko Akiba, Gerald K. LeTendre, and Alexander W. Wiseman, "Worldwide Shadow Education: Outside School Learning, Institutional Quality of Schooling, and Cross-National Mathematics Achievement," *Educational Evaluation and Policy Analysis* 23, no. 1 (Washington, DC: American Educational Research Association, Spring 2001): 1–17.

22. Connie Coutellier, "Today's Camps," 1. At http://www.KidsCamps.com [accessed May 16, 2001].

23. Ibid.

24. U.S. General Accounting Office and Health and Human Services Division, *Public Education: Commercial Activities in Schools*, GAO/HEHS OO-156, Washington, DC, September 8, 2000, 26–27.

25. Casey Banas, "Schools Weigh Allegiance to 1 Soda Brand," *Chicago Tribune,* MetroDuPage, April 23, 1998.

26. Alex Molnar and Joseph A. Reaves, *Buy Me! Buy Me!* (Tempe, AZ: Education Policy Studies Laboratory, Arizona State University, September 2001).

27. U.S. General Accounting Office and Health and Human Services Division, *Commercial Activities in Schools,* 15.

28. Kate Zernike, "Coke to Dilute Push in Schools for Its Products," *New York Times*, March 14, 2001.

29. Haar, *The Politics of the PTA,* 14. Like school districts, the National PTA and some of its affiliates are seeking corporate support to supplement their revenues.

30. Constance L. Lays, "Today's Lesson: Soda Rights," *The New York Times,* Business Day, May 21, 1999.

31. "School Administrator Calls for District Principals to Increase Coke Sales," *Not for Sale,* the newsletter of the Center for Commercial-Free Public Education, Winter 1999, 3.

32. Zernike, "Coke to Dilute Push in Schools," 11.

33. U.S. General Accounting Office and Health and Human Services Division, *Commercial Activities in Schools*, 30.

34. Ibid., 31.

35. Governmental Accounting Standards Board, press release, "GASB Expands on Financial Reporting Guidance for Fundraising Foundations and Similar Organizations," May 28, 2002. At www.gasb.org [accessed November 18, 2002].

36. For the National PTA's explanation of its position, which prevailed with the GASB in 1995, see Haar, *The Politics of the PTA*, 10–11.

37. For arguments in favor of restrictions on private spending for public education, see Terry M. Moe, *Schools, Vouchers, and the American Public* (Washington, DC: Brookings Institution Press, 2001). For an argument severely critical of the restrictions, see John L. Merrifield, *The School Choice Wars* (Lanham, MD: Scarecrow Press, 2001).

CHAPTER 6

# Foundation Support for Public Education

In chapter 1, "cost" was defined as a "resource sacrificed or foregone to achieve a specific objective." This definition is not limited to government costs; it is all-inclusive. Here, we focus on foundation contributions to K–12 education. These data are essential if our objective is to understand the resources utilized for K–12 education.

Ostensibly, referring to voluntary contributions as "costs" seems to be a contradiction; if someone gives you a ticket to a football game, your natural reaction is that your ticket to the game was "free." And so it was to you, but the cost of the ticket to the donor was a resource that was essential to the objective, that is, watching the game. This is why contributions to education are economic costs; they are resources "sacrificed or foregone to achieve a specific objective." Who absorbs the cost of the resources is a different issue.

An example may help to clarify the rationale for including foundation contributions to public education. The arts in the United States are supported mainly by private contributions and purchases, but government support is also a factor. If we wish to know whether there is adequate support for the arts, we must take into account both the private and the government contributions. The same principle applies to public education; to assess the adequacy of support, we must include the support from both sectors. In this context, the issue is the amount of resources devoted to public elementary and secondary levels of instruction, not the amounts spent by government or spent at government sites.

## FOUNDATIONS: AN OVERVIEW

As used here, "foundations" are nonprofit, tax-exempt organizations operating under Internal Revenue Service (IRS) regulation 501(c)(3). Foundations must be devoted to charitable purposes, such as improving education or health care. According to the Foundation Center, the nation's leading database on philanthropy, there were more than 56,600 active foundations in the United States in 2002, an increase of more than 6,000 over the number in 2001.[1] In view of the number of foundations, the variations in their charitable objectives, and the differences in their terminology and ways of categorizing their objectives, it is impossible to provide a precise estimate of their support for elementary and secondary education. Nevertheless, there are data that provide useful clues to foundation funding for elementary and secondary education.

Based upon a national sample of foundation grants of $10,000 or more, the Foundation Center reported that foundations made 22,063 grants to "education" in 1999.[2] These grants totaled $2.8 billion and constituted more than 24.4 percent of the value of all foundation grants during that year. Of this $2.8 billion, 15 percent was designated for higher education, 6 percent for elementary and secondary education, and 3.4 percent for assistance that might or might not have gone to both.[3] Assuming that the 3.4 percent was divided equally between precollege and higher education, foundations provided $467,600,000, or 16.7 percent, to higher education, and $215,600,000, or 7.7 percent, to elementary and secondary education.[4] These estimates do not include grants under $10,000, grants to individuals, and nondiscretionary grants of community foundations. They also do not include nongrant projects funded directly by the foundations, instead of through grants to other organizations.

Public schools are the beneficiaries of contributions and support from five kinds of foundations:

- Philanthropic foundations are grant-making organizations active in one or more fields without any inherent geographical restriction. Several of the largest are active worldwide in several different fields, such as education, health care, nutrition, civil rights, and the environment.

- Corporate foundations are 501(c)(3) philanthropic organizations established and controlled by the founding corporations. Corporate foundations are often limited by choice to geographical areas served by the company, fields like safety in which the company has a strong interest, or the welfare of company employees. For example, corporate foundations often provide scholarships to the children of company employees.
- Community foundations are local foundations devoted to a variety of charitable endeavors; however, "local" may be a region, a state, or even a larger area.
- School district foundations are foundations organized and controlled by the school districts they serve. They are very similar to the foundations established and controlled by institutions of higher education.
- Local education foundations (LEFs) are foundations devoted to education but are not controlled by any school district. LEFs solicit funds from government grants, businesses, and individuals and in turn spend the funds on public education.

There is an important distinction between "public" and "private" foundations. To be a public foundation, at least 33 percent of the income must come from the public in the form of memberships, fees, and sales of foundation services. Private foundations are also 501(c)(3) organizations, but less than 33 percent of their income comes from public support. However, private foundations must spend approximately 5 percent of their revenues every year, or they will be subject to penalties by the IRS. The public purpose of the requirement is to avoid larger and larger accumulations of wealth that are not subject to either market discipline or political accountability.

## PHILANTHROPIC FOUNDATIONS

Although all foundations are "philanthropic" in the sense of being nonprofit organizations formally dedicated to charitable causes, the term "philanthropic foundations" is generally applied to grant-making foundations that are not formally affiliated with any other organization. In

2001, 56,600 philanthropic foundations (89.3 percent of all foundations) gave grants of approximately $29 billion to a variety of causes, programs, and institutions.[5] The assets of the five largest foundations ranged from $21.1 billion (Bill and Melinda Gates Foundation) to $9.7 billion (David and Lucile Packard Foundation).[6]

Table 6.1 shows the grants for elementary and secondary education made by the 50 largest U.S. foundations in 2000. Most are philanthropic foundations, but absent a study of their governance structures, we cannot provide a precise breakdown on this issue.

**Table 6.1. Top 50 U.S. Foundations Awarding Grants for Elementary and Secondary Education, circa 2000**

| *Foundation Name* | *State* | *Dollar Amount* | *No. of Grants* |
|---|---|---|---|
| 1. Bill & Melinda Gates Foundation | WA | $276,172,311 | 96 |
| 2. The Annenberg Foundation | PA | 87,739,513 | 64 |
| 3. Walton Family Foundation, Inc. | AR | 47,717,901 | 108 |
| 4. J. A. & Kathryn Albertson Foundation, Inc. | ID | 31,807,323 | 173 |
| 5. The Ford Foundation | NY | 25,411,527 | 62 |
| 6. Wallace-Reader's Digest Funds | NY | 24,669,000 | 19 |
| 7. Lilly Endowment Inc. | IN | 21,675,335 | 12 |
| 8. The Joyce Foundation | IL | 16,478,176 | 43 |
| 9. Ross Family Charitable Foundation | NY | 15,776,306 | 2 |
| 10. The Brown Foundation, Inc. | TX | 14,495,641 | 49 |
| 11. Carnegie Corporation of New York | NY | 13,982,500 | 52 |
| 12. The William and Flora Hewlett Foundation | CA | 12,957,000 | 29 |
| 13. The Skillman Foundation | MI | 12,541,625 | 18 |
| 14. Bank of America Foundation, Inc. | NC | 11,628,650 | 103 |
| 15. W. K. Kellogg Foundation | MI | 10,734,025 | 43 |
| 16. The Freeman Foundation | NY | 10,252,882 | 51 |
| 17. The Spencer Foundation | IL | 10,100,268 | 109 |
| 18. Peninsula Community Foundation | CA | 10,028,259 | 186 |
| 19. The Starr Foundation | NY | 8,974,800 | 83 |
| 20. The Pew Charitable Trusts | PA | 8,546,000 | 23 |
| 21. Robert R. McCormick Tribune Foundation | IL | 8,484,262 | 100 |
| 22. The Edna McConnell Clark Foundation | NY | 8,324,300 | 26 |
| 23. The James Irvine Foundation | CA | 8,232,500 | 16 |
| 24. John D. and Catherine T. MacArthur Fdn. | IL | 8,147,000 | 34 |
| 25. Oberkotter Foundation | PA | 7,993,605 | 21 |
| 26. The Rockefeller Foundation | NY | 7,822,377 | 17 |
| 27. Marin Community Foundation | CA | 7,737,074 | 38 |
| 28. Stuart Foundation | CA | 7,193,692 | 29 |
| 29. The Ahmanson Foundation | CA | 7,186,000 | 85 |
| 30. The David and Lucile Packard Foundation | CA | 6,942,255 | 69 |
| 31. Connelly Foundation | PA | 6,750,131 | 68 |
| 32. The Milken Family Foundation | CA | 6,491,955 | 14 |
| 33. John S. and James L. Knight Foundation | FL | 6,462,000 | 28 |

*(Continued)*

| | | | |
|---|---|---|---|
| 34. Charles Stewart Mott Foundation | MI | 6,336,667 | 35 |
| 35. The Abell Foundation, Inc. | MD | 6,257,509 | 36 |
| 36. The San Diego Foundation | CA | 6,077,737 | 25 |
| 37. Open Society Institute | NY | 5,766,723 | 24 |
| 38. The San Francisco Foundation | CA | 5,546,190 | 80 |
| 39. The Annie E. Casey Foundation | MD | 5,442,640 | 48 |
| 40. The Greater Kansas City Community Foundation and Affiliated Trusts | MO | 5,422,268 | 64 |
| 41. Citigroup Foundation | NY | 5,398,250 | 115 |
| 42. Cisco Systems Foundation | CA | 5,323,570 | 17 |
| 43. Boston Foundation, Inc. | MA | 5,318,752 | 90 |
| 44. The Michael R. Bloomberg Family Foundation Trust | NY | 5,250,000 | 2 |
| 45. The Lynde and Harry Bradley Fdn., Inc. | WI | 5,249,510 | 44 |
| 46. Houston Endowment Inc. | TX | 5,135,000 | 18 |
| 47. The Prudential Foundation | NJ | 5,122,000 | 13 |
| 48. Z. Smith Reynolds Foundation, Inc. | NC | 5,079,110 | 41 |
| 49. The Rhode Island Foundation | RI | 5,065,894 | 40 |
| 50. Howard Heinz Endowment | PA | 5,045,000 | 28 |
| Total | | $862,293,013 | 2,590 |

Note: This table is based on grants of $10,000 or more awarded by a national sample of 1,015 larger U.S. foundations (including 800 of the 1,000 largest ranked by total giving). For community foundations, only discretionary grants are included. Grants to individuals are not included in the file. The search set includes all grants to recipient organizations classified in this topic area and grants to other recipient types for activities classified in this topic area. Grants may therefore be included in more than one topic table; e.g., a grant to a university for its arts program is included in Education, Higher Education, and Arts.

Source: The Foundation Center (copyright 2002).

As a matter of interest, the Carnegie Foundation (1905) and the Ford Foundation (1956) have had a significant impact on precollege education ever since they were founded. This is especially true of the Carnegie Foundation, which was partly responsible in 1905 for establishing the "Carnegie unit," a measure of time in class that is still widely used in the college admissions process. From 1985 to 2000, the Carnegie Foundation was the major source of funding for the National Board for Professional Teaching Standards (NBPTS), a national system for certifying teachers who are presumed to exercise a superior level of skill and knowledge in their teaching field.[7]

In March 2000, Microsoft Chairman Bill Gates and his wife announced a $350 million gift over three years to finance a variety of educational initiatives in 30 school districts nationwide.[8] The goals of the grants include leadership training and technological instruction for superintendents, principals, and teachers. These sizable contributions to public schools followed $500 million committed to public schools by the Annenberg Foundation, and more than $400 million for training superintendents, principals, and teacher union leaders in urban school systems committed since 1999 by the Eli Broad Foundation.[9]

Many foundations do not publish the grants they have made, and even when they do, categorizing them can be problematic. For example, the philanthropic foundations have given very substantial amounts for "civil rights" projects that are education-based or education-related, such as grants to challenge the use of tests that are deemed to discriminate against minorities. In 1999, the top 50 philanthropic foundations gave over $266 million for "civil rights and social action" projects and programs, of which $85,694,544 came from the Ford Foundation in 306 grants.[10] Because of their relationship to education, a significant share of these grants could also be categorized as grants for elementary and secondary education. The leading recipients of foundation largesse are shown in table 6.2.

**Table 6.2. Top 50 Recipients of Foundation Grants for Elementary and Secondary Education, circa 2000**

| *Recipient Organization* | *State* | *Dollar Amount* | *No. of Grants* |
|---|---|---|---|
| 1. Northwest Educational Service District No. 189 | WA | $45,012,830 | 1 |
| 2. Children's Scholarship Fund | NY | 28,865,000 | 24 |
| 3. Alliance for Education | WA | 27,701,000 | 20 |
| 4. Greater Philadelphia First Foundation | PA | 25,300,000 | 1 |
| 5. Coalition of Essential Schools, Bay Area | CA | 18,853,964 | 9 |
| 6. Spokane School District No. 81 | WA | 15,860,000 | 1 |
| 7. Ross School | NY | 15,751,306 | 1 |
| 8. Chicago Annenberg Challenge | IL | 15,400,000 | 4 |
| 9. Institute of Computer Technology | CA | 14,500,000 | 2 |
| 10. New Visions for Public Schools | NY | 13,724,974 | 19 |
| 11. Council of Chief State School Officers | DC | 10,442,500 | 12 |
| 12. Bay Area School Reform Collaborative | CA | 10,315,000 | 6 |
| 13. Rural School and Community Trust | DC | 9,775,000 | 4 |
| 14. United Way of America | VA | 9,000,000 | 1 |
| 15. Evergreen School District | WA | 8,959,808 | 1 |
| 16. School Futures Research Foundation | CA | 8,433,920 | 1 |
| 17. Communities in Schools | VA | 8,411,141 | 19 |
| 18. University of Minnesota Foundation | MN | 8,235,790 | 4 |
| 19. Idaho State Board of Education | ID | 8,186,798 | 13 |
| 20. University of Washington Foundation | WA | 8,032,581 | 6 |
| 21. Harvard University | MA | 7,537,127 | 14 |
| 22. Texas Leadership Center | TX | 7,220,200 | 4 |

*(Continued)*

| | | | |
|---|---|---|---|
| 23. University of Chicago | IL | 7,182,430 | 14 |
| 24. Kennewick School District | WA | 7,030,400 | 1 |
| 25. Academy for Educational Development | DC | 6,922,734 | 2 |
| 26. National Council of La Raza | DC | 6,752,627 | 1 |
| 27. Central Indiana Educational Service Center | IN | 6,615,000 | 1 |
| 28. High Tech High | CA | 6,395,373 | 1 |
| 29. Houston Annenberg Challenge | TX | 6,149,990 | 6 |
| 30. Public Education Network (PEN) | DC | 5,897,648 | 12 |
| 31. Project GRAD | TX | 5,895,000 | 11 |
| 32. Stanford University | CA | 5,664,148 | 5 |
| 33. Milken Community High School of Stephen Wise Temple | CA | 5,513,880 | 1 |
| 34. Florida Department of Education | FL | 5,499,727 | 1 |
| 35. Spence School | NY | 5,380,000 | 7 |
| 36. Foundation for Educational Administration | NJ | 5,100,000 | 1 |
| 37. Center for Collaborative Education-Metro Boston | MA | 5,064,021 | 3 |
| 38. Big Picture Company | RI | 5,051,000 | 6 |
| 39. Developmental Studies Center | CA | 5,049,540 | 8 |
| 40. Switzerland County School Corporation | IN | 5,000,000 | 1 |
| 41. Warren County Metropolitan School District | IN | 5,000,000 | 1 |
| 42. Alaska Council of School Administrators | AK | 4,974,112 | 1 |
| 43. New Technology Foundation | CA | 4,934,800 | 1 |
| 44. Kinkaid School | TX | 4,845,644 | 12 |
| 45. Boston Plan for Excellence in the Public Schools Foundation | MA | 4,790,926 | 14 |
| 46. Schools of the 21st Century Corporation | MI | 4,550,000 | 3 |
| 47. EdVisions | MN | 4,430,000 | 1 |
| 48. Community Studies | NY | 4,405,220 | 3 |
| 49. Bellingham School District No. 501 | WA | 4,326,400 | 1 |
| 50. Washington Department of Public Instruction | WA | 4,284,458 | 3 |
| Total | | $478,224,017 | 289 |

Notes: Elementary and secondary education grants are also included. This table is based on grants of $10,000 or more awarded by a national sample of 1,015 larger U.S. foundations (including 800 of the 1,000 largest ranked by total giving). For community foundations, only discretionary grants are included. Grants to individuals are not included in the file. The search set includes all grants to recipient organizations classified in this topic area and grants to other recipient types for activities classified in this topic area. Grants may therefore be included in more than one topic table; e.g., a grant to a university for its arts program is included in Education, Higher Education, and Arts.

Source: The Foundation Center (copyright 2002).

About 4 of the 50 recipients in table 6.2 are private schools; another 36 are public schools, or public school districts, or pass-throughs for public schools; and about 10 appear to be oriented toward both public and private schools or are uncertain. These figures constitute a major change from the previous year, when 20 of the 50 largest recipients were private schools and 20 were public schools or public school districts.

## CORPORATE FOUNDATIONS

In 2000, 2,018 corporate foundations were 3.5 percent of all active foundations.[11] Their assets of $15.9 billion were 3.2 percent of all foundation assets, and their $3.1 billion giving was 10.8 percent of all foundation giving.[12] In addition, there was a tremendous outpouring of support by corporations and corporate foundations in response to the terrorist attacks on the United States on September 11, 2001. Higher corporate contributions undoubtedly resulted from the robust economic growth in late 1999 that began to decline in 2000. Nevertheless, corporate cash contributions to precollegiate education have been increasing since the publication of *A Nation at Risk* in 1983.

In addition to the contributions by corporate foundations, many corporations make charitable contributions directly from pretax corporation funds, resulting in even larger overall contributions. The American Association of Fundraising Counsel (AAFRC) estimated that Americans (individuals, bequests, corporations, and foundations) donated $212 billion to charity in 2001.[13] During the previous year, more than $28 billion went to education, although the AAFRC report did not estimate the total for pre-college education; however, several other news items indicated that pre-college institutions received a significant amount of the total:

- $18 million from Price Charities (Costco stores) for a teaching and learning laboratory at three San Diego inner-city schools.[14]
- In May 2000, the Toyota USA Foundation announced its approval of grants totaling $790,000 to fund seven education programs designed to improve the teaching of K–12 mathematics and science throughout the United States.[15]
- In 1998, the Albertson Foundation in Boise, Idaho, pledged $110 million in grants to Idaho's 626 public schools—about $176,000 for every one of the state's public schools, or about $22 for each of the 481,176 students in Utah.[16]
- The Gateway Foundation is administering grant applications for its online computer training for 75,000 teachers over the next five years. The goal of its "Teach America" grant program is "to show the nation's K–12 teachers how to make more effective use of technology in the classroom."[17]

- Approximately 100,000 teachers in the United States (300,000 more worldwide) were the beneficiaries of training programs sponsored by Intel Corporation, which donated $100 million, and Microsoft Corporation, which donated 400,000 copies of software (estimated retail value of $344 million).[18]

We have not tried to estimate the value of the corporate services that are contributed to public education, but it is obviously significant in some cases. Since 1994, the International Business Machines Corporation (IBM) has invested $70 million for "improving children's academic performance and upgrading teacher training, providing new ways to use technology to link schools and homes, and developing more effective professional and classroom tools for teachers."[19] In addition to grants, IBM reported, "On any given day, there are 30 or 40 people in the IBM research lab working on solving problems in Reinventing Education projects," such as rewriting "Learning Village," an IBM software tool used by schools in IBM's Reinventing Education program.[20] Due to the absence of data, however, it is impossible to quantify the value of its contributed services as distinguished from its investment in entrepreneurial activities.

Although corporate foundations are also 501(c)(3) organizations that are frequently active in precollege education, their grants tend to be noncontroversial. The parent corporations want to foster favorable attitudes toward the corporation and/or its products or services. Promoting educational reforms that antagonize a sizable number of potential customers has a negative effect on this objective. Furthermore, many corporate foundations are limited to geographical areas in which the foundations conduct business, or to a limited group of beneficiaries, such as corporate employees.

## COMMUNITY FOUNDATIONS

Community foundations typically support activities in more than one field. They are an especially useful funding mechanism for corporations that wish to support philanthropic projects, but do not want to establish their own corporate foundation for doing so. Like public school foundations, community foundations support projects that serve specific communities, but "communities" may include regions or even entire states. Unlike the practice in school district foundations, boards of directors of community foundations are recruited from civic and business leaders in the areas served by the foundations and are independent of the school districts they serve.

The Foundation Center reported that 560 community foundations, with assets of $30.4 billion, distributed $2.2 billion to recipients in 1999.[21] We have not tried to estimate community foundation contributions to public education; the difficulty of ascertaining their contributions to public education rendered the effort impractical. The overall amount is probably not very large in the total picture, but it is undoubtedly very important in some of the recipient districts.

## SCHOOL DISTRICT FOUNDATIONS

School district foundations are growing in importance as a significant source of school district revenue; the number of school district foundations is increasing rapidly, as are the amounts they raise for public schools.[22] These amounts cannot be evaluated solely on the basis of their magnitude. Because the foundations have more discretionary funds than the schools they support, the foundations are able to utilize their funds in ways that are not available to the recipient school districts.

School district educational foundations, in which some control is exercised by the school district, are not easily distinguished from local education foundations (LEFs). LEFs provide community support to local schools and school districts. Nevertheless, LEFs are not necessarily affiliated with a school district. Some studies refer to school district foundations and local education foundations simply as school foundations. A 1998 study estimated that there were more than 2,000 LEFs nationwide, but the number is undoubtedly much higher in 2003.[23]

Two events triggered the growth of public school foundations in California, where they are widely utilized. First, in 1971, in *Serrano vs. Priest,* the California Supreme Court directed the state legislature to establish and implement a school finance system that would ensure that all public school expenditures per pupil were within $100 of the state-determined average base revenue limit. The base revenue limit is the amount of general-purpose revenue each school district receives from state funds and local property taxes. Base revenue limits are established legislatively every year and most are funded through a combination of state funds and local property taxes.[24] The second event was the 1983 passage of Proposition 13, an initiative that set school district property taxes according to a state formula. With the state formula in place, the state provided the additional revenue necessary to bring the district to its revenue limit for the basic per-pupil state aid. Statewide, each school district's revenue was increased by the same dollar amount per pupil.[25] The result was that affluent school districts could not generate much more tax revenue per pupil than poor districts; however, to take advantage of their greater wealth, the affluent districts often established foundations to provide a tax-deductible way to contribute resources to the districts.[26] As often happens, many affluent California school boards opposed the idea of achieving funding equality by leveling down what they could spend on their schools. Of particular concern was the distribution of categorical aid for meeting the special needs of some schools and districts. Only noncategorical aid is included in the state revenue limit.[27]

By 1987, California had 122 active public school foundations, a considerable increase from the 40 school foundations that existed in 1981–82.[28] A study of 113 local education foundations in California concluded that in 1987–88 "most foundations successful in the amounts raised per pupil in average daily attendance are located in small, affluent communities and support elementary [school] districts."[29] Of the 113 foundations sampled in that study, one foundation raised enough to increase the cost per pupil in average daily attendance ($5,266 in 1987) by $544, another $503, and still another raised $407 over the government-allocated cost per pupil. All but 13 foundations contributed less than $100 to the per-pupil cost in average daily attendance.[30]

In 1992, 323 California school district education foundations had net revenues of more than $29 million during the 1992 tax year.[31] When added to the net revenue contributed from other school-based fundraising organizations, discussed later in this chapter, a total of $97 million was contributed to California public schools, an average per-pupil contribution of approximately $19 for each of California's 5.1 million students in public schools in 1992.[32] When the $97 million is attributed only to the schools for which the funds were raised, the amount raised per elementary student was $98, and $48 for junior and senior high students.[33]

Of the 1,001 school districts in California in 2001, 500 had at least one educational foundation; cumulatively, these foundations raised more than $55 million statewide to help finance public education.[34] The richest school district foundation in Los Angeles County raised the equivalent of almost $400 per student districtwide; meanwhile many other school districts in the county did not even have a school district foundation. Although the Los Angeles Unified School District (LAUSD) tries to limit spending differences between its schools to no more than $200 per student, funding inequalities have continued in that district and elsewhere in Los Angeles County and the state. In Pasadena, a nonprofit group raised more than $1 million and helped win grants that generated $6 million more for Pasadena's public schools in 2000. Other foundations in the county raised $153 per student in Beverly Hills, $145 in Manhattan Beach, and $15 in Culver City.[35]

Because California was the first state to experience widespread establishment of school district foundations, and leads the nation in the number of school district foundations, the data from California may presage developments elsewhere on the subject. One striking fact about California school district foundations is that they appear to raise more revenue for schools than other types of nonprofit organizations. In 1992 California LEFs raised $28.9 million, PTAs $27.7 million, and booster clubs $19.3 million.[36]

Michigan, as well as other states and the federal government, has adopted a school-aid formula that favors school districts with large concentrations of children from low-income families.[37] At the same time, however, school districts in Michigan that have established foundations also tend to be better funded than nonfoundation districts; at least, that was one of the conclusions reached in a 1999 study of 153 school district foundations in Michigan.[38] In Michigan, "local education foundations were generally found in mostly white suburban and rural school districts . . . and averaged a mere $17,024 in 1994–95 among districts responding to the survey."[39] Wayne State University professor Michael F. Addonizio, who conducted the survey, speculates that "the rise of local educational foundations in relatively high-expenditure and high-income districts may offset, to some degree, the equity effects of the state's school aid system."[40]

In contrast, there is already a "tremendous disparity in spending among districts" in New York.[41] According to a study in 2001, the recent development of school district foundations—which supplement school revenues by $17 per pupil—"exacerbate, albeit to a very small degree, an already highly inequitable school finance system."[42]

The potential of public school foundations is evident from their development in higher education. Interestingly enough, several corporate philanthropic foundations are modifying their historic emphasis on higher education in favor of supporting education below the college level. For example, executives at the Estee Lauder Companies, Inc., donated $1 million to the Bronx High School of Science in New York City. In April 1998, the Brooklyn (New York) Technical High School announced its campaign to raise an endowment fund of $10 million.[43] And in 2000, the historic Boston Latin School announced its fundraising goal of $60 million, the most ambitious financial crusade of any public school in the nation.[44]

The University Laboratory High School, a public high school affiliated with the University of Illinois, raises almost half of its annual budget ($2,727,000 in 2001–02) from alumni and parents. State aid allocated on the same basis as for other public schools also accounts for almost half, and about $500,000 is from foundation grants. By August 2001, the University High Foundation had raised $420,000 toward its endowment goal of $2 million. At the reunion of University High's class of 1952, it announced gifts of $500,000, $250,000, and another commitment of $50,000, all from the class of 1952.[45] From its inception, the University High Foundation had been assisted by the University of Illinois Foundation, one of the leading public university foundations in the United States.

Although the total number of school district foundations and their resources cannot be ascertained precisely, their growth is impressive.[46] Guidestar is an online (http://www.guidestar.com) research organization that provides financial information on more than 700,000 501(c)(3) organizations. Using "school district foundation" as the keyword, Guidestar's search engine turned up 163 responses; "school foundation" brought up 866 when accessed July 20, 2001. The vast majority were public school district foundations. Obviously, these two searches did not exhaust all of the titles and not all public school foundations are registered with Guidestar. Furthermore, many of the organizations that support public education are unincorporated and need not report to the Internal Revenue Service if their gross annual receipts are less than $25,000. Except in smaller school districts, the districts without foundations may soon be exceptions instead of the common practice.

## THE PUBLIC EDUCATION NETWORK (PEN) AND LOCAL EDUCATION FUNDS (LEFs)

In contrast to school district foundations, the Public Education Network (PEN) and its affiliated Local Education Funds (LEFs) are education assistance and reform organizations that are not controlled by the school districts they serve. Although there were a few local education funds prior to the 1980s, the number of such funds and the amounts they have raised for public education have been increasing steadily. Since 1980, the Ford Foundation has provided most of the seed money needed to launch LEFs, and in 1987 it was instrumental in launching the Public Education Network (PEN). Referring to itself as the largest independent school reform organization, PEN strives to "create positive, lasting change in public schools."[47] Essentially, PEN is a national organization comprised of local education foundations established to improve public education in their geographical areas. Although most LEFs serve only one school district, several serve multiple districts, and the West Virginia affiliate serves the entire state. Based in the District of Columbia, PEN is governed by a 20-member board of directors, drawn largely from foundations, LEFs, and nonprofit organizations with a similar emphasis on public education. In 2002, PEN employed 31 staff members to carry out its agenda.

LEFs work with public school systems, especially urban school districts with a significant population of disadvantaged students. As of November 2002, PEN reported that 77 LEFs were operating in 30 states and the District of Columbia, serving "more than 8.9 million children in 12,600 schools in over 500 school districts in high poverty areas."[48] Many local education funds serve more than one school district; for example,

Denver's Public Education and Business Coalition serves 57 schools in eight districts.[49] Funds are raised and spent locally for mini-grants for teachers, parent and citizen involvement, academic enhancements, technology access, reading/writing improvement, student counseling, professional development, technical assistance, and other programs deemed beneficial to schools and/or entire school districts. Some LEFs even create community coalitions to support school bond campaigns.

In the 1990s, PEN affiliates dramatically increased their fundraising for public school programs. Generally speaking, the larger the school district, the more likely it is to have a local education fund. In 1998, PEN reported that LEFs in its network serve "nearly 5 million children in more than 250 school districts."[50] In 2001, the Ford Foundation, a longtime donor to foundations for public education, estimated that "[local education] funds have funneled more than a billion dollars" to nearly 300 school districts since the early 1980s.[51] In 1999, LEFs served districts that enrolled approximately 11.4 percent of the 46.3 million pupils then in U.S. public schools. About half of the students in PEN districts were eligible for free or reduced-price lunches, and more than 70 percent were children of color.

LEFs sponsor or participate in a variety of programs (300 in 2001), most of which are "local partnerships." The partnerships are between school districts and various community groups, national reform organizations, vendors to school districts, and other local entities interested in efforts to improve public education. PEN distributes most of its revenues to LEFs, but the LEFs raise most of their funds locally from their own efforts. Excluding endowments, their total budgets in 1997 were approximately $52 million, received from the sources shown in table 6.3. Table 6.4 shows the ways in which LEFs spent the $60 million they raised in 1999.

In 1999, 47 LEFs employed 505 employees; only 4 of the 47 did not employ a full-time staff member. The LEF budgets comprised less than 1 percent of their districts' budgets, but the percentages are likely to increase, as they have since the formation of LEFs in 1983. In general, the revenues and staff fluctuated with the size of the district. Regardless of the amounts, however, LEF funds are significant because they can bypass school district bureaucracies and procedures when that would be necessary to implement their proposed changes. The amounts

**Table 6.3. Sources of Funding for LEFs**

| *Source of Funds for LEFs Affiliated with PEN* | *Percent* |
|---|---|
| Foundations, including PEN | 42 |
| Government agencies | 20 |
| Corporations | 17 |
| Other private sources | 10 |
| Individual donors | 8 |
| Miscellaneous | 3 |
| Total | 100 |

Source: Elizabeth Useem, *Local Education Funds: What They Do, How They Do It, and the Difference They Make,* Public Education Network, 1998, 3.

are significant in some school districts and will be in more districts in the future as foundations and business donors pay more attention to elementary and secondary education. Obviously, LEFs underscore the importance of examining district revenues and costs on a district-by-district basis; comparisons of local district costs to state and/or national averages can be very misleading.

LEFs also pose the danger of double-counting school district costs. For example, in 2000–01, 33 foundations, corporations, and federal government agencies donated $27 million to PEN; in turn, PEN distributed $19 million to LEFs through grants from those funds.[52] Not all funds are

**Table 6.4. LEF Allocations to Programming in 1999**

| *Program* | *Percentage of Combined Resources* |
|---|---|
| Teacher professional development | 20.6 |
| Parent/family involvement | 11.7 |
| Public engagement/advocacy | 10.7 |
| Literacy/reading development | 7.3 |
| Administrator/leadership training | 6.8 |
| School to career | 6.3 |
| Technology and education | 5.9 |
| Content standards | 3.2 |
| Higher education participation | 2.9 |
| School accountability | 2.8 |
| School finance | 2.5 |
| Dropout prevention | 2.2 |
| School-health integration | 2.0 |
| Education and race | 1.0 |
| Student assessment | 1.0 |
| Other | 23.5 |

Source: Findings from the *PEN Annual Survey 1999*, p. 3.

distributed at once; planning grants, followed by an assessment of program effectiveness, are often a prerequisite to subsequent funding. Nevertheless, PEN/LEF revenues often follow this path: Ford Foundation (or a different philanthropic foundation) provides grants to PEN, which then makes grants to LEFs from the grant. The grants from PEN have ranged from $30,000 over three years to $1.9 million over three years.[53] Only the foundation grant to PEN or the PEN grants to LEFs therefrom should be counted as costs or contributions to public education.[54]

## SUMMARY

Perhaps the most important conclusion to be drawn from the foregoing discussion is that evaluations of school district efficiency that do not consider the contributions and the costs absorbed by nongovernment parties will often lead to erroneous results. Another key issue hopefully resolved by GASB Statements Nos. 14 and 34 is the extent to which government statistics on the costs of education should show third-party contributions or absorptions of costs. Still another is whether public policy should restrict contributions that exacerbate fiscal inequity among school districts and among schools within districts. Finally, it must be emphasized that external pressure was necessary to bring about more accurate reporting of private costs. This situation is likely to prevail in school districts as a result of GASB requirements and perhaps of increasing foundation scrutiny. In July 2002, three well-respected Pittsburgh foundations discontinued their grantmaking to the Pittsburgh public schools they had previously supported with combined donations of over $11.7 million in the last five years.[55] Foundation officials cited "a sharp decline of governance, leadership and fiscal discipline."[56]

It remains to be seen whether the developments in Pittsburgh were an isolated incident or part of a trend toward increased accountability in philanthropic contributions to K–12 education.

## NOTES

1. Steven Lawrence, Foundation Center press release, "Foundation Center Releases New Report on Grantmaking Resources in 2000 and Beyond," June 2002.

2. Foundation Center, "Distribution of Foundation Grants by Subject Categories, circa 1999." At http://fdncenter.org/fc_stats/pdf/04_fund_sub/1999/10_99.pdf [accessed November 12, 2002].

3. Ibid.

4. Foundation Center Statistical Services, *Foundation Giving Trends* (Washington, DC: Foundation Center, 2001). At http://www.fdncenter.org [accessed November 12, 2002].

5. Loren Renz and Steven Lawrence, *Foundation Growth and Giving Estimates: 2001 Preview* (Washington, DC: Foundation Center, 2002), 6.

6. Ibid., 7.

7. This NBPTS claim has been vigorously challenged. See Dale Ballou and Michael Podgursky, *Teacher Pay and Teacher Quality* (Kalamazoo, MI: Upjohn Institute, 1997). However, Ballou and Podgursky agree that NBPTS is a significant innovation in terms of its prominence and the resources devoted to it.

8. Sam Howe Verhovek, "Gates Foundation $350 Million to Education Programs Over the Next 3 Years," *The New York Times,* March 1, 2000, A20.

9. The Broad Foundation at http://www.broadfoundation.org/employment/assocdir.shtml [accessed November 7, 2002].

10. Foundation Center, "Top 50 Foundations Awarding Grants for Civil Rights and Social Action, circa 1999." At http://fdncenter.org/fc_stats/pdf/04_fund_sub/1999/50_found_sub/sub_r_99.pdf [accessed November 12, 2002].

11. Renz and Lawrence, *Foundation Growth*, 6.

12. Ibid., 5.

13. American Association of Fundraising Counsel press release, "Charitable Giving Reaches $212 Billion," 1-2. At http://www.aafrc.org/press3.html [accessed November 12, 2002].

14. Louis James, "Improving Education? Donated Millions Poured into Public Schools with Few Results," *Foundation Watch* (Washington, DC: Capital Research Center, September 2000): 2.

15. "Corporate Giving," *Philanthropy News Digest* 6, no. 18, May 2, 2000.

16. Andrew Trotter, "$80 Million Gift to Boost Technology in Idaho Schools," *Education Week* 17, no. 38 (June 3, 1998): 6.

17. "Private Funding Initiatives Provide Big Grants for Education," *School Improvement Report*, June 2000, 6.

18. Andrew Trotter, "Intel, Microsoft to Launch Major Training Program for Teachers," *Education Week* 19, no. 20 (January 26, 2000): 5.

19. Andrew Trotter, "Reporter's Notebook: IBM Invests Millions More in 'Reinventing Education,'" *Education Week* 20, no. 41 (June 20, 2001): 16.

20. Andrew Trotter, "IBM Attracts Praise for 'Reinventing Education,'" *Education Week* 20, no. 16 (January 10, 2001): 16.

21. Renz and Lawrence, *Foundation Growth*, 6.

22. Brian O. Brent, "Expanding Support through District Education Foundations: A Tale of Two States." Paper presented at the annual conference of the American Education Finance Association, Albuquerque, NM, March 2002, 6.

23. P. deLuna, "Local Education Foundations: Right for Many Schools," *Phi Delta Kappan* 79, no. 5 (1998): 385–389.

24. Judith Ann Adams, "The Effect of Local Education Foundations upon Fiscal and Program Equity in Selected Districts in the State of California" (Ed.D. diss., University of Colorado at Denver, 1991), 20.

25. Eric Brunner and Jon Sonstelie, "Coping with Serrano: Voluntary Contributions to California's Local Public Schools," 4. A shorter version of this paper was published in *Proceedings of the 89th Annual Conference on Taxation, National Tax Association* (Syracuse, NY, 1997), 372–381.

26. Adams, "Effect of Local Education Foundations," 138.

27. Brunner and Sonstelie, "Coping with Serrano," 6.

28. Adams, "Effect of Local Education Foundations," 46.

29. Ibid., iv.

30. Ibid., 136.

31. Brunner and Sonstelie, "Coping with Serrano," 13.

32. Ibid., 14.

33. Ibid., 15.

34. See Sue Fox, "Private Fund-Raising for Schools Runs Gamut," *Los Angeles Times*, April 15, 2001. At http:www.latimes.com/cgi-bin/print.cgi [accessed April 16, 2001].

35. Ibid.

36. Ron Zimmer et al., *Private Giving to Public Schools and Districts in Los Angeles County* (Santa Monica, CA: Rand, 2001), 88. Although devoted mainly to private giving to school districts in three Los Angeles counties, the Rand study is a good overview of private giving to public schools and school districts. See also Brunner and Sonstelie, "Coping with Serrano."

37. U.S. General Accounting Office, *School Finance: State and Federal Efforts to Target Poor Students*, GAO/HEHS-98-36, Washington, DC, January 1998.

38. Michael F. Addonizio, "New Revenues for Public Schools: Alternatives to Broad-Based Taxes," in *Selected Papers in School Finance*, 1997–1999, (Washington, DC: National Center for Education Statistics, 1999).

39. Ibid., 9.

40. Ibid., 9.

41. Brent, "District Education Foundations," 7.

42. Ibid., 21.

43. "News in Brief, a National Roundup," *Education Week*, June 17, 1998, 4.

44. Pamela Ferdinand, "True to Their Public High Schools," *Washington Post,* March 1, 2000.

45. Dave Porreca, "Spouse of Late Alum Virginia Downs Borem, '31, Doubles Uni Endowment," *Alum Uni* 6, no.1 (Fall/Winter 2000–01): 4. The school has a fundraising operation that many colleges would envy.

46. Kathy Mickey, in "Foundations Play Role in Schools' Computer Programs," reported that nationally, foundations have been established in about 20 percent of the country's 16,000 school districts, (NY) *Journal News*, July 18, 2000. Brent in "District Education Foundation" estimated there were 4,000 school foundations, 1.

47. Public Education Network, *Annual Report 1998,* Washington, DC, 1998, 17.

48. Public Education Network [at-a-glance], Washington, DC, November 2002, 1.

49. Beth A. Brophy, "Powerful Allies: Local Education Funds as 'Conveners and Brokers' for School Reform," *Ford Foundation Report*, Spring 2001, 31–33.

50. Public Education Network, *Annual Report*, 16.

51. Brophy, "Funds as Conveners and Brokers," 31.

52. PEN, 2001 *Year in Review,* Washington, DC, 4.

53. Public Education Network at http://www.publiceducation.org/about [accessed July 11, 2001].

54. Data on PEN and its LEFs are taken from Public Education Network, *Public Education Funds: A Report on the Public Education Network and Findings from the Annual Members Survey, 1999*, Washington, DC: Public Education Network, 2000.

55. Carmen J. Lee and Jane Elizabeth, "Foundations Yank City School Grants," *Pittsburgh Post-Gazette,* July 10, 2002. At http://80-web.lexis-nexis.com [accessed November 14, 2002].

56. Ibid.

CHAPTER 7

# Public School Costs in Higher-Education Budgets

This chapter and the next are devoted to a discussion of government costs that are not included, or not included completely, in conventional summaries of the costs of public education. Some examples may help to clarify our rationale for these chapters.

- School district A pays professor X at university Y to provide in-service training for district teachers on released time at district facilities.
- School district B employs professor X to provide the same instruction, but X is paid from state, not district, funds for his work.
- Teachers in school district A individually pay university Y for a course taught by professor X; the course includes the same contents as are included in the previous examples. The teachers receive salary credit for the course, but the school district does not pay anything to professor X.
- Teachers in school district A are paid stipends to take a summer course from professor X paid for by the National Science Foundation (NSF).

In the examples set forth, teachers receive instruction in the same content from the same instructor, but the cost of instruction is paid for by four different sources. From an economic point of view, the same resources are utilized to pay for the same service, but the different ways of paying for the service have different implications for the government cost of public education. The problem is how to treat these situations so as to present a consistent approach to the costs of public education.

Essentially, this chapter and the next are devoted to the costs of public education that are carried on the budgets of other public agencies. This chapter is devoted to the costs of public education that are conventionally treated as costs of higher education. Three major categories of the costs of public education absorbed by institutions of higher education can be identified:

- The costs of teacher education. As used here, "teacher education" includes preparation for managerial and/or supervisory as well as teaching positions in public schools.
- The costs of educational research and development on K–12 matters.
- The costs of remedial instruction at K–12 levels.

## THE COSTS OF TEACHER EDUCATION

Our threshold question is whether teacher education is a cost of public education. We divide this question into two parts: The cost of preemployment education and the cost of teacher education during employment.

As a practical matter, the cost of preemployment training for a specific occupation is ordinarily absorbed by the trainees and/or the future employers of the trainees. Other things being equal, the longer the training period, the more employers must pay for the services of the trainees. Training to be a physician, including four years of premedical education, extends over an eight-year period; this is one of the reasons why physicians are paid more than nurses, whose preemployment training is four years or less. Health maintenance organizations (HMOs) aside, the physicians' employers are the patients or HMOs who utilize their services; the fees must be large enough to compensate physicians for the expenses of medical education, as well as eight years of foregone income. Other factors, such as the talent level involved, strongly affect physician compensation, but the duration of professional education is one of the most important.

A bachelor's degree is the norm for beginning teachers. From then on, the vast majority of U.S. teachers are paid solely on the basis of their years of service and the amount of college and university credit they have received. School districts vary in how much they pay for seniority and academic credit, but very few districts pay teachers on any other basis; however, teachers do not pay the full costs of their professional education. In 1996–97, tuition and fees accounted for only 19.0 percent of the revenues of the two- and four-year degree-granting public universities, and 27.9 percent of the revenues of the private two- and four-year degree-granting ones.[1] Of course, the student share of the cost for the entire institution does not apply equally to all academic and professional programs; the student share will be higher in some and lower in others.

Teacher education programs tend to cost less per student. Nevertheless, some institutions of higher education are able to generate a surplus, the equivalent of profits, on their teacher education programs. Interestingly enough, taxpayers paid for 16.7 percent of the revenues of private universities in 1996–97.[2] Although the costs of teacher education programs in degree-granting universities vary considerably, clearly there is a significant amount of government support for teacher education programs in private as well as public institutions.

In-service teacher education certainly is a cost if we follow the common private-sector practice of treating training costs as a cost of the enterprise. For example, IBM spends tens of millions annually for training its employees. Airlines pay the costs of training pilots and mechanics to work in new kinds of airplanes. Automobile companies do the same for training mechanics on their new models. Among department stores, the cost of training salespersons, whether newly employed or longtime employees, is a cost of doing business. The U.S. Department of Defense pays the training costs for everyone in the armed services after induction. Ordinarily, a new soldier's first assignment is to undertake a lengthy training program. In these and countless other occupations, the costs of occupation-specific training are absorbed by the person or enterprise that utilizes the training.

We do not take a position on the extent to which governments at various levels should subsidize teacher education. This is an important but much-neglected issue, as is the broader issue of the extent to which governments should subsidize occupation-specific education generally. Generally speaking, government support for occupation-specific education in the U.S. has been the result of political pressure by interest groups that want government to subsidize education for certain occupations. Be that as it may, our focus here is on the costs of teacher education, regardless of its professional utility.

There are several ways to estimate the costs of teacher education in higher education. All involve difficult problems and a substantial range of error. One way is to determine the number of professors of education (including the ranks below full professor) employed in U.S. institutions of higher education. The American Association of Colleges of Teacher Education (AACTE) is the national organization of the schools of education in the U.S. In 2000, its member institutions, comprising approximately 70 percent of all teacher education programs in the U.S., employed "professional education staff" as follows:

19,061 full-time education faculty
6,878 part-time education faculty, full-time institution faculty
18,061 part-time education faculty only[3]

If the above numbers are adjusted upward to reflect the fact that only 70 percent of all teacher education programs was included in the AACTE/NCATE Joint Data Survey, we get the following results:

| | 70% | 100% (estimated) | FTEs |
|---|---|---|---|
| Full-time education | 19,061 | 27,030 | 27,030 |
| Part-time education, full-time institution faculty | 6,878 | 9,826 | 3,275* |
| Part-time education only | 18,061 | 25,800 | 8,600* |
| | | Total FTEs | 38,905 |

*Three part-time = one FTE (full-time equivalent)

Although popular opinion equates "education courses" with courses on pedagogy, that is, methods and techniques of teaching, the education faculty devoted to teaching methods courses constitutes less than one-half of the full-time faculty in education, and two-thirds of the part-time faculty. In the state universities, which generally support the largest schools of education, the other subjects offered by education faculty include graduate and upper-level undergraduate courses in the following:

- Curriculum
- Educational psychology

- School finance
- Preparation of principals (elementary, middle school, secondary)
- Preparation and training of superintendents (including deputy, associate, and assistant superintendents)
- Preparation of curriculum directors and subject matter specialists (mathematics, science, special education, reading, etc.)
- Tests and measurements
- School transportation
- School construction
- Management of school facilities
- School services, e.g., food services
- Legal issues and problems
- Collective bargaining with unions of school district personnel
- Human resource management
- School bonding issues
- Ethnic issues, such as Afrocentric curricula
- Multicultural education
- Extracurricular activities, e.g., athletics, plays, clubs
- Philosophy of education
- The politics of education

As noted above, many education courses are devoted to managerial education, including the education of superintendents, business managers, curriculum directors, other central office personnel, principals, and assistant principals. The costs of this training are included in the costs of teacher education faculties, so we do not count these costs as an additional item.

The amounts paid for faculty salaries and benefits are by no means the total government expenditures for teacher education by institutions of higher education. To the costs of salaries and benefits of education faculty, we must add the costs of teaching facilities, administrative personnel and facilities, office space, libraries, secretaries, graduate assistants, custodians, librarians, supplies, equipment, communications, travel—the list goes on and on.

In applying for federal grants in education, institutions of higher education are allowed a percentage of their direct costs for overhead. Most institutions claim that their overhead costs are from 30 to 60 percent of their direct costs in implementing federally funded projects. Their direct costs include secretarial/clerical help, travel and per diem, copying, publications, communications, supplies, equipment, consultants, and rent, in addition to the salaries and benefits of project personnel. Consequently, their overhead percentage would be much higher if it is based solely upon the salaries and benefits of project staff. We have estimated noncompensation costs to be twice as much as the costs of salaries plus benefits for education faculty.

The following adjustments are treated as a wash in our calculations of costs. One is the tuition paid for graduate and undergraduate education courses. The state legislatures and cities appropriate various amounts to their institutions of higher education to make them more affordable. Nationwide, in 1996–97, tuition and fees accounted for $24.7 billion (19 percent) of the $130 billion revenues of degree-granting public institutions of higher education.[4] In addition, income from philanthropic foundations, alumni organizations, endowments, and other nontax sources of revenue amounted to $6.3 billion, 4.8 percent of the $130 billion in revenues. The government's share of the revenues from teacher education was approximately 25 percent of the expenditures.

Another adjustment is necessary, because teacher education typically costs less than most other professional programs; little or no special equipment is needed and large classes are often possible. However, counter-considerations include the fact that a substantial percentage of education courses are at the graduate levels, where academic salaries tend to be higher and class sizes tend to be lower than at the undergraduate level. On the other hand, most departments, schools, or colleges of education operate full-time in the summer, whereas this is seldom the case in other professional programs in higher education. Year-round operation obviously supports a higher overhead rate than an academic year operation.

To simplify the discussion, we have treated the costs of faculty members who are not based in the departments of education but who nevertheless teach or conduct research on public school matters as equal to the costs of education faculty members who do not focus on public school issues. Undoubtedly, these adjustments do not precisely offset each other, but treating them here as offsetting should bring us closer to the reality, whatever that turns out to be.

How much are education faculty paid? Although the average salary for all institutions and all fields excluding medicine in 1999–2000 was $56,308 in private and $58,313 in public institutions, the averages for professors of education were less than the average for all faculty, as shown in table 7.1.

We have not adjusted the figures to take account of the number of faculty in each specialty, either within schools of education or externally, but we have made an adjustment to take into account the fact that twice as many public as private institutions responded in the *Chronicle of Higher Education*'s survey on faculty salaries. Consequently, our final average salary for all education professors is $51,103. Assuming that private institutions of higher education prepare about one-tenth of the nation's teachers, we have reduced 38,905 by 10 percent to 35,015, the total number of FTE education faculty at public institutions of higher education. However, because this average salary of $51,103 does not include fringe benefits, we have arbitrarily increased the salary average by 25 percent, which we regard as a conservative estimate of the costs of fringe benefits in higher education. The results are some rather large numbers, as shown in table 7.2.

**Table 7.1. Estimated Compensation of Professors of Education**

| *Field of Specialization* | *In Private Colleges and Universities* | *In Public Colleges and Universities* |
|---|---|---|
| Counselor education | $54,045 | $52,661 |
| Curriculum and instruction | 52,735 | 50,535 |
| Education | 49,137 | 54,369 |
| Educational administration and supervision | 55,249 | 56,221 |
| General teacher education | 44,348 | 50,802 |
| Health and physical education | 44,310 | 48,713 |
| Reading teacher education | 47,184 | 51,878 |
| Special education | 47,619 | 52,978 |
| Teacher education, specific academic and vocational programs | 46,840 | 49,893 |
| Technology and industrial arts | — | 53,237 |

Source: *The Chronicle of Higher Education*, May 12, 2000, A20.

**Table 7.2. Estimated Taxpayer Cost of Teacher Education**

| *Estimated Taxpayer Cost* | *Type of Teacher Education* |
|---|---|
| $35,015 | FTE education faculty employed by public colleges and universities |
| 63,879 | Average salary ($51,103) + fringe benefits ($12,776) at 25% of salary |
| 2.24 billion | Salaries and benefits of education faculty in public institutions of higher education |
| 4.48 billion | All other expenditures for teacher education in public institutions |
| 6.72 billion | Total for 1999–2000 |

Source: *The Chronicle of Higher Education,* May 12, 2000, A20.

## WHO PAYS FOR TEACHER EDUCATION?

In some respects, government support for in-service teacher education follows the pattern of support for pre-service professional education. Teachers absorb some of the costs through tuition and fees, and school districts pay teachers higher salaries based on the amount of academic credit amassed by the teachers. In the private sector, however, the employers usually pay more of the cost of in-service training. One reason is that private-sector employers usually benefit from the training that they subsidize, and do not subsidize it otherwise. Although school districts sometimes pay tuition and fees for teachers seeking additional academic credit, the usual practice is for teachers to pay the tuition, fees, and incidental expenses of in-service courses, with the districts paying higher salaries as the teachers receive additional credit. Inasmuch as the cost of graduate teacher education programs is partly subsidized by government, students need to pay less than the real cost of their graduate work, and do not require as much payment by school districts to be compensated for the costs of their graduate courses.

To illustrate, suppose the cost of an education course in a public university is $10,000, and the state appropriations reduce the cost to the university by $5,000. Consequently, the university need charge students only enough tuition to recoup $5,000, and the higher salaries paid to teachers taking the course need compensate them for only $5,000 of out-of-pocket costs.

Note that taxpayer support of teacher education is present in both public and private institutions, and for in-service as well as pre-service programs. Parenthetically, school districts frequently do not exercise close control over the kind of course work that receives salary credit. In fact, teachers frequently receive salary credit for courses that are convenient and inexpensive, courses that prepare teachers to be school administrators, or courses that prepare teachers to enter an occupation outside the field of education. It is doubtful that many private companies pay for in-service education that prepares the trainee to leave the company.

Generally speaking, the higher the tuition, the lower the percentage of students in the teacher education programs. Ivy League institutions graduate few students who become public school teachers.

## EDUCATIONAL RESEARCH

A 1998 study indicates that the education professoriat devoted 11.1 percent of its time to educational research.[5] As is generally the case in other disciplines, the faculty teaching load typically reflects the research expectations of the institution; however, in the field of education, on average, full-time instructional faculty work ten hours per week in classroom instruction.[6] In universities with strong graduate schools, faculty usually teach one or two courses per week, usually meeting once a week for two to three hours. At the other extreme, faculty in community colleges teach 12 hours or more per week, and significant research is not expected. The reality is, however, that in graduate schools of education, as in graduate schools generally, professors often overestimate the amount of their time devoted to research. The more time they devote to research (which cannot be monitored), the less time they can be required to teach or perform other professorial duties that can be monitored.

Efforts to increase federal expenditures for educational research and development illustrate the practical importance of the issue. Every year, the American Educational Research Association (AERA) urges larger federal appropriations for educational research and development. Its assumptions are that funding for educational research consists largely of the amounts spent for it by the federal government, and that the industry percentage of expenditures for educational research and development is far below the percentages for this purpose in other industries. These assumptions, however, do not take into account the released time for educational research in institutions of higher education, public and private, or the amounts contributed or spent by philanthropic foundations and for-profit companies. When such released time is taken into account, the expenditures for educational R & D are much greater than is acknowledged by the proponents of increased expenditures for it. If total spending for educational research and development is substantial, there may be no reason to increase the government's share, even though it contributes only a small portion of the total. The issue here is not whether there should be more or less funding for educational R & D; our point is that more accurate and more complete information on the issue is needed.

Parenthetically, we note that the educational researchers frequently cite the situation in the pharmaceutical industry, in which some large companies spend over 20 percent of their revenues for research and development. These references, however, never suggest that educational research should adopt the incentive structure of for-profit industries. The educational researchers want the money but not the assumption of risk associated with research in the private sector.

Conceptually, at least, we should include the student resources devoted to doctoral dissertations (mainly the value of graduate student time) as resources devoted to educational research. Historically, doctoral dissertations were supposed to be evidence that the student was capable of conducting research at a high level. Doctoral students were required to pass tests in foreign languages (usually French and German for students seeking a Ph.D. in education) to demonstrate their ability to read research in non-English countries. Because most doctoral students in education sought higher-level positions as school administrators instead of academic careers, most graduate schools of education eventually adopted the Ed.D. (Doctor of Education), which did not require proficiency in foreign languages, as an alternative for practitioners.

The issue here is not the quality of the research in doctoral dissertations. It is the amount of resources devoted to educational research. Academics characterize doctoral dissertations in their universities as "research," but do not count it as research in estimating the resources devoted to educational research. The inconsistency leads to substantial underestimates of the resources devoted to public education.

Of course, some institutions offer a doctoral degree without a dissertation requirement, and among many others, characterizing the dissertations as "research" is quite a stretch. Furthermore, many dissertations are devoted to topics in higher education or nursery schools or other topics that do not involve K–12 public schools, at least directly; however, many dissertations in fields other than education (for example, law, psychology, taxation, economics) are devoted to public education issues.

In 1999–2000, 245 institutions of higher education awarded 6,830 doctoral degrees in education, the largest number awarded in any discipline.[7] Since we have already included the cost of faculty time and facilities, only student time should be added to the costs of K–12 education that are associated with higher education.

Most doctoral candidates in education are midcareer teachers or school administrators, such as principals and assistant principals. Some are doctoral students full-time, but the most common pattern is part-time during the school year and full-time during the summer. It usually takes more than a year, and sometimes several years after a master's degree, to complete the requirements for a doctoral degree. In short, virtually every factor affecting estimates of the student costs is subject to significant uncertainty; hence our estimate of the cost of student time may be substantially lower or higher than the actual cost. We must reiterate, however, that the quality of doctoral dissertations or the research that goes into them is irrelevant to the cost. Just as we count the salaries paid to poor teachers in estimating the costs of education, we must also count the costs of poor research in estimating the costs of educational research.

Institutions of higher education awarded 6,830 doctoral degrees in education in 1999–2000. Let us assume that the value of doctoral student time is equal to $50,000, our conservative estimate of the average teacher salary plus benefits for one full year. On this assumption, the cost of doctoral students' loss of work for one year would be $341,500,000, not a large amount in the total picture. Nevertheless, it is large enough to suggest a valuable resource that is underutilized in the education reform movement.

Our interest in the statistics on doctoral degrees in education is twofold: (1) Their bearing on how much is spent on educational research and development, and (2) What the statistics can tell us about the real costs of public education. Unfortunately, the data are not very enlightening on either issue. We did not seek a breakdown between Ph.D.s and Ed.D.s because the categories do not mean very much anymore. Some Ph.D.s are not research-oriented, and some Ed.D.s are. Furthermore, the standards of what constitutes "research" vary widely between and within institutions. Our guess is that 3 to 5 percent of the doctoral degrees in education involved serious research.

The amounts spent in higher education for "educational development" in public education are probably not very substantial. Several for-profit learning companies active in K–12 education, such as Edison Schools and Sylvan Learning Centers, spend a significant amount for development, but the amounts are miniscule in the overall picture. Similarly, nonprofit organizations, such as Educational Testing Service (ETS), budget for research and development, but there appears to be no systematic testing industry data on the amounts. However, the research and development costs of for-profit educational companies already include expenditures for better instructional equipment, textbooks, audiovisual aids, distance learning, bleachers, buses, desks, athletic gear, lockers, uniforms, gymnasium apparatus, school construction, and other products and services provided by the for-profit sector for public education. Because some of these expenditures are devoted to products and services that are sold in noneducational as well as educational markets, their R & D costs cannot be allocated completely to K–12 education.

## REMEDIAL EDUCATION

As used in this study, "remedial education" refers to educational services intended to teach basic skills that are normally taught and learned in K–12 education. In effect, therefore, expenditures for remedial education, by whatever title, are expenditures for elementary and secondary education.

The largest costs of remedial education are those of school districts using federal (Title I) funds authorized by the No Child Left Behind Act of 2001 and it predecessors. These costs are routinely included in estimating the costs of public education. The costs of remedial education that are not included as expenditures of public schools are mainly the costs of remedial education provided by institutions of higher education and by for-profit companies. We begin with our estimates of these costs of remedial education in institutions of higher education.

Large-scale remediation in U.S. higher education first emerged in the City University of New York (CUNY) in 1969. CUNY is a system of higher education that enrolls over 200,000 students on 20 campuses in all 5 boroughs of New York City. Another 150,000 students take adult and continuing education courses. As a result of minority student strikes and takeovers of several university facilities in the late 1960s, the CUNY board of trustees voted to allow any graduate of a city high school who could pass a tenth-grade test of basic skills to enroll in a CUNY facility. This policy, and similar ones elsewhere, have been labeled "open admissions."

The predictable result of open admissions was a huge influx of students who could not read or write well enough to handle regular college work. In order to avoid a situation in which large numbers of students would have to drop out within a short time after admission, the CUNY trustees initiated a large-scale remedial program. The implications of the remedial program for the city's K–12 schools were largely ignored, partly because K–12 schools were governed by a different board of trustees. The City University of New York maintains the remedial programs, but since 2000, they have been available only in CUNY's two-year colleges. Just as the prominence of open admissions in New York City triggered similar policies elsewhere, the transfer of such programs to two-year colleges is likely to strengthen the movement away from remediation in senior colleges and universities elsewhere.

## THE EXTENT OF REMEDIAL EDUCATION IN HIGHER EDUCATION

In 1995, the National Center for Education Statistics (NCES) conducted the most extensive survey of remedial education to date. In its survey, NCES defined remedial education as follows:

> For the purposes of this study, we define remedial education to be courses in reading, writing, or mathematics for college students lacking those skills necessary to perform college-level work *at the level required by*

> *your institution.* "Throughout this [NCES] questionnaire, these courses are referred to as 'remedial'; however, your institution may use other names such as 'compensatory,' 'developmental,' or 'basic skills,' or some other term." Please answer the survey for any courses meeting the definition above, regardless of name; however, do not include English as a second language (ESL) when taught primarily to foreign students. Do not include remedial courses offered by another institution, even if students at your institution take these courses.[8]

Inasmuch as virtually everyone agrees that reading, writing, and arithmetic are essential for citizenship and productive occupational roles, the NCES definition is based upon the widest possible consensus regarding the components of remedial education. Some of the highlights of the NCES survey are that:

- Seventy-eight percent of the institutions of higher education that enrolled freshmen offered at least one remedial course in reading, writing, or mathematics.
- Ninety-nine percent of public two-year institutions offered remedial courses in the three subject areas.
- The average number of courses offered was 2.1 for reading, 2.0 for writing, and 2.5 for mathematics; however, the averages were much higher in two-year institutions.
- Twenty-nine percent of incoming freshmen enrolled in at least one remedial course.
- As of 1995, the number of students taking remedial courses had remained the same or increased slightly during the past five years.
- Placement tests were used to select students who need remedial education in about 60 percent of the institutions.
- About half of the public two-year institutions provided remedial services to local business and industry, whereas only 5 percent of the other institutions offered such services.
- Only about one in four institutions reported any limits on the length of time students could take remedial courses.
- Twenty-five percent of all institutions offered remedial courses in subjects other than reading, writing, and mathematics.[9]

Generally speaking, the results of the NCES survey were consistent with the studies of remedial education by the Southern Regional Education

Board (SREB) from 1988 to 1995;[10] however, the SREB surveys included data on faculty participation not available in the NCES survey. The SREB survey found that on average, four faculty members at each institution taught reading, six taught writing, and seven taught precollege mathematics. About half of the remedial education faculty were part-time; also, about half were employed to teach only remedial courses.[11]

Neither the NCES nor the SREB study presented any data on the costs of remedial education; however, a different SREB study explained why it was very difficult to generate reliable data on the costs of remedial education.[12] Consequently, the SREB researchers turned to studies of the costs of remedial education in Maryland, Florida, and Texas. David W. Breneman, one of the researchers, attempted to estimate the national costs by extrapolating from the estimated costs in Texas and Maryland. In Texas, the costs of remedial education were 2.25 percent of state funds for higher education. In Maryland, 1.2 percent of its educational and general funds were spent for remedial education. If the Maryland and Texas percentages are applied to the 2000 state expenditures for public higher education across the United States, the costs of remedial education in institutions of higher education ranged from $900 million to $1 billion.[13]

The fact is, however, that institutions of higher education have strong incentives to under-report their expenditures for remedial education. Furthermore, although the states provide over half of the funds for remedial education in public institutions of higher education, there are substantial expenditures for it that would not show up in the estimates in Texas and Maryland. The very fact that the expenditures for remedial education in private institutions were not included in the NCES and SREB studies is a major omission, since a considerable amount of these expenditures are funded by government. Actually, as Breneman recognized, there are several plausible ways to estimate the costs of remediation, and the different ways result in very different outcomes. The cost of remedial education may be twice as high (adjusted for inflation) as his $1 billion estimate.

Several factors conducive to underestimation are applicable to Breneman's estimates of the national cost of remedial education in higher education. For example, if the overhead costs—more university bureaucracy, more red tape, more institutional publications, more classrooms—are included, the estimates would be substantially higher. However, even prior to the emergence of large-scale remedial education in higher education, there was widespread concern about the duplication of courses between higher and secondary education, as well as the "dumbing down" of courses in higher education. To the extent that these criticisms are valid, we cannot attribute the costs of remedial education to open enrollment, but the costs per se would not be affected.

Although the expenditures for remedial education in higher education in any given year are spent for the benefit of students who attended K–12 schools in the past, the expenditures are a cost of K–12 education in the years in which the expenditures are made. The important point is the level of instruction, not the grade level of the students. For that matter, most remedial education in higher education is devoted to recent immigrants, recent high school graduates, and/or recent dropouts to qualify them for entry-level jobs or regular college courses (which often include components of remedial education, albeit not labeled as such).

A 2000 study of remedial education in Michigan illustrates the complexity of estimating its costs. The study utilized five different ways of estimating the costs of remedial education in higher education and in business settings. Table 7.3 shows that these five different ways resulted in a range of costs from $311 million to $1.148 billion, with an average of $601 million; however, these figures do not include the very substantial private costs generated by remedial education.

The strategies differed in their economic assumptions, the number of persons requiring remedial education, how "remedial education" was defined, and in other ways, but the estimate deemed most reasonable by Greene was consistent with the studies by Breneman and others. Greene

**Table 7.3. The Costs of Remedial Education in Michigan**

| | *Estimated Costs for Each Strategy (in millions)* | | | | |
|---|---|---|---|---|---|
| *Type of Institution* | *1* | *2* | *3* | *4* | *5* |
| Community colleges | 65 | 65 | 80 | n/a | 65 |
| Four-year colleges | 24 | 24 | 17 | n/a | 24 |
| Businesses | 222 | 400 | 436 | n/a | 1,059 |
| Total (in millions) | $311 | $489 | $533 | $523 | $1,148 |

Average of five estimates: $601 million, not counting private costs.

Source: Jay P. Greene, *The Cost of Remedial Education: How Much Michigan Pays When Students Fail to Learn Basic Skills* (Midland, MI: Mackinac Center for Public Policy, 2000), 9–16.

pointed out that all of the five strategies may underestimate the costs of remedial education because they do not include:

- The costs of remedial education in courses not explicitly labeled as such.
- The costs of technology to compensate for employees' lack of basic skills.
- The costs of remedying work habits and attitudes that should have been learned in precollege education.
- The extent to which college-level work includes courses normally taken by high school students.
- Expenditures by vocational schools due to inability to distinguish expenditures for teaching basic skills from expenditures for job-specific skills.
- The capital costs of providing remedial education.
- The incidence of the failure of remedial education.[14]

Table 7.4 shows results from an Ohio study where the percentage of high school graduates taking remedial courses increased. The increase in enrollment in remedial mathematics resulted in almost 3,000 more students taking remedial courses. The study also found that remedial work was being transferred from the state's public senior colleges and universities to its community colleges and branch campuses. The percentage of students in the main campuses taking remedial work declined by over 50 percent in the last 20-year period. These figures appear to reflect a nationwide trend; hence the overall costs of remedial education in higher education may be declining even if the number of students enrolled in remedial work does not change appreciably. The reason is that the cost per student in community colleges and branch campuses is less than it is in four-year and graduate institutions.[15]

**Table 7.4. Percent of Students Taking Remedial Mathematics and English in Ohio Institutions of Higher Education**

| | *Percent in 1978–79* | *Percent in 1998–99* |
|---|---|---|
| Remedial mathematics | 23 | 26 |
| Remedial English | 16 | 22 |

Source: "Let's Try That Again: Remediation in Ohio's Public Universities," *Policy Note* (Columbus, OH: Buckeye Institute, August 2001), 1.

## SUMMARY

Because they are fundamentally costs of elementary and secondary education, the costs of remedial education for college school students should be counted as a cost of elementary and secondary education. Similarly, 80 percent of the costs of teacher education should be considered costs of public education, since approximately 80 percent of students in teacher education programs teach in public schools. In addition, most of the higher-education expenditures for educational research on elementary and secondary education are not but should be regarded as costs of public education.

This study does not assign a specific percentage of the costs of higher education to K–12 education, but the shortfall appears to fall within a range of 4 to 8 percent of the official cost of the latter. In 2001, that amount would have been between approximately $17 billion and $34 billion.

## NOTES

1. U.S. Department of Education, National Center for Education Statistics, *Digest of Education Statistics 2001,* NCES 2002-130, Washington, DC, 2002, 378–379.
2. Ibid., 379.
3. AACTE/NCATE, *Joint Data Survey*, Washington, DC, 2000.
4. U.S. Department of Education, *Digest of Education Statistics 2001,* 374.
5. U.S. Department of Education, National Center for Education Statistics, *Background Characteristics, Work Activities, and Compensation of Faculty and Instructional Staff in Postsecondary Institutions: Fall 1998,* Linda J. Zimbler, NCES 2001-152, Washington, DC, 2001, 40.
6. Ibid., 42.
7. U.S. Department of Education, *Digest of Education Statistics 2001*, 320. The study defined "doctor's degrees" as "the highest academic degree and requires mastery within a field of knowledge and demonstrated ability to perform scholarly research. Other doctorates are awarded for fulfilling specialized requirements in professional fields, such as education (Ed.D.)."
8. U.S. Department of Education, National Center for Education Statistics, *Remedial Education at Higher Education Institutions in Fall 1995,* NCES 97-584 (Washington, DC: Government Printing Office, October 1996), iii.

9. Ibid., iii–v.

10. Southern Regional Education Board, *Remedial Education in College: How Widespread Is It?* (1988); They Came to College? A Remedial/Developmental Profile of First-Time Freshmen in SREB States (1991); and Ansley A. Abraham Jr., *College Remedial Studies: Institutional Practices in the SREB States* (1992). Atlanta, GA: Southern Regional Education Board.

11. Abraham, *College Remedial Studies*, 21–24.

12. Ibid., 25–26.

13. David W. Breneman, "Remediation in Higher Education: Its Extent and Cost," in *Brookings Papers on Education Policy,* 2000. This is perhaps the best study available on the cost of remedial education.

14. Jay P. Greene, *The Cost of Remedial Education: How Much Michigan Pays When Students Fail to Learn Basic Skills* (Midland, MI: Mackinac Center for Public Policy, 2000), 9-16. See also: David Breneman and William Daarlow, *Remediation in Higher Education* (Washington, DC: Thomas B. Fordham Foundation, July 1998); Ronald Phipps, *College Remediation: What It Is, What It Costs, What's at Stake* (Washington, DC: Institute for Higher Education Policy, December 1998). It is surprising that these last two studies do not take the private costs of remediation into account in contending that remediation is a wise expenditure of government funds.

15. "Let's Try That Again: Remediation in Ohio's Public Universities," *Policy Note* (Columbus, OH: Buckeye Institute, August 2001), 1.

CHAPTER 8

# The Educational Costs of Noneducational Agencies of Government

This chapter is devoted mainly to the answers to two questions: First, how much do noneducational agencies of government spend on elementary and secondary education? And second, to what extent, if any, should the costs of noneducational government agencies be allocated to public education, and if such allocations are appropriate, how shall they be measured or estimated?

Our answer to the first question focuses on elementary and secondary schools supported by the U.S. Department of State and/or operated by the U.S. Department of Defense, and education in federal, state, and local prisons, and juvenile justice facilities. To be sure, the costs of these programs should not be included as costs of pupils in average daily attendance in regular K–12 public schools, but they are relevant to how much is being spent for elementary and secondary education. Similarly, because the education of Indian children is implemented through the Bureau of Indian Affairs, the funding for it is not included in estimates of the costs per pupil in average daily attendance.

The issues raised by the second question can be illustrated by court cases on school district budgets. Assuming that these cases would not arise in the absence of public education, should we allocate the costs of judges, juries, and judicial facilities in such cases to public education? From an economic and accounting point of view, data on the kinds of cases that utilize our judicial system are important from a public policy standpoint. As will be evident, the same issue arises in other government services.

## U.S. DEPARTMENT OF DEFENSE ELEMENTARY/SECONDARY SCHOOLS

Table 8.1 shows the federal agencies that have fiscal and/or administrative responsibilities for American elementary and secondary students under the aegis of the U.S. Department of Defense or the U.S. Department of State. The abbreviations shown have been adopted by the agencies.

The cost of schools for the dependent children of U.S. military personnel stationed at various bases within and outside the United States is one of the largest costs of elementary/secondary education by a noneducational government agency. Most of the school-age children among overseas Americans in 2001–02 attended schools established, authorized, and controlled by the U.S. Department of Defense.[1] However, most civilian agency dependents abroad attend nongovernment schools of various kinds, which are supported in part by the U.S. government under a program administered by the Office of Overseas Schools of the U.S. Department of State. In 2001–02 there were 182 such American-sponsored schools in 130 countries.[2] Most of these nongovernment, independent schools are financed principally through parental tuition payments, although gifts and contributions also provide some assistance.

Nearly 74,000 students attend Department of Defense Dependents Schools (DoDDS) overseas and about 33,000 students attend Department of Defense Domestic Dependent Elementary and Secondary

**Table 8.1. Federal Agencies That Support Elementary and Secondary Schools for American Military and Civilian Personnel, 2001–02**

| *Agency* | *Acronym* | *U.S. Students* | *Budget* |
|---|---|---|---|
| 1. Department of State Overseas Schools | OS | 28,000 | $7 million |
| 2. Department of Defense Education Activity | DoDEA | HQ/CSS* | 73.7 million |
| Dependents Schools (Overseas) | DoDDS | 74,000 | 871.7 million |
| Domestic Dependent Elem. & Sec. Schools | DDESS | 33,000 | 355.1 million |
| Junior Reserve Officer Training Corps | JROTC | varies | 235 million |

*Headquarters and Consolidated School Support

Source: At http://www.state.gov/www/about_state/schools/omission.html and http://www.odedodea.edu/budget01/summarya02.html [accessed April 30, 2002].

Schools (DDESS) in the United States.[3] First administered by the military, the two separate but parallel systems were brought together in 1994 under the Department of Defense Education Activity (DoDEA), now governed by civilian managers. DDESS schools educate the children of service personnel who are employed in federal institutions that are not taxed to support public education. For instance, a large military base will draw many pupils from the families of military and civilian personnel, but the base is not taxed to support public education as the facilities of a private company would be.

The DoDEA operates 227 public schools in fourteen foreign countries, seven states, Guam, and Puerto Rico. Approximately 8,800 teachers serve DoDEA's more than 107,000 students.[4] Enrollment fluctuates annually with changes in the numbers of military personnel with school-age children. The Department of Defense budget for fiscal year 2001 (October 1, 2001, to September 30, 2002) included over $1.3 billion for the operation of its elementary and secondary schools for children of its servicemen and -women.[5]

The online DoDEA *Budget Book for Fiscal Year 2001* calculates that the annual per-pupil cost for DoDDS (overseas) elementary/secondary students was $9,838 in school year 1999–00, and the per-pupil cost for DDESS (domestic) elementary/secondary students was $8,796. These per-pupil costs include only costs identified as operation and maintenance and do not include the costs of new construction or capital improvements. Personnel costs for more than 13,000 full-time equivalents (principals, teachers, aides, counselors, psychologists, instructional specialists, school clerical and custodial staff) make up 69 percent of the operation and maintenance budget.[6] The costs of new and replacement textbooks, and of school supplies and equipment, are also included in the per-pupil costs.

Excluded from the per-pupil costs in DoDEA schools are several costs unique to DoDEA schools as reported in the online *Budget Book*. For example, the DoDDS teachers in foreign countries receive a living-quarters allowance—a cost that is rarely absorbed by school districts in the United States. In addition, DoDDS funds the transfer of a teacher and his/her household to a teaching vacancy in another location (for example, from Germany to Japan). During the 1999–2000 fiscal year, DoDEA paid the tuition for 2,082 eligible Department of Defense students to attend non-DoDDS schools in approximately 100 countries where there were no DoDDS schools available. Approximately 2 percent of the budget, or $20.5 million, was allocated for such tuition payments in FY 2001.

Likewise, the DoDEA pays the tuition and/or transportation costs for DDESS students enrolled in public schools operated by local education agencies in the United States. During the 1999–2000 fiscal year, DoDEA paid the tuition payments for 2,082 students under this program.[7]

Similarly, if nonmilitary dependents are enrolled in a DoDDS where space is available, the DoDEA receives the tuition payment from the parents. Such tuition payments appear as "Reimbursables" in the DoDEA budget. The DoDEA budget does not include the costs of the military personnel who serve on the Education Councils to advise the civilian school management.

Like conventional school districts, the DoDEA budget includes a separate budget for the costs of capital outlay, interest, and debt service. For FY 2001, the military construction budget for both overseas and domestic school construction and renovation was $36 million. In addition, the DoDEA procurement budget is to be used for capital purchases that exceed $100,000.

Actual expenditures for the operation of the DoDEA schools are submitted to the Office of the Secretary of Defense. Operating from its offices in Arlington, Virginia, the DoDEA provides budget information to the public through its website, and has done so since FY 1999. The DoDEA is a Department of Defense field activity under the direction, authority, and control of the Deputy Assistant Secretary of Defense for Military Community and Family Policy.[8]

Let us review briefly the reasons why the costs of DoDEA schools are included in this study. The pupils in the DoDEA schools transfer from and to U.S. public and private schools; in fact, these students may attend DoDEA schools for only a small fraction of their years in elementary/secondary school.[9] Furthermore, they are included in the state and national testing programs that form the basis of various evaluations of public education in the U.S.[10] Because pupils who have attended DoDEA schools are included in these testing programs, the federal government's cost of educating them should not be excluded from estimates of the total costs of public education, even though these costs do not affect the per-pupil costs in the continental U.S. non-DoDEA schools.

The cost of the Junior Reserve Officers Training Corps (JROTC) programs in U.S. secondary schools must also be added to the educational costs absorbed by the Department of Defense. The cost of this program was approximately $235 million in 2002, and when this is added to the cost of the DoDEA program, the Department of Defense spends well over $1.4 billion per year on elementary and secondary education.[11] Because the Junior ROTC program was provided to private as well as public schools, the total cost should be reduced to get a more accurate estimate of the public school cost. Although private school enrollments have been 10–12 percent of public school enrollments in recent years, the cost allocation to private schools might be less because most private school enrollments are in elementary schools.

The National Center for Education Statistics collects the data for elementary and secondary education expenditures by the Department of Defense Education Activity. However, none of these expenditures are included in the NCES estimates of the per-pupil costs of public education.[12]

## EDUCATION IN PRISONS, CORRECTIONAL INSTITUTIONS, DETENTION CENTERS, AND JUVENILE JUSTICE FACILITIES

Generally speaking, two systems of justice are operative in the United States. One is for adults in "prisons" and one for juveniles in "correctional institutions." However, the age that determines what system governs particular cases varies, so that many detainees in prisons would be juveniles in other states. Similarly, many detainees in facilities for juvenile offenders would come under the jurisdiction of the adult systems in other states.

Although federal programs are quite uniform, the state programs vary, depending upon state legislation. Our primary interest is in the costs of K–12 education that are not included in the NCES publications on the costs of public education. Obviously, the cost of such programs cannot be factored into the cost per student in average daily attendance unless the programs are administered through local school districts, as some of them are. In fact, we cannot even assert that the cost figures are approximations of the real governmental and/or nongovernmental cost of elementary/secondary education in prisons and/or correctional institutions. In any event, prison education should be included in the cost of achieving widely accepted national educational goals, such as universal literacy.

Our objective is to convey some idea of the magnitude of elementary/secondary education for incarcerated persons. We use elementary/secondary education to refer to the academic level of instruction, not the age level of the persons who are being educated. It is not the case, however, that elementary/secondary education in the juvenile justice system is completely independent of school district operations. On the contrary, it is often implemented by school districts and state education agencies, and when it is, the costs are reflected in their financial reports.

## EDUCATION OF FEDERAL PRISONERS

In the federal prison system there is a high level of internal consistency from prison to prison. For instance, all federal prisons are governed by the same policies, and the facts and figures do not, or do not as often, mix disparate statistics whose "averages" are merely statistical artifacts without practical utility.

One of the major consequences of the explosive growth in the federal prison population is its impact on the Bureau of Prisons' education programs. President George W. Bush's proposed 2002 federal budget included $4.7 billion for correctional activities, an increase of approximately $360 million over the 2001 budget.[13] This level of funding would assist at least 34 percent of all inmates in educational programs in obtaining a high school diploma or General Educational Development (GED) certificate, at least seven months prior to their release.[14] Thus, the educational programs in federal prisons are intended to enable approximately 50,000 of 142,000 federal prisoners to leave prison with a high school diploma, including the GED.[15]

Each Bureau of Prisons facility offers educational programs authorized by federal legislation. The programs include a focus on basic skills, such as reading, writing, calculating, speaking, listening, problem solving, and job and life skills. English as a second language is mandatory for non-English-speaking prisoners. The Literacy Program, also known as the GED Standard, is required for each inmate who does not have a high school diploma or a GED. The only exceptions to this rule are individuals with disabilities, illegal aliens, and pretrial inmates. The objectives of the program are to provide those inmates who need it with a GED credential and to maintain electronic education files of inmates in the program.

To attain a GED, inmates must participate in at least 240 instructional hours, beginning within four months of incarceration.[16] Any time absent from the program is added to the 240 total. Any inmate who does not achieve a GED within the 240-hour period may stay enrolled in the program. Wardens may approve incentive programs for inmates completing the literacy program—for example, cash awards or certificates. Another incentive is that inmates cannot ordinarily be paid more than entry-level compensation unless they have a GED or high school diploma.

Although the GED/high school diploma program is the largest educational program in federal prisons, other federal education programs emphasize job and life skills. Some higher-education courses are also available. The programs are intended to help inmates function as self-supporting, responsible individuals upon release; unfortunately, despite a wide array of services and incentives, one of every three federal inmates is incarcerated again within three years after being released.[17]

Obviously, the costs of education in federal prisons include some costs like those in public schools and exclude others such as transportation costs. One issue is how much, if any, of the noneducational costs of incarceration should be charged to prison education. For example, if any of the costs of prison construction are allocated to prison education, the costs of prison education would rise considerably, even though debt service and interest do not affect the costs of education in federal prisons. At the same time, federal prisons spend a great deal more than public high schools to follow up on the performance of their students; nothing comparable to parole exists in the public schools. These differences help to explain why per-pupil costs in prisons can vary widely from the per-pupil costs in school districts.

The fact that the Bureau of Prisons has assumed a leadership role in educating and training federal inmates to attain a GED, a high school diploma, or employment training raises several questions. Many inmates, perhaps a majority, are dropouts from the public schools. Do the educators in federal prisons know more about how to teach basic skills such as reading? Or does incarceration provide incentives and exclude distractions in ways that public schools cannot match? These are intriguing questions that are outside the scope of this study.

## EDUCATION OF INCARCERATED YOUTH IN STATE PRISONS

According to the U.S. Justice Department, an estimated 9,100 youths (2 percent of the total jail population) under the age of 18 were held in adult jails in 1999.[18] The costs of education for incarcerated youth also includes the costs of education for youth in court-ordered juvenile detention centers and in training schools. Ascertaining the costs is practically impossible, but the following data underscore the magnitude and complexity of the cost issues.[19]

- In 1999, law enforcement agencies made an estimated 2.5 million arrests of persons under 18 years of age.
- An estimated 108,900 were in residential treatment centers for crimes such as murder, manslaughter, forcible rape, robbery, aggravated assault, and drug offenses.
- Juvenile offenders were held in 3,711 residential facilities, 1,182 public and 2,529 private.
- Males made up 87 percent of the juveniles in residential placement, females the remaining 13 percent.
- Minorities accounted for 62 percent (39 percent blacks) and whites 38 percent of the juveniles in residential placement facilities.[20]
- At the end of 2000, state and federal prison authorities had 1,381,892 inmates under their jurisdiction; 621,149 adults were awaiting trial or serving a sentence in local jails.
- At the end of 2000, 6.5 million adults were on probation, incarcerated, or on parole—3.1 percent of all U.S. adult residents.[21]

The arrangements governing incarceration and education in state prisons are diverse in every way. States differ in how they define "juvenile" and what state agency has jurisdiction over juvenile offenders. In most states, the jurisdiction of the juvenile court ends at age 17, but age 16 also triggers the change from juvenile to adult court in about one-fourth of the states.[22] The upper age limit for jurisdiction of juvenile offenders differs among states.

A survey of 20 state-level juvenile justice education programs revealed that the state administrative structure for the delivery of educational services for incarcerated juveniles varied as follows:

- Special school district with the juvenile justice agency
- Juvenile justice agency
- No special school district
- The LEA
- State education agency
- A separate state agency
- Combined juvenile and adult agency, operated as a special school district [23]

The same study indicated that in every state, the teachers in the juvenile justice system were required to be certified by the state education agency.[24] This seems to be the only important aspect of education in the juvenile justice system that does not vary widely among the states.

## THE COST OF ELEMENTARY/SECONDARY EDUCATION IN STATE PENAL INSTITUTIONS

Differences in terminology render it impossible to place much confidence in comparisons or summaries of the educational programs in correctional institutions. Not surprisingly, a 1999 survey of 20 state juvenile justice agencies reported that "in 25 percent of the states surveyed, there was no way to calculate the per-pupil cost of education."[25] The study director, Bruce I. Wolford, reported that "the average level of funding in fourteen states was $5,984 with a range of $2,259 to $9,000. In the other six states, the per-pupil cost was not known."[26] If the average per-pupil funding for the 14 responding states were used as the average for all 50 states, the result would be to add approximately $283 million to the cost of public education; however, even this figure would be a gross underestimate if infrastructure and overhead costs were included in the estimates.

The Wolford study also surveyed states regarding their funding for educational services for juvenile offenders. The states utilized multiple sources of funds to support education in their juvenile justice systems. All utilized federal funds; thirteen utilized juvenile justice funds, nine utilized funds from the state education agency, and nine utilized other state or local funds.

## SPECIAL EDUCATION SERVICES FOR INCARCERATED YOUTH

The Individuals with Disabilities Education Act (IDEA) mandates the provision of special education services for students between the ages of 3 and 22 with disabilities, even if they reside in a juvenile correction facility. Estimates indicate that about 32 percent of all juveniles in correctional facilities qualify for special education compared to 9 percent for all children.[27] In most states, state education agencies provide these services in correctional facilities. The most common special education categories in juvenile facilities are for students with learning disabilities, emotional disturbances, and mental retardation. Funding for these services is resolved by the designation of the agency responsible for providing the services.[28]

Several court decisions have upheld the states' obligation to provide special education services for juvenile offenders in a timely manner. A 1995 Connecticut case held that school districts are responsible for providing a free and appropriate public education, as well as for identifying and evaluating students with disabilities in juvenile facilities. In contrast, a 1995 South Carolina case held that its state Department of Justice is the responsible agency.[29] In Alabama and South Carolina, separate school districts for juvenile correctional education are managed by the state Department of Juvenile Justice. In New Hampshire, statutes delegate this responsibility to the local school districts. In Florida, state law mandates that the inmate's district of residence provide special education services during the period of incarceration.[30] These rulings illustrate the variations in correctional education for juveniles among the states.

Federal funding for federal and state inmates is also authorized by the Adult Education and Family Literacy Act, part of Title II of the Workforce Investment Act of 1998. This legislation authorizes adult basic and secondary education programs and allows states to spend up to 10 percent of the state's grant for educational programs in correctional facilities. Also, in FY 2000, the National Literacy Act, as amended, provided $15 million for education in correctional institutions.[31]

In state and local prisons, adults as well as juveniles are receiving educational services normally provided in elementary and secondary schools. Unfortunately, the variations and complexities of service provision render it practically impossible to estimate the real costs within a reasonable margin of error. The data that are available are suggestive, but do not provide a basis for a comprehensive estimate of the costs of education in prisons or correctional institutions. For that matter, comprehensive data on its benefits as well as its costs are lacking. This is one reason why federal and state appropriations for prison education have been declining since 1994. For instance, prisoners first became eligible for federal educational assistance in 1965, when Title IV of the Higher Education Act of 1965 authorized Pell Grants for low-income prisoners otherwise eligible for such grants. By 1982, 45 states conducted higher-education programs in prisons. These programs were eliminated by the Violent Crime Control and Law Enforcement Act of 1994 and have not been reauthorized, despite claims that they have been highly effective in reducing recidivism, hence prison costs.[32] Be that as it may, the states have not made up the shortfall in federal aid, and in view of the budgetary pressures on the states, they may be unwilling to do so for several years to come.

## EDUCATION SERVICES THROUGH THE BIA

In 2001, the federal government spent $488 million on Indian education.[33] These funds, provided by the U.S. Department of the Interior through the Bureau of Indian Affairs (BIA), were distributed by formula to local school districts or schools operated by the BIA for 185 elementary and secondary schools and 25 tribal community colleges.[34] In addition, the BIA provided approximately $281 million for the planning, design, construction, maintenance, and rehabilitation of Bureau-funded school facilities and the repair needs for employee housing.[35] When combined with other federal funds intended to attract and train Indian teachers and administrators, fund construction projects, and support special education, the federal government spent over $600 million for Indian education in 2001.[36]

In FY 2001, the U.S. Department of Education provided funds through two programs for Indian students. One, appropriations through Title VII—Indian, Native Hawaiian, and Alaska Native Education—included about $116 million for formula grants to address the special educational and cultural needs of Indian children. Title VII involved 1,146 local education agencies and tribal schools serving more than 448,000 students.[37]

Title VIII—Impact Aid of the ESEA—is the second federal program for Native American youth. In 2000, this program provided over $1.1 billion for carrying out programs of financial assistance to federally affected schools. Impact Aid funds are available to local school districts whose total student enrollment was composed of at least 50 percent children living on Indian lands.[38] Impact Aid helps to take the place of the local revenue that does not materialize when students who reside on Indian reservations attend public schools. Because Indian reservations are exempt from local property taxes, local educational agencies have pupils to educate but lack access to the primary source of revenue that ordinarily comes with pupils.

According to the 2002 federal budget, Impact Aid payments, which support Department of Defense as well as Indian schools, include these five categories:

**Basic support payments.** Payments were made on behalf of approximately 1.2 million federally connected students enrolled in about 1,360 local educational agencies to assist the LEAs in meeting their operation and maintenance costs. The average per-student payments were approximately $750.

**Payments for children with disabilities.** Payments in addition to those provided under the Individuals with Disabilities Education Act (IDEA) were provided on behalf of approximately 53,000 federally connected students with disabilities in about 830 local educational agencies. Average per-student payments were approximately $940.

**Facilities maintenance.** Funds were used to provide emergency repairs for school facilities that serve military dependents and schools for Indian students.

**Construction.** Formula payments were provided to approximately 155 local educational agencies with large proportions of federally connected students who are military dependents or who reside on Indian lands.

**Payments for federal property.** Payments were made to approximately 250 local educational agencies in which real property owned by the federal government represents 10 percent or more of the assessed value of real property in the local educational agency.[39]

Over $40 million is available to qualifying schools for federal property payments. For example, the Kadoka School District in South Dakota was eligible for such payments because part of the district's land in Washabaugh and Jackson Counties is owned by the Department of Defense and used as a bombing range.[40]

## THE EDUCATIONAL COSTS IN OTHER STATE AGENCIES

To simplify the issues, let us assume a state budget in which 40 percent of the state expenditures is explicitly allocated to the provision of public education. As previously noted, some of the litigation that arises in the state judicial system would not have arisen in the absence of public education. Example: Lawsuits alleging that the formula for state aid to school districts violated the equal protection clause of the 14th Amendment. The work of state officials, such as the state legislators, treasurer, comptroller, and auditor, is also devoted in part to matters directly involving public schools. In all such cases, should we allocate some of the costs of these officials and agencies to public education?

It appears that such allocation is essential if we are to ascertain the real cost of public education. To illustrate why, consider the following example. Some school districts have security guards who are employed and directed by school officials; the costs are shown as costs of operating the school districts. In other school districts, security personnel from the police department are utilized; they are ultimately responsible to police officials. Although they are expected to work in schools, their school assignment is carried as a cost of the police department, not of the school district.

To facilitate the analysis, let us assume that the costs and functions of security personnel are the same, regardless of whether they are carried as a cost of the school district or the police department. On the above facts, we cannot say that one of the districts is more efficient than the other; the government costs are the same in both cases. And because our objective is to show the resources utilized as well as the real government costs, our approach is to treat security personnel utilized in public school districts as a cost of public education, regardless of what public agency absorbs the costs of such personnel. Alternatively, we might treat the cost of police in public schools as a cost of public safety even if paid for by the school district, but this approach assumes that the police would be needed even if there were no public schools, an assumption that cannot be sustained in some situations.

## STATE OVERHEAD EXPENDITURES FOR PUBLIC EDUCATION

Ideally, the most accurate way to estimate the state overhead costs of public education would be to determine the expenditures required for public education, agency by agency, and then add the dollar amounts. This approach would be desirable, because state agencies and officials with similar titles may devote very different percentages of their budgets to public education. For example, some state labor boards deal only with school district labor problems; other boards with the same title may have jurisdiction over labor relations in all state and local public agencies; and still others have no jurisdiction over school district labor relations. Because it is practically impossible to assess the public education workload of scores of state agencies, a simpler and admittedly cruder approach is required.

Essentially, our approach is similar to the approach utilized to estimate the federal cost of public education. We first determine the percentage of total state expenditures that is spent for public education. This percentage is then applied to the executive, legislative, and judicial costs of state government. The cost of state agencies devoted to a particular service, such as health, transportation, parks, and welfare, is not part of the base amount to which the percentage is applied. The dividing line is not always clear, because most state agencies probably have some interaction with public education, but the idea is to include in the base only the state's noneducational agencies that devote a significant share of their resources to public education. These costs are "the overhead cost" of public education. The overhead cost is not to be confused with the cost of state departments of education. Instead, it is the public education share of the cost of state agencies that exercise significant responsibilities applicable to two or more services provided by state or local public agencies.

The state governments spent $144 billion for "governmental administration" in the 1998–99 fiscal year; the category includes financial administration, judicial and legal expenditures, general public buildings, and other government administration.[41] The National Association of State Budget Officers has calculated that elementary and secondary education accounts for 22.2 percent of total state spending.[42] When this percentage is applied to the costs of governmental administration, the result is that $32 billion is the state overhead cost of elementary/secondary education. Because the costs of assistance to, and regulation of, private schools are included in this amount, the result could be reduced by 10 percent to provide an estimate of the state overhead costs attributable to public schools only.

One reaction to this procedure is that the costs allocated to education should be zero. If the state governments did not subsidize public education, they would still have governors, legislatures, and courts, with all of the costs associated with their operations. The fact that the states allocate some of their revenues to public education does not add to the costs of the other state agencies. On this view, we would count only the costs of collecting taxes earmarked for education as a cost of education.

The problem with this argument is that it leads to the conclusion that there are zero costs of state administration, except for the expenditures that are earmarked for a specified service. For example, in the typical situation, the governor is the official ultimately responsible for several services: prisons, public safety, hospitals, highways, and so on. In each case, it can be argued that none of the costs of state administration can be attributed to any particular service, because the costs of state administration would exist whether or not the state provided the service. Inasmuch as we cannot allocate any of the costs of state administration to any particular state service, the costs would be zero—which is obviously not the case.[43]

The same issue applies to other government costs, such as the costs of the judicial system. Let us assume that 2 percent of its cases deal with public education. Inasmuch as the state judicial system would exist even if public education did not, it can be argued that none of the costs of the state's judicial system should be allocated to education. This leads to the conclusion that state services do not affect the costs of our judicial systems. Each state service would contend that none of the costs of the judicial system should be charged against it, because the expenditures for the judicial system would still be necessary.

Perhaps a comparison of the costs of revenue administration will help to explain the reasons for our contrary conclusion. Private schools absorb the costs of informing parents about the fees and charges, collecting and accounting for revenues, notices of payments due and delinquencies, and efforts to collect in case of delinquency. In contrast, the tax system absorbs these costs for the public schools. In our view, to be explained more fully in the following chapter, revenue collection and administration are costs of public education, even though the costs do not appear on school district or state education department financial statements.

Although not every decision made in private schools must also be made in the public schools, or vice versa, clearly, many important decisions must be made in both, and the procedures for making them are a cost in both, regardless of whether or how the cost is shown on the financial statements of public schools. In this connection, it must be emphasized that there is more than one legitimate way to show the costs of an enterprise. For certain purposes, a government or company may wish to show its costs on a geographical basis; for other purposes, it may wish to show them on a functional basis (production, distribution, sales, legal, etc.), and other ways of presenting the costs are frequently utilized. For this reason, there is no inherent reason to question the legitimacy of our suggested way of estimating the costs of public education. Needless to say, the specifics probably require substantial refinement and adjustment to serve as a basis for educational policymaking.

In principle, the legitimacy of an approach to costs should be based upon the way it is to be utilized. This study is intended to show the actual costs of public elementary and secondary education in order to facilitate better-informed consideration of educational policy. In any case, we should not be surprised that government operation of a service involving more than one in four persons in the entire population generates a substantial share of the administrative costs of state governments, which have the legal responsibility for providing and/or regulating the service.

Some data on state legislation support our approach to the state overhead costs of public education. Faith E. Crampton has tracked state legislation on school finance for several years. Her research shows that the number of bills enacted on school finance increased from 127 in 1994 to 563 in 1999.[44] The total number of bills introduced is not available, but it is undoubtedly several times the number that were enacted. Although an important category of education legislation, education finance is only one of several broad categories of such legislation. Furthermore, some legislation not explicitly "educational," such as the sales and income tax rates, has a much greater impact on education than most legislation explicitly categorized as "educational." We can safely assume that the implications of such legislation for education require a considerable amount of legislative attention.

Regardless of whether schools are private or operated by government, issues such as the following must be resolved:

- When must students enroll in schools?
- What will be the requirements, if any, to hold a teaching, school support, or administrative position?
- How is school construction to be financed?
- What requirements must be met to fire teachers?
- How are school governance bodies elected or appointed?
- What individuals or agencies are responsible for oversight of school governance?
- Who is responsible for preparing the school budget and approving it?
- When and by whom will there be an audit of school expenditures?
- What tests, if any, are pupils required to take?
- What will be the graduation requirements?
- What will be the terms and conditions of employment?
- What will be the number of days in the school year and the duration of the school day?

In private schools, the costs of resolving these issues are costs of operating the school. Not so, or not necessarily so, in public schools. Most of the foregoing issues, and they are far from exhaustive, are resolved partly by school boards and partly by the state legislatures. For example, the legislatures sometimes mandate the limits on class size; the school districts do not spend any time resolving the issue of maximum class size. State law may provide that in order to be eligible for state aid, school districts must require a minimum number of school days and a minimum pupil day. Sometimes the state mandates resolve the issues completely, and sometimes they resolve only certain aspects of them. The aspects that are not resolved by state law are resolved by local school districts, and the costs of the latter are reflected in the costs of the district personnel who make or recommend the relevant policies and decisions. Needless to say, there are enormous variations from state to state on how many matters are resolved at the state level; California unquestionably leads the way, if we can call it that, on the extent of state regulation of public schools.

When a state legislature resolves educational issues, there are costs, just as there are when private schools resolve them. State legislators must devote time to resolving the issues, and they utilize support services in the decision-making process. The costs of this process, however, are not counted as costs of public education.

Should they be? If public schools did not exist, the legislatures would not be incurring these costs, or would not be incurring most of them. This conclusion is supported by the fact that the overwhelming majority of state statutes applicable to K–12 education are not applicable to private schools. For instance, state legislation on the following subjects is not usually applicable to private schools:

| | |
|---|---|
| Class size | Support personnel |
| Collective bargaining | Teacher retirement |
| Contracting out | Teacher leaves of absence |
| School boards | Teacher salaries |
| School day/school year | School district budgeting |
| School transportation | Teacher tenure |

A few statutes might not change, or change very much, in the absence of public schools. For example, private schools must follow the same procedures relating to special education as public schools; schools that do not follow the statutory mandates are not eligible for state/federal funding for special education students. State statutes and regulations on pupil health and safety would not be affected, nor would the civil rights statutes.

Granted, if all K–12 education were private (an unrealistic outcome not advocated here), some new legislation would be required; for instance, the statutes and regulations relating to raising and distributing funds to school districts would have to be replaced by a different system of distributing state funding for K–12 education. Also, the sheer size of the private education sector would probably lead to new legislation relating to private schools. Nevertheless, granting all the qualifications and exceptions, it is hardly debatable that the legislative costs of K–12 education would be reduced drastically in the absence of public schools.

We have not tried to estimate the overhead costs attributable to local governments. Public school districts are regulated primarily by state governments. In fact, many school districts are not a part of any other local government. Large urban school districts dependent on local governments for revenues would be exceptions, but local overhead costs replace rather than supplement state and federal overhead costs. In any event, our objective is acceptance of the principles involved, not a precise estimate of the overhead costs of education.

What is the scope of state regulation that would exist in the substantial diminution of public schools? There is no clear-cut answer to this question. On the one hand, the forces seeking a larger market share for private schools are usually the forces seeking less regulation of private schools. For this reason, it might appear that any success in achieving a larger market share is likely to be accompanied by success in avoiding more government regulation. The contrary view is that the way to enable private schools to obtain a larger market share is for them to accept much greater governmental regulation than exists at present.[45] In our view, the private schools that need more government support (they already receive some, a fact ignored in voucher controversies) would be willing to accept more government regulation on some issues, but not on others. For example, denominational schools might be willing to accept more regulation of school construction, but they reject government support if it requires government control of the curriculum. This is why more government support for private education will not necessarily be tied to substantially more government regulation of private education. In American politics, there is widespread reluctance, if not outright opposition, to increased government regulation of denominational organizations of any kind.

## NOTES

1. U.S. Department of State, "Overseas Schools Advisory Council Worldwide Fact Sheet—2000–2001," Washington, DC, 2001, 1. At http://www.state.gov/www/about_state/schools/ [accessed May 1, 2002].

2. Ibid., 2.

3. U.S. Department of Defense Education Activity, "DoDEA Demographics," *Budget Book for Fiscal Year 2001*, Washington, DC, 2002, 1. At http://www.odedodea.edu/budget01/pdf/budgetbook2001.pdf [accessed May 1, 2002].

4. U.S. Department of Defense Education Activity, "DoDEA Facts 2002," 1. At http://www.odedodea.edu/communications/dodeafacts2002.htm [accessed May 1, 2002].

5. U.S. Department of Defense Education Activity, "DoDEA Demographics," *Budget Book for Fiscal Year 2001*, 2.

6. Ibid.

7. Ibid., 1–2.

8. Ibid.

9. Richard Buddin, Brian P. Gill, and Ron W. Zimmer, *Impact Aid and the Education of Military Children* (Arlington, VA: RAND, 2001), 83–84.

10. One study that analyzes the overall high performance of DoDEA students on the National Assessment of Educational Progress (NAEP) is Claire Smrekar, James W. Guthrie, Debra E. Owens, and Pearl G. Sims, *March toward Excellence: School Success and Minority Achievement in Department of Defense Schools* (Washington, D.C.: National Educational Goals Panel, 2001).

11. U.S. Department of Education, National Center for Education Statistics, *Federal Support for Education: Fiscal Years 1980 to 2002,* Charlene Hoffman, NCES 2003-0068, Washington, DC, 2002, 34. At http://www.nces.ed.gov/pubs2003/2003006.pdf [accessed November 12, 2002].

12. U.S. Department of Education, National Center for Education Statistics, *Digest of Education Statistics 2001,* NCES 2002-130, Washington, DC, 2002, 423–428.

13. Office of Management and Budget, *Administration of Justice,* Washington, DC, 2001, 7. At http://www.whitehouse.gov/omb/budget/fy2002/bud17.html [accessed August 24, 2001].

14. Ibid.

15. U.S. Department of Justice, Bureau of Justice Statistics, *Prison and Jail Inmates at Midyear 2001,* Allen J. Beck, Jennifer C. Karberg, and Paige M. Harrison, Washington, DC, April 2002, 2. At http://www.ojp.usdoj.gov/bjs/pub/pdf/pjim01.pdf [accessed October 10, 2002].

16. Bureau of Prisons, *Program Statement: Literacy (GED Standards)*, PS 5350.25, Washington, DC, 1997, 1–6. At www.bop.gov/progstat/5350_25.html [accessed July 12, 2001].

17. Tamar Lewin, "Inmate Education is Found to Lower Risk of New Arrest," *New York Times,* November 16, 2001.

18. U.S. Department of Justice, Office of Juvenile Justice and Delinquency Prevention, *Juvenile Offenders and Victims: 1999 National Report,* Howard N. Snyder and Melissa Sickmund, Washington, DC, 1999, 208.

19. Bruce I. Wolford, *Executive Summary: Juvenile Justice Education: Who is Educating the Youth?* (Richmond, KY: Training Resource Center, Eastern Kentucky University, May 2000), i.

20. U.S. Department of Justice, Office of Juvenile Justice and Delinquency Prevention, OJJDP Annual Report 2000, Washington, DC, 2000, 69–71. At http://www.ncjrs.org/pdffiles1/ojjdp/188419.pdf [accessed July 12, 2001].

21. U.S. Department of Justice, *Statistics 2002*, 16.

22. U.S. Department of Justice, *1999 National Report*, 104–108.

23. Wolford, *Executive Summary: Juvenile Justice Education*, 7.

24. Wolford, *Executive Summary: Juvenile Justice Education,* 4–5.

25. Ibid., i.

26. Ibid., 6.

27. Mary M. Quinn, Robert B. Rutherford Jr., and Peter E. Leone, *Students with Disabilities in Correctional Facilities* (Arlington, VA: Council for Exceptional Children, December 2001), 1. At ERIC Clearinghouse on Disabilities and Gifted Children, #E621.

28. Rowand T. Robinson, and Mary Jane K. Rapport, "Providing Special Education in the Juvenile Justice System," *Remedial and Special Education* 20, no. 1 (January/February 1999): 19–26.

29. Ibid., 3, 7.

30. Ibid., 3, 7.

31. U.S. Department of Education, Office of Correctional Education, *Mission of the Office of Correctional Education,* Washington, DC, 2002, 1. At http://www.ed.gov/ovae [accessed October 10, 2002].

32. "Prison Break," *New Republic,* October 21, 2002, 7.

33. U.S. Department of Education, *Digest of Education Statistics 2001,* 423.

34. U.S. Government Printing Office, Superintendent of Documents, *Budget of the United States Government, Fiscal Year 2002,* Washington, DC, 2001, 79.

35. U.S. Government Printing Office, Superintendent of Documents, *Budget of the United States Government, Fiscal Year 2002, Appendix,* Washington, DC, 2001, 593.

36. U.S. Government Printing Office, *Budget 2002,* 64.

37. U.S. Government Printing Office, *Budget 2002, Appendix,* 353.

38. See website at http://www.ed.gov/offices/OESE/ImpactAid/new.html, "Impact Aid," 4.

39. U.S. Government Printing Office, *Budget 2002, Appendix*, 347–348.

40. Ibid., 347.

41. U.S. Census Bureau, *United States State and Local Government Finances by Level of Government: 1998–99*, Washington, DC, 2002, 3. At http://www.census.gov/govs/estimate/9900.html [accessed November 16, 2002].

42. National Association of State Budget Officers, *State Expenditure Report 2001,* Washington, DC, 2002, 2. At http://www.nasbo.org/Publications/PDFs/nasbo2001exrep.pdg [accessed November 16, 2002].

43. We are indebted to James L. Payne for suggesting this point, which is especially relevant to the costs of tax collection in chapter 9.

44. Faith E. Crampton, "Financing Education in the Twenty-First Century: What State Legislative Trends Portend," *Journal of Education Finance* 27, no. 1 (Summer 2001): 482–483. Convention, not logic or economics, explains why these legislative costs are not categorized as costs of public education.

45. For an argument that private schools should and will accept those outcomes, see Terry M. Moe, *Schools, Vouchers, and the American Public* (Washington, DC: Brookings Institution Press, 2001).

CHAPTER 9

# Funding Costs of Public Education

Tax funds do not flow effortlessly into government coffers. The operation of any tax system involves numerous costs. These costs are, in effect, the "fundraising costs" of public institutions, analogous to the overhead costs of private companies or the fundraising costs of charitable institutions. In order to make a correct estimate of the true cost of public education, therefore, the costs associated with the operation of the tax system need to be included. Our objective is not to produce a precise estimate, but to introduce an important but frequently overlooked issue in school finance.

## ADMINISTRATIVE COSTS

All taxes involve administrative costs, which stem from the actions required to determine and collect an individual's tax obligation. All else being equal, the more it costs to administer the tax, the less efficient it is. This is true regardless of who bears the cost of administration. If the cost is borne by the taxpayer, as is often the case for income taxes, the loss of consumer utility goes beyond the dollar amount that ultimately is paid to the government. The more time it takes to fulfill taxpayer obligations, the greater is the consumer's loss and the more difficult it will be for the public sector to make up the loss through the provision of public services. If the cost is borne by the public sector, higher costs also result in fewer resources available for providing public services.[1]

---

This chapter draws heavily on an analysis prepared by economist James L. Payne for the Education Policy Institute; however, the authors are solely responsible for the content here.

This point is especially important if one wishes to make a comparison between tax-funded education and private education. Generally speaking, the fundraising costs of private schools automatically appear in their budgets, while these same costs are excluded from the budgets of public schools. For example, in a private school, the cost of reminding parents to make payments, following up on the reminders, and keeping track of the payments is simply one of the costs of school administration and is included in the school budget. A similar function has to be performed for public schools supported by property taxes. Taxpayers have to be notified and reminded to pay, and records have to be kept of their payments. However, the administrative costs associated with these activities do not appear in the school budget. They are borne by agencies outside the school, such as the county treasurer's office.

It is only since the 1960s that scholars in the field of taxation have begun to study the costs and burdens associated with the operation of tax systems. In ignoring the costs of the tax system, academics have lagged as badly as the politicians. Economists theorized in the abstract about a welfare state that was assumed to have no overhead costs in raising funds for public purposes (and as a result, their models gave a highly exaggerated picture of the value of government programs). As a result of recent research, however, policymakers are now more aware that the operation of any tax system entails substantial overhead costs that should be included in any cost-benefit analysis of public services.

Until very recently, the costs of raising government revenues were not a prominent political issue in national politics. The issue was not wholly ignored, but it was rather marginal until the 1996 federal elections, when Republican presidential candidate Steve Forbes proposed a highly simplified flat tax on income. He proposed a tax return that should take only a few minutes to prepare. Although revenue issues still predominate, the costs of tax collection, including the time devoted to the process by taxpayers, are a much more prominent issue than in the past.

A moment's reflection indicates that the taxpaying process raises important questions for our study. Obviously, if education were funded privately, the costs of raising revenues for it would not be a significant cost of government. No special taxes for education would be required to pay for education, and the cost of government regulation and oversight would be minimal. Our analytical problem would be greatly simplified if this were the case, but it is not and will not be in the foreseeable future. For this reason, the government costs of raising revenues to pay for public education are relevant to our study.

Because the fundraising costs of public schools are not directly accessible, it becomes a challenging task to identify and estimate them. These costs include the cost of running local agencies involved in the property tax system, such as assessors' and treasurers' offices, as well as state and federal tax collection agencies. They also include the burdens of the tax system that fall on the private sector. These burdens may be much larger than the government costs of the tax collecting agencies.

One daunting problem is that all levels of government, especially the state and federal, raise their revenues by several different taxes, charges, fees, and other involuntary payments to government. The tax collection (perhaps "revenue collection" is a better term) costs vary widely, not only among these different taxes, but also for the same tax from place to place and time to time. Of course, our estimates will be highly tentative, with no claim whatsoever of precision in the real world. Nonetheless, the basic point that there are costs to tax collection and that these costs should be factored into the real costs of public education seems unassailable. The costs of public education begin long before school districts receive their revenues. Our approach is to make rough estimates of the costs of getting and collecting income and property taxes and to use these estimates to arrive at an overall estimate of the costs of raising the revenues for public education.

Our focus on income and property taxes is based upon their dominant roles in funding public education. In 2001, property taxes accounted for 73 percent of local revenues, far ahead of sales and gross receipts taxes (16 percent), individual income taxes (5 percent), and corporate and other taxes (6 percent).[2] Because local revenues are expended primarily for public elementary and secondary school systems, the costs of collecting property taxes must be considered. In 2001, income taxes (personal and corporate) accounted for 57 percent of federal revenues and about 40 percent of state revenues; hence their collection and disincentive costs are also major issues.[3] Sales taxes will be disregarded, since they are a major component of education funding only at the state level, where they generate less than one-third of the funds for public education. It must be emphasized, however, that each level of government levies some taxes that are the primary source of revenue at other levels. For example, some dependent school districts receive funds from sales taxes, and 39 states utilize state property taxes.[4] We believe, however, that a sense of the magnitude of the costs of raising revenues for public education is demonstrable without greater precision in the analysis.

Obviously, our approach to the costs of collecting revenues for public education raises the basic allocation of cost issues discussed in previous chapters. One can plausibly argue that the costs of tax collection would not diminish, or would not diminish very much, if there were no public schools. For example, the federal government would continue to utilize the federal income tax as its main source of revenue. As previously noted, however, this argument leads to the unsustainable conclusion that there are no costs to tax collection; every government service could claim that the tax system would remain in place even if its services were abolished. To avoid this outcome, we have allocated the costs of tax collection in proportion to the service revenues raised by a tax. If half of the revenues of a tax go to public education, then half of the costs of collecting the tax will also be allocated to education.[5]

## THE COSTS OF COLLECTING PROPERTY TAXES

Although property taxes account for almost two-thirds of public school revenues nationally, there are large differences in the percentage from state to state and sometimes between school districts in the same state.

In an effort to establish the magnitude of the collection costs of property taxes, economist James L. Payne undertook an examination of the systems of Spokane County, Washington, and Bonner County, Idaho.[6]

Spokane County is an urban county, including the city of Spokane, with a population of 361,000 and property tax revenue of $261 million. Bonner County is a rural area, with a population of 27,000 and property tax revenue of $24 million.

Using published budget figures and interviews with administrators and budget officials, Payne began by outlining the three main units in a local property tax system. First, the assessor's office sets values to property, sends out notices of these valuations, and deals with citizen disputes concerning these valuations. (In Bonner County, this function appears as two separately funded activities, assessment and property revaluation, both of which function in the same physical office.)

The quasi-judicial body where taxpayers appeal the decisions made by the assessor is generally called a board of equalization. (In Bonner County, the county commissioners also serve as the board of equalization to hear assessment protests.) In addition to the local board of equalization, there are higher levels of appeal, including a state board of equalization as well as the courts. The costs of these higher levels of appeal are ignored in Payne's analysis, since they appear to be quite small in the overall picture.

Finally, every property tax system has a tax collection agency that sends out notices of taxes due, records payments, pursues delinquencies, and, ultimately—with the assistance of local law enforcement officials—seizes property of defaulting taxpayers. Generally, this collection function is carried on by the local treasurer. Since this office also has other functions, such as receiving nontax payments and managing investments, Payne asked officials to estimate the fraction of tax-related work carried on by the treasurer's office. This was put at 60 percent by the Spokane treasurer's office, and 80 percent by the Bonner County treasurer. These figures were used to allocate a proportion of the treasurer's office expenses to the tax system.

The results of the tabulations of administrative costs are shown in tables 9.1 and 9.2. In Spokane, administrative costs totaled $4.7 million, or 1.81 percent of property taxes collected. In Bonner County, costs were $1 million, or 4.15 percent of property taxes collected. The greater efficiency of the Spokane system would seem to reflect economies of scale.

**Table 9.1. Administrative Costs of Property Tax System in Spokane County, Washington, 1997**

| *Agency* | *Cost* |
|---|---|
| Assessor's Office | |
| Budgeted expenditures | $2,554,990 |
| Overhead costs not in budget | 660,000 |
| Board of Equalization | |
| Budgeted expenditures | 8,388 |
| Overhead costs not in budget | 30,000 |
| Treasurer's Office | |
| 60% of budgeted expenditures | 827,632 |
| Overhead costs not in budget | 538,000 |
| Total administrative cost | 4,619,010 |
| Total property taxes collected | $261,104,370 |
| Administrative cost as a fraction of total taxes collected | 1.81% |

Source: James L. Payne, *Fundraising Costs of Public Education*, paper prepared for the Education Policy Institute, Appendix, table A1, August 14, 2001.

**Table 9.2. Administrative Costs of Property Tax System in Bonner County, Idaho, 1997**

| *Agency* | *Cost* |
|---|---|
| Assessor's Office | |
| Budgeted expenditures | $166,066 |
| Benefits and overhead | 187,343 |
| Revaluation, budget | 224,637 |
| Benefits and overhead | 169,266 |
| Treasurer's Office | |
| 80% of budgeted expenditures | 89,895 |
| Benefits and overhead | 167,133 |
| Total cost | 1,004,340 |
| Total property tax collected | $24,224,542 |
| Administrative cost as a fraction of taxes collected | 4.15% |

Source: James L. Payne, *Fundraising Costs of Public Education*, paper prepared for the Education Policy Institute, Appendix, table A2, August 14, 2001.

## COMPLIANCE COSTS

In addition to the work performed by government tax agencies, tax systems involve effort, time, and money on the part of the taxpayers who have to deal with them. This burden is the compliance cost of the system. Ideally, a survey of taxpayers should be utilized to estimate the compliance costs. Although many surveys have been made of taxpayer behavior in connection with income tax systems, Payne was unable to identify any survey of taxpayer compliance costs in a property tax system. His estimates of the compliance costs in the two counties are shown in tables 9.3 and 9.4.

In a property tax system, compliance costs occur at four points. The first is the taxpayer response to the assessment notice, which sets the value of the property for tax purposes. Interviews with officials in the assessors' offices indicated that a surprisingly high number of taxpayers question their assessments. In Spokane it appeared that about 10 percent of assessments are challenged, or at least queried; in Bonner County, the figure appears to be over 20 percent.

Naturally, the time each taxpayer devotes to these challenges will vary. In a few cases, it might involve only one telephone call; at the other extreme, the taxpayer might spend weeks discussing his assessment problem with friends, advisors, and professionals. One important variable in this picture is whether the taxpayer contacts the assessor's office by telephone or in person. Naturally, the latter method involves a greater expenditure of time (unless the assessor's telephone is always busy—which is not unusual at the height of the tax season). It appears that in Spokane, the majority of the challenges are made by telephone, while in Bonner County the majority are personal visits. For his analysis, Payne assumed

**Table 9.3. Compliance Costs of Property Tax System in Spokane County, Washington, 1997**

| *Taxpayer Activity* | *Number of Cases* | *Cost Per Case* | *Total Cost* |
|---|---|---|---|
| Questioning/Challenging Assessment | | | |
| Assessor level | 20,000 | $26.60 | $532,000 |
| Questioning/Challenging Assessment | | | |
| Board of Equalization | | | |
| Initial contacts | 5,000 | 26.60 | 133,000 |
| Full petitions | 600 | 1,250.00 | 750,000 |
| Severe delinquencies (foreclosures, seizures) | 2,700 | 1,250.00 | 3,375,000 |
| Total cost | | | 7,716,000 |
| Total property taxes collected | | | $261,104,370 |
| Compliance cost as a fraction of total taxes collected | | | 2.96% |

Source: James L. Payne, *Fundraising Costs of Public Education*, paper prepared for the Education Policy Institute, Appendix, table A4, August 14, 2001.

**Table 9.4. Compliance Costs of Property Tax System in Bonner County, Idaho, 1997**

| *Taxpayer Activity* | *Number of Cases* | *Cost Per Case* | *Total Cost* |
|---|---|---|---|
| Questioning/Challenging Assessment | | | |
| Assessor level | 7,600 | $26.60 | $202,160 |
| Questioning/Challenging Assessment | | | |
| Board of Equalization | | | |
| Full petitions | 70 | 1,250.00 | 87,500 |
| Tax collection | | | |
| Responding to notices | 32,600 | 13.30 | 433,580 |
| Initial delinquencies | 4,400 | 26.60 | 117,040 |
| Severe delinquencies | | | |
| (foreclosures, seizures) | 550 | $1,250.00 | 687,500 |
| Total cost | | | 1,527,780 |
| Total property taxes collected | | | $24,224,542 |
| Compliance cost as a fraction of total taxes collected | | | 6.31% |

Source: James L. Payne, *Fundraising Costs of Public Education,* paper prepared for the Education Policy Institute, Appendix, table A4, August 14, 2001.

that the average amount of time that a taxpayer takes in questioning an assessment notice at the assessor's level is two hours. This includes the time spent thinking about and preparing for the contact, the time spent making contact (driving, waiting, telephoning and getting a busy signal), and time actually spent discussing the problem with officials. To value this time, Payne used the nationwide hourly rate of $13.30.[7] This results in a cost of $26.60 for each case. Out-of-pocket costs, such as parking expenses, telephone bills, copying charges, and so forth, were included in this figure.

When the taxpayer fails to get satisfaction at the assessor's level, he appeals to the board of equalization. This appeal has two levels of involvement. First, there are preliminary contacts with equalization board staff, in which the taxpayer explains his situation and attempts to determine how and whether to pursue the dispute, and perhaps makes an initial request for a hearing. Most taxpayers drop out at this stage, learning that their case has little chance of success, or deciding that contesting the issue is not worth their time. For the purpose of assessing this burden, Payne treated it as requiring the same amount of time as the initial inquiries at the assessor's office. (In Bonner County, where the county commissioners serve as the board of equalization, the burden of these initial contacts was already included in the questioning process taking place in the assessor's office.)

Some taxpayers pursue their case at the board of equalization level and prepare a full petition to be considered by the board at a formal hearing. Although the actual hearing time was only 10 minutes to 1.5 hours, the cases generally involved considerable preparation. As officials made clear to taxpayers, it is pointless to go before a board of equalization with only the complaint that one's taxes are "too high." The taxpayer must develop empirical evidence to document the position that his property was overvalued. This often involved considerable research and complicated calculations due to the different methods of valuation (cost, market value, or income). In Spokane, the majority of appeals included independent assessments, paid for by the taxpayer. Taxpayers with large homes, as well as business taxpayers, often hired accountants and attorneys to develop the paperwork for their case. In cases with millions of tax dollars at stake, the taxpayers were willing to spend substantial amounts to prepare their argument for a lower valuation. Payne estimated that the average cost of taxpayer involvement in these cases is $1,250. This figure covers both the taxpayer's time in thinking about, discussing, and preparing the case, and all expenses for materials and professional services.

The third stage of the compliance process is the taxpayer's response to the notice of tax due, sent by the treasurer's office. The taxpayer normally responds to this by making payment. At a minimum, the costs involved at this stage include the time taken to write a check, prepare an envelope, perhaps copy the check and/or notice, and mail it. A surprisingly large number of taxpayers—around 10 percent—come to the treasurer's office to pay in person, either to get a receipt or to query or complain about a tax bill. Payne estimated the time/cost for taxpayers to be one hour, or $13.30. (Taxpayers who do not pay at this stage and become delinquent are assumed to bear no burden.)

The next stage of the collection process is the pursuit of delinquencies. According to tax collection officials, about 10 percent of tax bills remain unpaid at the end of the statutory period and become delinquent. These "initial delinquencies" are pursued by notices, letters, and telephone calls, and most of them are eventually cleared up. The taxpayer burden here was assumed to be the same as for questioning assessments, two hours, or $26.60. When a delinquency has passed a statutory period, the property becomes subject to foreclosure and seizure action by the tax collector acting through the courts and police. These "severe delinquencies" generally involve considerable taxpayer involvement, as the taxpayer acts to hold on to his property. Taxpayer activities at this stage include retaining lawyers to resist foreclosure, meeting with local officials to arrange for delays, and special payment plans. This burden was set at $1,250, the same as for a formal assessment appeal.

With these values ascribed to the different phases of the taxation process, Payne estimated the taxpayer compliance burden, as shown in tables 9.3 and 9.4.

Tables 9.3 and 9.4 show that the Spokane jurisdiction had a lower relative cost (2.96 percent, compared to 6.31 percent for Bonner County). The most likely explanation for this difference is that the Bonner County tax system is more accessible to citizens. They are more likely to know the (locally elected) assessor, treasurer, and commissioners, and feel less inhibition about going to county offices. In the city of Spokane, protesting a tax or tax assessment is more difficult, and more forbidding, so more citizens—even if dissatisfied—simply do not act upon their complaints about the tax system.

Compared to an income tax with all its complexities, a property tax is extremely straightforward. The definition of property, and the ownership of property, are simple concepts, and there is very little opportunity for tax avoidance or evasion. As a result, we would expect that a property tax system would have much lower compliance costs than an income tax system.

Payne's data bear this out. In Spokane County, the monetary value of these compliance burdens on citizens amounted to over $1.5 million, or 2.96 percent of total taxes collected. In Bonner County, they amounted to $1.5 million, or 6.31 percent of taxes collected. For the overall estimate of compliance costs under property taxes, Payne used the average of these two values, or 4.64 percent.

This figure is much lower than the 26.4 percent compliance cost that Payne calculated for the federal income tax system, but it is not negligible. Citizens make a significant investment of time and money in dealing with property taxes. A survey of local assessors' offices by the Washington State Department of Revenue found the "number of telephone calls and visits from property owners to the assessors' offices following revaluation is so great in some counties that it is often difficult to accommodate property owners in the 30 days before they must file an appeal."[8]

## THE COSTS OF COLLECTING STATE REVENUES

In 1998–99, state governments provided $169.3 billion in public school revenues.[9] Of seven main functional categories of state spending, elementary and secondary education is the largest state expenditure, utilizing more than 35 percent of general fund spending.[10] Along with other receipts, state income taxes paid by individuals are paid into the state's general fund. The cost of collecting these taxes is lower than the cost of collecting federal income taxes for two reasons. First, 43 states levy state personal income taxes as a percentage of the taxpayers' federal income tax obligations.[11] Furthermore, as noted above, the state income tax codes are much simpler than the federal code. Most state personal income tax laws provide for an optional standard deduction and allow the taxpayers to utilize their federal itemized deductions as their state deductions. In addition, the government cost is reduced if employers collect most of the revenue for the tax. These factors suggest that the percentage cost of collecting state income taxes is about one-fourth the percentage cost of collecting federal income taxes.

State sales taxes and excise taxes raised 49 percent of state revenues in 1997.[12] State sales taxes cost more to collect per dollar of revenue than either property or income taxes. Thus, individual income and sales taxes accounted for 82 percent of state revenues in 1997; by adjusting the costs to reflect the amount raised by each kind of tax, and applying the percentage to the remaining sources of state revenues, one could estimate the cost of collecting state revenues for public education.

## THE COSTS OF COLLECTING FEDERAL REVENUES

In fiscal year 1998–99, federal revenues accounted for 7.1 percent of the revenues for public education.[13] In 1985, Payne estimated that the federal government cost of revenue collection was 0.61 percent of the revenue collected.[14] Although Payne's estimate is not as recent as is desirable, it may be on the conservative side for several reasons. First, the Internal Revenue Code is more complex than it was in 1985; this means more government and taxpayer time, more utilization of lawyers and accountants, and higher costs of collection on both the government and the taxpayer sides. Second, Payne did not include various costs which in toto would have raised the percentage by a significant amount. For example, his analysis did not take into account the congressional expenses devoted to tax matters or the tax-related expenses of the presidency and other executive offices, including the Office of Management and Budget (OMB). For these and other reasons, Payne's estimate appears to be realistic even if the percentage of federal costs that he included has declined since 1985. Assuming that the federal government cost of collecting federal revenue in FY 1998–99 was 0.61 percent of the total, the cost of collecting federal taxes for education in that year would have been $1.49 billion—not a huge amount in the overall picture, but more than a trivial one. It should be emphasized, however, that if our analysis is valid, the federal revenues for public education are much larger than the NCES estimates; hence the costs of collecting federal revenues for education would correspondingly be more than $1.49 billion.

To arrive at a single number that expresses the overhead cost of raising school tax funds nationwide, we can combine the property and income tax figures in a 2:1 ratio, which is roughly the proportion of property taxes to income taxes in the school tax mix (as already noted, excise and sales taxes are excluded from this analysis). This yields an overall figure of 36.2 percent and means that to raise $1.00 in taxes for the public schools, an additional cost of 36.2 cents for tax collection must be included. This is the factor that should be added to published budget figures to arrive at a more realistic estimate of the cost of public education. For example, suppose total revenues for public elementary and secondary schools are $300 billion. Our admittedly highly tentative estimate of the cost of raising these funds through the tax system is 36.2 percent of this amount, or nearly $109 billion. Hence, the actual total cost of public primary and secondary education would be $409 billion.

Obviously, this estimate of the fundraising costs of public education involves many large uncertainties. Its purpose is not so much to establish the precise cost of collecting school tax funds, but rather to dispel the prevailing assumption that these costs are zero.

## THE COST OF CONFLICT

Democratic theory says that citizens should pay their taxes cheerfully, but someone seems to have forgotten to tell taxpayers this. They often resent having their money wrested away from them, and as a result, they often resent the people deemed responsible for the taxes that must be paid. Understandably, when a school system is funded by taxes, it generates an underlying reservoir of opposition. This opposition poses an enduring problem for public schools. At any moment, the critics may comprise a majority, and defeat a needed funding measure, thus leaving the school in a financial crisis. Another possibility is that this critical bloc may elect, or help elect, school boards or other officials hostile to expenditures for public schools.

Conflict within the schools is an even more daunting problem. Because public education is funded through taxes, everyone in the community has a right to complain about anything that goes on in the schools, and school officials are legally and morally bound to consider their complaints. As a result, public schools are repeatedly embroiled in public disputes that sap everyone's energy.

Unfortunately, the public disputes often escalate into a community-wide struggle. Factions are formed, and charges are traded back and forth. If teacher tenure or competence is involved, the teacher will turn to the union for support, thus further escalating the conflict. Protesting taxpayers and parents will become watchdog bodies.

It is important to realize that this unsatisfactory outcome is not necessarily the result of poor management or inadequate leadership. By turning to the tax system for funding, American educators inadvertently brought a great deal of social conflict into the schools. Public education was founded partly to "Americanize" the huge number of immigrants arriving in the U.S. in the latter half of the nineteenth and early part of the twentieth centuries. Today, however, scores of differing ethnic, religious, and cultural groups, all of which feel equally qualified to express and act upon their displeasure about various aspects of public education, present a much different situation. Although the cost of social conflict in the schools is not necessarily included in school district financial statements, it could be very substantial. Interestingly enough, as early as 1962, Milton Friedman warned that our political system could not withstand the divisive tendencies inherent in public education.[15]

## LOTTERY REVENUES

Although lottery revenues for education are included in the foregoing analysis, a brief discussion of them illustrates the gap between the political rhetoric and the realities of educational revenues. In the early years of our nation, government-sponsored lotteries were frequently utilized to finance various public services. By 1900, however, every state prohibited lotteries, and the prohibitions remained in effect until 1964.[16] In that year, New Hampshire adopted a lottery to fund public education. Since then, 37 states and the District of Columbia have adopted lotteries. In 1997, gross state lottery revenues were over $35 billion and net lottery revenues exceeded $12 billion.[17] Almost half of the state lotteries allocate all or some of the lottery revenues to public education. In the other states, lottery revenues are allocated to the state's general fund; these funds may or may not be used to increase appropriations for public schools.

Reliance on lottery revenues for public education is subject to criticism for the following reasons:

- Lottery revenues are highly unstable, often requiring sudden adjustments in school district budgets.
- Lotteries have a negative impact on economic growth. Consequently, lotteries can result in a decline in sales, excise, and/or income taxes; some states appear to have lost $0.23 in other revenues to gain $1 in lottery revenues.[18]
- Lottery revenues replace, not supplement, other revenues for education. Other public services, not education, are the beneficiaries of lottery revenues earmarked for education. Their benefits are the additional revenues made possible by earmarking lottery revenues to education, and the fact that the noneducation services benefit

> from their higher-priority claim to revenues from the state's general fund. Actually, lotteries often function to conceal legislative unwillingness to raise taxes for education, rendering it more difficult to do so after a lottery plan is enacted.

Perhaps the single most telling criticism of state lotteries to raise revenues for any public service is their inefficiency as a means of raising revenues. Lottery administration requires promotion, ticket selling, and accounting costs, often in conjunction with a new state bureaucracy that raises another set of problems. After payment of expenses, only about $11 billion out of gross lottery revenues of $32.1 billion in 1995 was available to fund public services.[19] In Florida, lottery legislation mandated that 50 percent of gross lottery revenues be spent for prizes and not over 12 percent for administration, thus leaving only 38 percent for education.[20] No alternative way of funding education costs as much as lotteries per dollar of net revenue.

As noted above, in most states lottery revenues supplant instead of increase revenues for education. In effect, they illustrate the pressure on legislators to raise more revenue without enacting higher taxes that are unavoidable. Inasmuch as no one is required to buy a lottery ticket, or needs one to survive, lottery revenues are viewed as a politically painless way of generating school revenues. However, public school organizations do not wish to depend on sources of revenue that can fluctuate widely from year to year. A resolution adopted by the National Education Association states that "the amount of aid must be generally predictable for long-range planning and specifically predictable for year-to-year planning."[21]

Low-income citizens provide a disproportionate share of lottery revenues; hence such revenues also conflict with the objective of paying for education through a progressive tax system. The revenues from lotteries are a minor source of revenues for education, but this is not the case with education revenues from state sales taxes, which are growing in importance as a source of revenue for public education. Despite efforts to mitigate their regressivity, sales taxes are inherently regressive inasmuch as their effectiveness depends upon their unavoidability—and only necessities are unavoidable.

## SUMMARY

The failure to include the costs of tax collection is one of the major reasons why the net benefits of tax-supported welfare programs are exaggerated. In private schools and private business generally, the costs of raising revenues to fund the enterprise are routinely included as a cost of doing business. Not so in public education, where the costs are allocated to the agencies that levy and collect taxes. The Internal Revenue Service (IRS) estimated that it cost $0.39 to collect each $100 of tax revenue in the year ending September 30, 2000. Because the federal government provides only about 7 percent of funding for public education, the estimated costs of levying and collecting taxes at the state and local levels should also be included in estimates of the costs of public education. Compliance costs by taxpayers should also be considered in these estimates.

All of the 37 states and the District of Columbia that allocate some lottery revenues directly to public education have extensive administrative, promotion, and advertising expenses. No alternative way of funding education costs as much as lotteries per dollar of net revenue. Lottery revenues have replaced, not added to, general revenues for education.

## NOTES

1. David H. Monk, *Education Finance: An Economic Approach* (New York: McGraw-Hill, 1990), 137. An NEA publication makes essentially the same point. See "Administrative and Compliance Costs," in Research Division, NEA, *Tax Options for States Needing More School Revenue* (Washington, DC: National Education Association, 1994), 15.

2. Michael Fitzpatrick Lorelli, *Special Report: State and Local Property Taxes* (Washington, DC: Tax Foundation, 2001), 2–3. At http://www.taxpolicycenter.org/TaxFacts/state/rates.cfm [accessed November 4, 2002].

3. Internal Revenue Service, Form 1040 Instructions, 2. At http://www.irs.gov/pub/irs-pdf/i1040.pdf [accessed November 14, 2002].

4. Lorelli, *Special Report,* 3.

5. On this issue, we have followed the approach taken in James L. Payne, *Costly Returns* (San Francisco: ICS Press, 1993), especially 121–122.

6. All of the following data on the costs of revenue collection in these two counties are taken from the paper submitted by Payne to the Education Policy Institute. None of Payne's figures has been changed.

7. Calculated from *Statistical Abstract of the United States,* 1997, tables 635 and 666. This figure pertains to 1994.

8. Washington State Department of Revenue, "Improving Property Tax Administration in Washington State" (1992 Report to the Legislature), 6.

9. U.S. Department of Education, National Center for Education Statistics, *Digest of Education Statistics 2001,* NCES 2002-130, table 158. Revenues for public elementary and secondary schools, by source and state: 1998-99 (Washington, DC: U.S. Department of Education, 2001), 179.

10. National Association of State Budget Officers, *State Expenditure Report 2001* (Washington, DC: National Association of State Budget Officers, 2002), 2–3. At http://www.nasbo.org/Publications/PDFs/nasbo2001exrep.pdf [accessed November 12, 2002].

11. Tax Policy Center, Individual Tax Rates, 1–3. At http://www.taxpolicycenter.org/TaxFacts/state/rates.cfm [accessed November 4, 2002].

12. Lorelli, *Special Report,* 3.

13. U.S. Department of Education, *Digest of Education Statistics 2001,* 179.

14. Payne, *Costly Returns,* 123.

15. Milton Friedman, *Capitalism and Freedom* (Chicago: University of Chicago Press, 1962).

16. Percy E. Burrup, Vern Brimley Jr., and Rulon R. Garfield, *Financing Education in a Climate of Change*, 7th ed. (Boston: Allyn and Bacon, 1999), 133–134.

17. Ibid, 134.

18. Mary O. Boog, Paul M. Mason, and Stephen L. Shapiro, "The Cross Effects of Lottery Taxes on Alternative State Tax Revenue," *Public Finance Quarterly* 21, no. 2 (1993): 123–140.

19. Peter Keating, "Lotto Fever: We All Lose!" *Money* 5 (1996): 142–149.

20. S. A. MacManus and C. J. Spindler, "Florida's Lottery: How Long Education's Sacred Cow?" *Florida Policy Review* 4, no. 2 (1989): 1–4. Parenthetically, it should be noted that the teacher unions in Florida supported the establishment of the state lottery for education in 1986. One can only speculate on whether Florida teachers have ever been aware of the fact that their dues were instrumental in the enactment of lottery legislation that was contrary to their interests.

21. "Resolution, A-14 Financial Support of Public Education," *NEA Handbook 2001–2002* (Washington, DC: National Education Association, 2002), 277.

CHAPTER 10

# Disincentive Costs

The largest overhead cost of a tax system is normally the *tax disincentive cost*. This is the effect that taxation has on discouraging productive economic activities. This cost stems from the elementary principle that a tax on any activity will, by raising its price, act as a deterrent or disincentive to that activity. A tax on labor will discourage people from working, a tax on homes will discourage homebuilding, and so on.

Though elementary, this principle is often overlooked. One reason why this cost was overlooked for so long—and is still overlooked by many—is that people are inclined to assess public policies in terms of their *intentions* instead of their *effects*. Since legislators do not intend to harm production and trade with their taxes, it is assumed that the taxes won't harm production and trade.

Another error that leads many to overlook the disincentive effect of taxation is the tendency to ignore the motivation of economic actors. Assume a community where every family has one and only one child. It has a system of school funding that is completely private and voluntary: each family pays an average of $5,000 for its child to attend a private school. Now consider a second community, identical in all respects except that it has a tax-funded school system: each family pays an average of $5,000 in taxes to the school system which educates its child. At first glance, these systems would seem to be economically identical, and it is difficult to see why the tax-funded system would entail any economic loss. But

---

This discussion draws heavily on an analysis prepared by economist James L. Payne for the Education Policy Institute; however, the authors (ML and CKH) are solely responsible for the content here. Although the chapter includes changes from Payne's analysis, most of the chapter follows Payne's paper and it follows Payne on the critical issues.

consider the motivation of the individual workers. In the private system, Jones the shoemaker has to earn enough money to enable his child to go to school. This means that the desire to educate his child *adds* to his motivation to work. Suppose, for example, that his normal income does not quite provide the amount he needs to send his child to a desired school. This situation will prompt Jones to work overtime and make perhaps five extra pairs of shoes a month to send his child to school.

Under the tax-funded system, the desire for education would not add to Smith's desire to work. Since his child will be educated regardless of his economic effort, he is not prompted by educational considerations to work overtime. As a result, the community has five fewer pairs of shoes, and is thus poorer than it otherwise would be. Worse still, the tax to raise money for the school is likely to be levied in some way on Smith's production of shoes. By taking away some of the fruits of his labor, it will discourage him from working as hard as he otherwise would. Hence, the effect of a tax-funded school system is to make the community poorer than it would be under a privately funded school system of the same scale and kind.

For the most part, educational finance has focused on the effects of various taxes on education. Does the tax raise sufficient revenue? Is it equitable? Easily administered? And so on. The effects of various kinds of taxes for public education on private-sector incentives have reached much less attention. As previously noted, however, the impact of taxes and tax systems is a highly controversial issue in politics and economics. For instance, payroll taxes discourage work; as such taxes rise, persons with choices may elect leisure over work, or turn to work that is not openly subject to taxes. To decide rationally whether the benefits of a policy are more valuable than its costs, policymakers need to know the costs as fully as possible.

A recent development in federal taxation should help to clarify the issue. In 1990, Congress passed a luxury tax on yachts as part of a plan to tax according to ability to pay. The upshot, however, was that the yacht-building industry experienced a drastic decrease in the demand for yachts, throwing workers in the yacht-building industry out of work and into unemployment compensation and other federally funded welfare programs. Congress repealed the tax in August 1993, because the costs turned out to be much greater than the benefits.

Looking at this situation, we can say that in enacting the yacht tax, Congress failed to take into account its disincentive effects. The same issue is at stake in the congressional controversies over efforts to reduce marginal tax rates. One way or another, the arguments for the tax reductions were arguments for reducing the disincentive effects of taxes; meanwhile the opponents of the reductions contended that the tax reductions would help the wealthy at the expense of the poor. As economist David Monk points out, however:

> The preference for taxing products where either the demand or the supply is relatively insensitive to price is one manifestation of a broader efficiency standard that is commonly applied to the evaluation of taxes. This broader goal is for the tax to affect as little as possible the working of the economy. Taxes that dramatically affect either the production or consumption behavior of individuals are considered undesirable.[1]

Monk's point explains why the disincentive effects of taxes for education should be considered in evaluating our system of funding it. Although the disincentive costs are not included in estimates of the government costs, they should be included in any comprehensive assessment of funding for public education. The disincentive costs should not be overlooked merely because academics ignore them or because we have only crude ways to assess them, or because they do not fit into the conventional accounting definition of "costs."

A critical issue is whether the government costs of public education are large enough to generate disincentive costs. At the federal level, the appropriations for public education are probably too small a part of the federal budget to generate any substantial disincentive effects. However, it must be emphasized that the total amount that taxpayers pay in taxes, not the amount paid to one level of government, is the critical factor in assessing disincentive effects. At the local level, the revenues for public education are much more than half of all locally generated revenues; if there are disincentive effects of local property taxes, educational funding is probably the main cause.

Corporate relocation or start-up decisions illustrate the importance of disincentive costs. In educational circles, it is often said that the presence of good schools is an extremely important consideration in business location decisions. Perhaps, but relocation experts regard a pro-business tax structure as a much more important inducement; in fact, states and communities often compete for new company plants through tax exemptions or commitments to lower taxes for lengthy periods of time.

In this connection, consider the location of new automotive plants in recent years.

| | |
|---|---|
| Spring Hill, TN | Saturn* |
| Canton, MS | Nissan |
| Smyrna, TN | Nissan |
| Georgetown, KY | Toyota |
| Decherd, TN | Nissan |
| Greer, SC | BMW |
| Lincoln, AL | Honda |
| Vance, AL | Mercedes-Benz[2] |

*Only unionized plant on the list

None of these choices appears to be based on the quality of education at the site; "good schools" are probably more a result than a cause of plant location. The critical point is that high levels of taxation discourage plant location; hence, whatever contributes to high levels is a legitimate area of public concern. Although taxes for public schools play a significant role in state and local taxation, their private-sector effects are important regardless of whether these effects are categorized as "costs" or in some other way.

Nationwide statistics indicate that about 45.9 percent of public elementary and secondary school funding comes from local property taxes, while most of the remainder comes from a combination of state and federal income taxes and sales and excise taxes.[3] For the purposes of this discussion, we confine our attention to taxes on property and income, and leave aside excise and sales taxes.

## DISINCENTIVE COST OF INCOME TAXES

Income taxes are the main source of federal and state revenues going to public education. Taxes on personal income, as well as taxes on corporate income and the income from capital gains, are included in "income taxes."

The first empirical studies of the disincentive cost of income taxes appeared in the 1970s.[4] Since that time, specialists in the economics of taxation have made numerous studies of this effect (which they usually call the "marginal excess burden of taxation" or "deadweight loss"). Partly because they are using different economic models, scholars have not arrived at a single estimate. The discrepancies also reflect the fact that the effect of an income tax varies considerably, depending on the type of taxpayer and type of income.

The disincentive effect is extremely high for taxes on the income from capital, because capital is such a mobile factor of production. A study of the capital gains tax by economists Roger Gordon and Burton Malkiel in 1981 found that the disincentive cost amounted to 123 percent.[5] In other words, to raise $1 through the capital gains tax causes a loss or waste of $1.23 in the overall economy. In the same study, they found that the tax on corporate income had a disincentive cost of 139 percent. A later study by Jane Gravelle and Laurence Kotlikoff put the disincentive cost of the corporation tax at between 84 and 151 percent.[6] Some economists have concluded that the taxation of capital income does so much harm to the economy that it does not raise any net revenue.[7]

Generally speaking, the disincentive costs for taxes on labor income are lower than those estimated for capital income. The main reason for this is that the supply of labor is less elastic than capital, that is, less likely to change dramatically in response to taxation. A 1981 study by Jerry Hausman found an overall disincentive effect for labor of 28.7 percent.[8] This overall figure masks a considerable variation of this effect for different kinds of workers. For low-wage married men, for example, the disincentive effect was 21.8 percent. For low-wage married women—who can more readily quit jobs if taxes take a bigger part of their paycheck—the disincentive effect was 58.1 percent.

In a 1987 study, Edgar Browning calculated the disincentive cost of labor taxation at between 31.8 and 46.9 percent.[9] This estimate is of particular interest because Browning's model, using what are known as "compensated elasticities," assumes that the tax money is used to supply something like schooling, which the taxpayer would otherwise be purchasing. It is, therefore, more appropriate for our purposes than models that assume government spending goes to some public good that does not substitute for something the taxpayer would purchase directly, like defense spending.

Some scholars have developed general models that attempt to assess the overall disincentive effect of the tax system on all types of income. One of the first of these "general equilibrium" models was put forward by Charles Stuart in 1984, who came up with an estimated disincentive effect of 24.4 percent. In 1985, a detailed, comprehensive model advanced by Charles Ballard, John Shoven, and John Whalley found a disincentive effect of 33.2 percent; that is, raising $1 through the tax system causes 33.2 cents in lost production.[10] Another comprehensive model developed by Dale Jorgenson and Kun-Young Yun came up with an estimate of 46.0 percent.[11]

Some recent work by Martin Feldstein, former chairman of the Council of Economic Advisors, suggests that these estimates may be much too low. Basing his calculations on the actual behavior of taxpayers in response to the 1986 tax reform, Feldstein found a disincentive effect of 165 percent.[12] This higher figure reflects something of a trend in the literature on disincentive effects; estimates of tax disincentive costs have tended to increase as economists have refined their models and improved their empirical foundations.

For present purposes, the Ballard, Shoven, and Whalley figure of 33.2 percent is probably the most comprehensive and accurate. Furthermore, this figure falls between the other estimates, and this makes it perhaps the most representative figure.

## THE DISINCENTIVE EFFECTS OF PROPERTY TAXES

In the 14,891 independent school districts in the United States (in 1998–99), 95 percent of local tax revenue was raised by property taxes. For this reason, reliance upon the disincentive costs of property taxes will result in reasonable estimates of the disincentive costs of local taxes for education if the estimating procedures are reasonably accurate.[13]

To weigh the economic effect of a property tax, it helps to review the general theory of disincentive effects. All taxes do not create a disincentive effect. For example, in ideal form, a head tax (also called a "lump sum" tax) is a fixed levy on each and every person. It must be paid whether taxpayers work or sleep, whether they are rich or poor, whether they have saved their wealth, or consumed it. Because the head tax is not tied to any economic activity, it does not discourage any, and, therefore, would have no disincentive effect on economic production. An income tax lies at the other extreme. It is usually tied to the productive economic activities that generate income—work, savings and investment, the invention and application of technology—and therefore it directly discourages them.

Lying between these two categories is a tax on property. For taxpayers owning a property on a permanent basis, such as a homeowner, a property tax approaches being a head tax. You pay it in a fixed amount, whether you have worked or slept, whether you are rich or poor, whether you have invested or consumed. Therefore, for such taxpayers, the property tax would not, in the main, seem to affect economic behavior. However, in other cases, the value of property is tied to income-producing efforts. If a farmer wants to earn more income he may have to build a bigger barn—which will increase his property taxes. Therefore, the property tax indirectly discourages him from earning more income.

A property tax also operates as an excise tax, raising the cost of owning homes, stores, and factories. As such, it would have some discouraging effect on the sale of, and hence the construction of, these properties. Economists are generally of the opinion that an excise tax reduces labor effort, the logic being that since the worker can buy less with his paycheck, it makes leisure relatively more attractive. But it does not seem that this effect is as great as a direct tax on labor. An excise tax falls only on some commodities, and therefore does not shrink the value of the paycheck across the board. In particular, it does not fall on savings and investment. Thus, a property tax bears only indirectly, or partially, on income.

These considerations suggest that for the property tax, we treat its disincentive effect as falling halfway between that of an income tax, which we have suggested is 33.2 percent, and a head tax, to which we have ascribed a value of zero.[14] That approach gives us a figure of 16.6 percent for the disincentive effect of a property tax. In other words, to raise $1 through the property tax causes the loss of 16.6 cents of economic production.

## WHO PAYS THE TAXES?

Although public policies are supposed to govern the kinds of taxes that are imposed, the political influence of potential taxpayers is often the decisive factor on this issue. The developments in Vermont illustrate this point.

In 1997, Vermont enacted the Equal Educational Opportunity Act of 1997. The act imposed a statewide property tax of $1.10 per $100 of equalized assessed valuation. Towns wishing to spend more were allowed to impose additional taxes, but the amounts raised this way were to be redistributed evenly among all of the participating districts. Although the local option was supposed to be a concession to districts that wanted to spend more than the statewide block grant, its political effect was to antagonize the higher-spending districts. In some, taxpayers established private foundations to avoid sharing their additional taxes with other school districts.[15]

As a practical matter, Vermont prefers property to income taxes because a great deal of property in the state is owned by taxpayers who do not live in the state, including large out-of-state ski corporations. An income tax would increase the tax burdens of state residents, because they would lose the revenue from the property of out-of-state taxpayers.

Another point of interest is who pays the taxes. Although the point is debatable, property taxes are generally progressive, because the lower-income taxpayers are less likely to own property subject to property taxes. Other taxes, however, tell a different story. Table 10.1 provides a breakdown of the sources of education funding in Michigan.

**Table 10.1. Funding Education in Michigan in 2000**

| *Source of Revenue* | *In Millions* |
|---|---|
| Tobacco/Liquor Taxes | $401.8 |
| Gambling Revenues | 712.0 |
| Property-related Taxes | 1,802.2 |
| Income Tax | 2,043.9 |
| Sales and Use Tax | 5,170.1 |

Source: Michigan Education Report, Spring 2001, 1.

More than 10 percent of Michigan's School Aid Fund is comprised of taxes on behaviors deemed undesirable, at least for children, including drinking, smoking, and gambling. But over a billion dollars in public school funding would be lost if adults ceased engaging in these activities. Generally speaking, sales taxes are most effective when levied upon items that cannot be avoided. Taxpayers can decide not to buy yachts, but they must buy food. This is why a tax on food is more effective at raising revenue. Taxes on food, however, are regressive, as are tobacco and liquor taxes. As a result, at least 55 percent of state aid to education is from regressive taxes. It would be safe to add the 7 percent from gambling taxes, since these taxes also tend to be very regressive.[16] Generally speaking, the regressivity of sales taxes tends to rise as income rises. The reason is that the higher the income, the lower the percentage of it that is spent on the basic necessities that all or most taxpayers must buy.

The public school organizations naturally prefer income and other progressive taxes, but as table 10.1 suggests, this preference can be very difficult to achieve. The upshot is that despite its concern for the economically disadvantaged, the public school establishment frequently supports regressive taxes on the basis that such taxes are the only feasible alternative under the circumstances.

## AMERICAN HERITAGE ACADEMY: A CASE IN POINT

On various occasions, tax issues relating to the cost of education come to a head in a single situation. Such was the case when a for-profit school, American Heritage Academy, was assessed a $75,000 impact fee in Cherokee County, Georgia. The impact fees in the county are one-time charges on new development; the charges are supposed to pay for roads, public safety, parks, and libraries.

American Heritage Academy planned to triple its capacity from 340 K–7 students to serve 800–900 students, including high school students. The school requested a waiver, pointing out that the addition would relieve overcrowding in the county public schools; it also requested that the Cherokee County Water and Sewage Authority grant a 50 percent reduction in the water and sewer tap fees that county public schools receive.

Impact fees in the county ranged from $1,832 for new homes, regardless of size, to $10,522 per 1,000 square feet for fast-food restaurants. Recent impact fees included:

| | |
|---|---|
| Golf course | $52,000 |
| Gasoline station | 44,000 |
| Hotel | 32,000 |
| Pizza restaurant | 27,000 |
| Church (under appeal) | 3,000 |

The academy's requests were rejected on the grounds that a school for profit should not be treated differently from any other for-profit business; as one commissioner put it, "there's no difference from the newest McDonald's."[17]

Arguably, the county government might have waived the fees on the grounds that the county would be better off economically if its schools were relieved of the burden of educating an additional 460–560 secondary students; in any event, the situation illustrates the difficulty of establishing a "level playing field" in public/private school competition.

When critics of educational vouchers decry the absence of a "level playing field," they are referring to the fact that public schools are regulated more highly than private schools, to the competitive disadvantage of the public schools. A "level playing field" in the business context means that government does not favor any company over its competitors. In the educational context, a "level playing field" is sometimes interpreted as converting private schools into public schools. This would eviscerate private school opportunities to offer educational choices not available in the public schools.

## A NOTE ON TAX EXPENDITURES

The tax systems of the modern state are characterized by numerous exemptions—or "loopholes"—which allow certain taxpayers or taxpaying units to escape the tax, or to pay a lower tax than other taxpayers. This tax relief can represent a subsidy to the entities involved, and therefore its effects need to be included when estimating the cost of operating those entities.

Public schools receive exemptions from many kinds of taxes, and this significantly lowers their on-budget, or apparent, costs. First, public schools are exempt from federal corporate income taxes, and this lowers their apparent costs vis-à-vis corporations. Since there are some taxpaying private corporations operating schools and providing other kinds of educational services, this is a significant issue. A correct comparison between public schools and a private educational corporation would have to include an estimated amount of the tax the public schools should pay. For example, if the private firm paid a federal corporation tax amounting to 2 percent of its gross revenue, then 2 percent of the revenue should be added to the costs of the public schools if the objective is a realistic comparison. On the other hand, since most private schools and colleges are exempt from corporation taxes, they are on the same footing as the public schools on this issue. Therefore, a comparison between the costs of the typical private school and a public school would not need to include the corporation tax issue.

Similar issues arise when considering the impact of exemptions from state and local taxes. Public schools are exempted from both sales taxes on the purchases they make and from property taxes that would normally fall on the lands and facilities they own. In effect, all other taxpayers in the jurisdiction are being forced to pay higher taxes in order to provide community services to the schools: roads, police and fire protection, public health services, and so on. Thus one could say that public school costs are understated to the extent of the exempted property and sales taxes. However, if a cost comparison is being made with private schools, it needs to be noted that these schools also enjoy various tax exemptions. Many private schools, especially denominational ones, are exempt from local property taxes. And, in some cases, they may be exempt from state and local sales taxes, at least for some purchases.

In summary, we can say that the tax-exempt status of public schools means that their real costs are significantly understated as compared to the costs of a private, profit-making school. This understatement of costs is less when public schools are compared to nonprofit educational institutions, because private nonprofit schools also enjoy tax exemptions similar to those enjoyed by public schools.

## TAX REFORM

Specialists in school finance constantly propose changes in the taxes utilized to raise revenues for education. For example, they often support utilizing state income taxes instead of local property taxes as the primary source of school revenues. Also, proposals to raise or lower or supplement property taxes are commonplace. Such proposals, however, assume the continuation of the existing tax system. In contrast, two widely discussed changes in the structure of taxation, the flat tax and a national sales tax, would lead to major changes in the tax system, provided that the changes replaced, not just supplemented, existing taxes. The qualification is crucial, since most of the supporters of either change would not support the changes as add-ons to our existing system of taxation.

The rationale for a national sales tax is that it would be a tax on consumption; hence, it would not have negative effects on productive activities; also a sales tax would make it possible to eliminate most of the IRS and the accountants, auditors, and tax lawyers who advise taxpayers on IRS issues. Citizens would be paid the entire amount they have earned; there would be no withholding of income taxes. In contrast, every time we bought goods or services, with whatever exceptions are carved out by Congress, there would be a visible tax bite. One important implication for education would be a sweeping reduction of hidden taxes. This would render it more difficult to raise federal taxes, and hence to increase federal spending for public education. Similarly, it would be difficult to raise the flat tax, which also appears to be only a remote possibility for many years to come.

A federal flat tax or sales tax that replaces most of the existing system would also lead to a huge reduction in the lobbying industry. Much of this industry is devoted to efforts to enact tax benefits of one kind or another. For example, the NEA's legislative program includes the following:

NEA supports

- reinstatement of the three-year period for recovery of members' retirement contributions;
- exemption from taxation and/or withdrawal penalties for Individual Retirement Account and 403(b) savings used for an individual's or his/her dependents' postsecondary education;

- exemption from taxation of educational scholarships, fellowships, or awards;
- exemption status within the tax code for professional business expenses, including continuing education, home office, home computers, educational travel, professional and union dues, and designation of such expenditures as "necessary" and "ordinary";
- full miscellaneous deductions for educational materials purchased by educators for classroom use;
- recognition in the tax code for dependent care expenses;
- full deductibility of interest on educational loans;
- exemption from tax liability for tuition remissions where available;
- exemption from taxation of employee benefits, including employer paid health and life insurance, legal services, and educational assistance;
- repeal of Internal Revenue Code provisions that jeopardize the availability or tax exemption of employee benefit plans, including the taxation of negotiated severance payments prior to separation from employment;
- deferral of taxation on retirement annuity contributions;
- expansion of Section 125 of the Internal Revenue Code to include group long-term health care insurance premiums;
- use of Section 125 plans for retired education personnel, with the respective retirement fund designated as the employer.

NEA opposes

- diminution of retirement income;
- taxation of public employee pension benefits.[18]

Like many other initially attractive ideas, the problem of how to go from the status quo to implementation appears to be insuperable. If existing taxes are to be replaced, the persons and companies that would be required to pay higher taxes as a result of the change are able to prevent it from happening. Phasing in these tax reforms means that existing taxes will not be phased out, and a complete changeover in one stroke appears to be beyond the realm of practical possibility.

## SUMMARY

Tax disincentive costs, which discourage productive economic activities, are the largest indirect cost of a tax system. These costs should be considered in any comprehensive assessment of funding public elementary and secondary schools, but they are ignored because they are not government costs. An awareness of tax disincentives is essential to understanding how the costs of public elementary and secondary education affect economic development.

## NOTES

1. David H. Monk, *Educational Finance: An Economic Approach* (New York: McGraw-Hill, 1990), 135.

2. Sue Anne Pressley, "The South's New-Car Smell," *Washington Post,* May 11, 2001.

3. This figure was drawn from data provided by the National Center for Education Statistics, for the year 1994. It includes bond revenue as local property tax income.

4. The first treatments were those of Michael Boskin in the 1975 *Journal of Public Economics* and of Edgar Browning in the 1976 *Journal of Political Economy*.

5. Roger H. Gordon and Burton G. Malkiel, "Corporation Finance," in Henry J. Aaron and Joseph A. Pechman, eds., *How Taxes Affect Economic Behavior* (Washington, DC: Brookings Institution, 1981), 178.

6. Jane G. Gravelle and Laurence J. Kotlikoff, "The Incidence and Efficiency Costs of Corporate Taxation When Corporate and Noncorporate Firms Produce the Same Good," *Journal of Political Economy* 97 (August 1989): 774.

7. Roger H. Gordon and Joel Slemrod, "Do We Collect Any Revenue from Taxing Capital Income?" in Lawrence H. Summers, ed., *Tax Policy and the Economy* 2 (Cambridge, MA.: MIT Press, 1988), 120.

8. Jerry A. Hausman, "Labor Supply," in Henry J. Aaron and Joseph A. Pechman, eds., *How Taxes Affect Economic Behavior* (Washington, DC: Brookings Institution, 1981), 61.

9. Edgar K. Browning, "On the Marginal Welfare Cost of Taxation," *The American Economic Review* 77 (March 1987): 21.

10. Charles L. Ballard, John B. Shoven, and John Whalley, "General Equilibrium Computations of the Marginal Welfare Costs of Taxes in the United States," *The American Economic Review* 75 (March 1985): 135.

11. Dale W. Jorgenson and Kun-Young Yun, "The Excess Burden of Taxation in the U.S." (paper prepared for presentation at the Coopers & Lybrand Foundation symposium, U.S. Tax Policy for the 1990s, New York, November 7–8, 1990), 18.

12. Martin Feldstein, "How Big Should Government Be?" *National Tax Journal* 50 (June 1997): 211.

13. Lawrence G. Walters and Gary C. Cornia, "Electric Utility Deregulation and School Finance in the United States," *Journal of Education Finance* 26 (Spring 2001): 346.

14. This conclusion parallels that of economist Carl Shoup, who advanced an intuitive assessment of the disincentive effect ("excess burden") of the property tax compared to an income tax. According to Shoup, "the real-estate tax as a whole does not produce much if any more excess burden, and may produce less." Carl Shoup, "The Property Tax versus Sales and Income Taxes," in C. Lowell Harriss, ed., *The Property Tax and Local Finance,* Proceedings of the Academy of Political Science 35, no. 1 (1983): 37.

15. Bruce D. Baker, "Balancing Equity for Students and Taxpayers: Evaluating School Finance Reform in Vermont," *Journal of Education Finance* 16 (Spring 2001): 438.

16. For an analysis of who pays lottery taxes, see Percy E. Burrup, Vern Brimley Jr., and Rulon R. Garfield, *Financing Education in a Climate of Change*, 7th ed. (Boston: Allyn and Bacon, 1999), 133–135.

17. Janet Frankston, "For-profit School Feeling Impact of Cherokee's Fees on Businesses," *Atlanta Journal and Constitution*, December 27, 2000.

18. National Education Association, "Legislative Program: Taxation," *NEA Handbook 2001–2002* (Washington, DC: National Education Association, 2002), 396–397.

CHAPTER 11

# Implications, Conclusions, and Recommendations

The casual observer might assume that requiring governments in the United States to report their expenditures accurately is not or should not be a difficult problem. Presumably, public expenditures are scrutinized by interest groups, media, and the public; hence, flagrant errors are likely to be detected and corrected. As we have seen, however, this assumption is unrealistic. Few citizens have any incentive to scrutinize government budgets or expenditures; those who do scrutinize them are usually more interested in achieving more tax benefits or subsidies than ascertaining the real costs of government services. As noted at the outset of this study, government officials at all levels tend to present information that shows agency performance in the best possible light. Independent analysis of government operation is essential, but it requires resources that taxpayer organizations do not have; the few that focus on tax reduction generally must choose among a host of public services that should be monitored.[1]

The reality is that remedying inaccurate government reporting requires long, arduous political initiatives that have little prospect of success. Significantly, GASB Statement Nos. 14 and 34 are the only recent major efforts to effectuate more accurate reporting on government financial matters. GASB is not a government agency; instead, it is a private organization that sets the accounting standards for private investors in government financial obligations. Essentially, the GASB reforms are being driven by the private sector, often over the opposition of public-sector officials. Investors in government bonds and lenders to government need accurate financial statements before committing funds. The fact that private action was essential to achieving the GASB reforms that are under way suggests that significant reforms initiated by government agencies are not likely.

In education, the problems of accurate reporting on costs are exacerbated because three levels of government (local, state, federal) are involved. Sometimes intrastate regional levels must be added to the mix. The producers at all of these levels wish to be perceived as efficient producers; hence most have strong incentives to exaggerate their achievement and avoid scrutiny of their costs. Furthermore, accurate reporting at one level does not necessarily lead to accurate reporting at the other levels, and lower levels of government cannot require accurate reporting of costs from the higher levels. Political factors and the doctrine of states' rights impede federal efforts to require accurate reporting by the states, and similar factors impede state efforts to mandate accurate reporting by local school boards.

As we point out in chapter 4, political leaders at all levels of government are prone to enact immediate benefits paid for by taxes that are imposed much later, so that the legislators who enacted the benefits are not required to raise the taxes required to pay for them. The obvious remedy would be to require that the present cost of future benefits be shown in government financial statements, as they are in the private sector. However, the very pervasiveness of the problem prevents an adequate solution to it; too many legislators wish to take or have taken credit for immediate benefits to be paid for by later cohorts of taxpayers. Very few legislators have not succumbed to this temptation, and nothing on the horizon suggests that matters will be different in the future.

In education, as with government services generally, a structural problem helps to explain why it will be very difficult to achieve more accurate reporting of government costs. Local school boards are the producers of public education. The boards are also supposed to represent consumers: parents, taxpayers, and the general public that wants public schools to provide good education at a reasonable price. Unfortunately, when the school board's producer role conflicts with its consumer protection role, the producer role is usually dominant. This is especially the case with information. The cost information that educational consumers need to evaluate the performance of their school boards would often be politically damaging to the boards; hence the information is frequently not forthcoming, and it becomes extremely difficult to obtain.

This structural weakness applies to most public services at all levels of government. In its role as defender of national security, the Department of Defense tries to persuade the American people that the department is fulfilling its role at a reasonable cost. At the same time, however, the department does not publicize cost overruns or the blunders by military personnel.

The lack of legislative oversight at all levels of government is also a consequence of this structural conflict. Congressional and state legislators, school board members, and school administrators who have promoted certain "reforms" do not encourage oversight that might challenge their effectiveness. Since 1966, Congress has appropriated $321 billion (in 2002 dollars) to improve academic achievement among low-income children, but there is virtually no evidence to conclude that the expenditures have led to significant improvement.[2] Nonetheless, members of the 107th Congress significantly increased federal spending on K–12 education, appropriating almost $22.5 billion to fund the 2002 reauthorization of the Elementary and Secondary Education Act (ESEA).[3] That amount included the fiscal year 2002–03 appropriation of $10.3 billion for ESEA Title I, a program of education for the disadvantaged only.[4] No member of Congress wants to be perceived as someone who has voted against appropriations intended to help low-achieving pupils.

The structural nature of the problem suggests that structural changes are essential to a solution. Perhaps more accurate government statistics on the costs of education will be achieved only as a benefit of reforms that apply to government services generally. In contrast, an "education only" solution will probably require a larger for-profit sector in K–12 education.

In the private sector, concealment of costs, or failure to recognize them, usually results in disaster for the enterprise. Of course, individual shareholders and corporate officers may benefit, or expect to benefit, from concealment of costs. As this is written, however, Congress and several state legislatures are considering more severe penalties for misinforming the public and/or regulatory agencies for failure to report financial data accurately. Note also that for-profit enterprises usually have a strong reason to identify all of their costs; the higher their costs, the lower their tax liability.

Most of the products and services we buy are purchased pursuant to prices that enable us to decide whether what we might buy is worth the cost to us. Prices are not the only consideration, but they are vital information. We can decide whether air travel, haircuts, college tuition, houses, dental work, auto repair, legal assistance, whatever, are worth the cost. Taxpayers cannot make an intelligent decision about whether public education is worth the cost, because they do not know the total cost or the cost to themselves as taxpayers. Of course, in some school districts, the property tax bills show the local expenditures for public schools. Taxpayers are not informed about the state and federal taxes and the private contributions allocated to education, and frequently the local property tax does not include all of the local costs of public education. It is fair to say that very few taxpayers, if any, have a reasonably accurate idea of either the total government cost or their contribution to the costs of public education. Occasionally, parents and taxpayers are aware of the cost of specific items, such as band uniforms or an additional teacher, but such information does not remedy the lack of information about the cost of many other items and/or the individual taxpayer cost.

Obviously, this point is not as applicable to private schools. Parents know their share of the costs, even if they are not aware of the total costs. And it is safe to say they will usually have a better idea of the total costs as well. For instance, when a denominational school asks parents to contribute more or to pay a higher tuition, the explanation for the increase will often refer to the increases in total costs. Inasmuch as parents enroll their children in private schools in the absence of information about the costs of public schools, or their share thereof, many more would probably choose the private option if it were available to them.[5]

Or would they? A huge advantage of public education to parents is that nonparents bear most of the costs. Thus, even if the total costs of public schooling are twice as much as the costs of a comparable education in private schools, most parents might still opt for the public school option because their out-of-pocket costs might be much less. By the same token, however, a voucher system could eliminate or reduce this potential public school advantage. Nonparents could be the main source of revenue for private school vouchers, and the double burden on parents who wish to enroll their children in private schools could be reduced by the amount of the voucher.

The fact that parents (as well as nonparents) would continue to pay for the education of all children raises different issues that are outside the scope of this study, but a few observations may be appropriate. From an economic perspective, public education, like health care, suffers from the fact that the producers are not funded by the consumers. Whenever this happens, there is less pressure on the producers to maximize efficiency. Where the producers operate in a competitive industry, the consumers know how much they have to pay, but do not know or care about the costs to the producers.

Compare briefly the information and decision-making costs of public education to those under parental choice in a market system. In the latter, parents would decide on the schools in which they will enroll their children. Needless to say, some would initially choose a school for poor reasons or none at all, but the issue is how often this would happen when competing schools expose the weaknesses of their competitors. In any case, the costs of getting the information needed to make the decision would not be much different than the costs of getting information about automobiles. On-site visits and discussions with neighbors about their experiences with competing schools would be easily arranged. Advertising would provide some information (and misinformation), but consumer information services would emerge, just as they already have for purchasers of cars or higher education and a host of other services and products. The possibility that many parents would make poor choices must be recognized, but governments have information costs and make poor choices, just as individual consumers do.[6] More important, competing companies frequently provide more and better monitoring of costs and quality than government agencies.

The belief that government agencies can just make the facts about public schools available and let parents come to their own conclusions about school quality is another illusion. The selection of the facts to be publicized and those to be ignored would generate intense controversy, such that school boards and government agencies generally would avoid realistic evaluations of school quality. Government agencies are not going to advise parents to enroll their children in better public school A than inferior public school B. The parents of pupils in school B will not want to transfer their children to school A, which will usually not be feasible anyway because of its distance, lack of space, or lack of transportation. If they do anything, the parents in school B are likely to put pressure on the board to improve B. To avoid such pressure, however, school boards will avoid disseminating information likely to lead to it. Furthermore, it would be perverse policy to reward a superior school by increasing its class size. In most districts, teacher union contracts would not allow any such arrangements. Even where this is not the case, classroom availability and distance from school would often render public school choice an exercise in futility.

The point here is an important but limited one. It is that the costs of information and decision making are typically omitted from estimates of the cost of public education. The costs of school boards would be an exception to this statement, but the costs of legislative committees on education, of negotiating on education legislation in the state capitols, and of public education's share of gubernatorial and congressional time and overhead, are not included in U.S. Department of Education reporting on public school costs. Neither the public nor the professional education community is accustomed to thinking about the costs of education this way, and inertia reinforces the status quo.

## EDUCATION AND THE MASS MEDIA

One of the most discouraging aspects of cost problems in education is the lack of media attention to them—and the misleading nature of their treatment when they do get any attention. The media devote an enormous amount of space and/or time to student tests and test results, but very little to the costs of education. As a result, there is minimal attention to improvements on the cost side; the sine qua non of political interest in better education is advocacy of more spending for it. Urging attention to the cost side runs the political risk of being characterized as "anti-education." In the media, government news releases on the costs of education are taken at face value. Reporting and editorializing about them consists of getting the reactions of "experts" who supposedly have conflicting views on the significance (but not the accuracy) of the estimates. The possibility that the cost estimates might be seriously flawed is not raised, and it is doubtful whether adequate space or time would be forthcoming if it were accorded recognition. The "experts" are frequently asked to state their position in one or two sentences, and most do not decline the invitation.[7] They are well aware that the media can easily get the quotes they need from others in the unlikely event that anyone declines the invitation.

Unfortunately, media treatment of educational issues is typical of media treatment of public policy issues generally, and the media are not going to change their modus operandi in order to accommodate insightful reporting on school finance issues. The fact that the overwhelming majority of media personnel has no expertise in public finance or school finance is also a factor in media failure to come to grips with cost issues, but it is open to question whether more media expertise would matter very much.

In conducting this study, we were unable to identify any mass media publications on the deficiencies in the NCES estimates of the cost of public education; even the leading educational journals, including the *Journal of Education Finance*, the professional journal on school finance, ignore the topic, for whatever reason. It is difficult to fault the media for its neglect of the issue when the professionals in the field pay so little attention to it.[8] To be sure, a few books discuss the problem of government misinformation generally, but none has focused on the government underestimates of the costs of public education.[9]

## INTRADISTRICT DISPARITIES

The average per-pupil expenditures, even if accurate, can be a very misleading figure if assumed to be equally applicable to all schools within a school district. In fact, the differences in per-pupil costs may be greater between schools in the same district than between the district and nearby districts. These facts have been known, if not widely recognized, since Patricia C. Sexton published *Education and Income* in 1964, and the reasons for the differentials are the same in 2002 as they were in 1964.[10]

In large school districts, teacher transfer policies are based upon or give great weight to seniority. As a result, teachers with the most experience, who are also the highest paid, are allowed to transfer from the least to the most desirable schools in their school districts. There is no mystery about which schools fall into these categories. Typically, the "least desirable" schools are characterized by low levels of student achievement, high drug and crime rates, high absentee rates among students and teachers, disrespect for teachers, the absence of parent support, dilapidated facilities, lack of school security; readers get the picture, although the particular mix of these characteristics varies from school to school. The most desirable schools are those which rank at the opposite end of the scale on these criteria.

When an opening materializes at a desirable school (through retirement, change of residence, promotion to an administrative position, etc.), union contracts typically provide that the most senior teacher who can fill the position and applies must be transferred to it. There are some variations, such as administrator choice among the three most senior teachers who apply, but the dominance of seniority is beyond dispute.

In addition to allowing the highest-paid teachers to transfer to schools in the most affluent neighborhoods, the system ensures that the very lowest-paid teachers will be assigned to the least desirable schools. The lowest-paid teachers are the new teachers, substitutes, temporary teachers, and probationary teachers. As a result, there can be a huge difference between the per-pupil costs in inner city and middle-upper-class schools in the same school district. Due to the publicity over compensatory education, the popular, but erroneous perception is that more money is paid per pupil in the inner-city schools; however, school boards and teacher unions do not wish to publicize the facts of the matter.

The basic reason school boards cannot remedy the situation is adamant union opposition to deviations from seniority. Generally speaking, teacher unions, like unions generally, are dominated by senior teachers. Even the less senior teachers accept seniority as the determinative criterion, first because they have nothing more attractive to put in its place, and second, because they expect to benefit from seniority themselves in the future.

The intensity of union opposition to deviations from seniority is illustrated by the fact that one of the longest teacher strikes in the history of U.S. education was partly over this issue. In a 59-day strike during the 1972–73 school year, the Philadelphia school board tried to assign the senior teachers to the schools with the lowest-achieving students. Needless to say, the ensuing teacher strike in Philadelphia was not conducive to similar efforts in other school districts.

The incidence of students in special education from school to school within a school district could also lead to differences in their per-pupil costs. The per-pupil costs of special education students are much higher than for regular students, and there are usually more special education students in the inner-city schools; however, because our educational policies support higher-than-average expenditures for special education students, their higher per-pupil costs are not perceived as an inequality deserving of criticism. The fact is, however, that significant inequities between schools are usually present even after expenditures for special education students are eliminated from the comparisons. The per-pupil expenditures may be substantially equal throughout the district if the expenditures for special education students raise the average in inner-city schools, but this tactic conceals the inequity applicable to regular students. The tactic simply cites a difference in per-pupil spending that is supported by public policy to conceal inequities that are not supported by it.

## ACCOUNTABILITY

When we employ a dentist, the fee includes the dentist's cost of dental education, the foregone income during dental school, rent or purchase price of the dentist's facilities, dental supplies and equipment, professional travel and publications, professional development, insurance, and, of course, adequate income for the dentist and dental assistants and secretaries. As patients, we know the cost to ourselves; hence we can decide whether the dental services are worth the cost.

In contrast, taxpayers do not know with reasonable accuracy how much is spent collectively or individually for public education. Nobody started out to establish such a system, but it is the one we have, with poor prospects of significant improvement in the near future.

Who benefits from the lack of clarity about the real costs of public education? This is tantamount to asking: What parties would be hurt by public awareness of the real costs? These parties include public school personnel and their organizations, especially the teacher unions. Their opposition to clarity is not based upon overt support for obfuscation; nobody adopts such a public position, but there is no public school support for any system that would clarify the cost issues raised in this study.

Proposed legislation on vouchers and/or charter schools sometimes would require payments based on a percentage of the average per-pupil cost in regular public schools. The focus of the controversies over such payments has not been on the amount of the payments; instead it has been over accountability for them. For example, the opponents of school choice contend that there is no accountability in school choice plans that include private schools, because private schools would be able to take public funds but need not open their books for public inspection. The unstated premise is that there is accountability in public education because its revenues and expenditures are supposedly matters of public record. This premise is highly debatable; an alternative and much more useful definition of "accountability" is that it requires knowledge of who is responsible for an action and the ability of higher authority or consumers to discipline or reward the actor if such action is appropriate.

Consider the situation facing taxpayers and parents. They do not know how much the public schools cost or their contribution to them, nor can they determine who is paying how much for education. They face major obstacles in finding out what government agencies or officials are responsible for various policies; if diligent enough to find out, they may be unable to ascertain whether the problems are due to the policymakers or the parties that implement the policies. If their local school board enacted the objectionable policies, or took an objectionable action, only one or two or none of the board members who took the action may be on the ballot in any given year. Unless the parents can organize a political collective, or join one, they will be unable to change the policies or their implementation. The board members and/or legislators responsible for originating poor policies may have moved on to higher positions, partly on the strength of the policies parents seek to change.

Where is the accountability in this situation? Even when it is possible to identify the public official(s) to be held "accountable," the responsible official(s) may be essential to support the citizen's positions on other issues of much greater importance to the latter. If holding legislators "accountable" means voting them out of office (where that is possible, since the responsible legislators may represent other jurisdictions), citizens may be adding to their losses by the pursuit of accountability in education.

The surprising aspect of accountability issues in education is the widespread assumption that there is "accountability" in public education but that it would not be present among private schools that enroll pupils in a voucher system. The unstated assumption is that because education is publicly funded, the citizenry can evaluate school performance and parents know how well their children are learning. In the real world, the assumption is not true for most parents, taxpayers, and policymakers. Much of what happens in local school districts has been mandated by state and federal legislators who are invulnerable to removal by dissatisfied voters, especially when the voters who elect them reside outside local school jurisdictions. Among those who have studied the matter, there is widespread agreement that the federal government has spent $125 billion in a futile effort to raise the levels of educational achievement by students from low-income families.[11] No elected official appears to have been voted out of office for continuing to support these huge expenditures without any solid evidence of their educational outcomes.

Consider another example. In 1975, Congress passed the Education for All Handicapped Children Act (Public Law 94-142), later renamed the Individuals with Disabilities Education Act (IDEA). In 1999–2000, local, state, and federal governments spent $78.3 billion to educate disabled children.[12] Even government officials and supporters of increased spending on education cannot tell us what has been accomplished by these huge expenditures for special education. Special education services are delivered pursuant to Individual Education Plans (IEPs), that is, agreements reached by parents and school authorities on the educational plan for each student categorized as requiring "special education." In 2002, 12 percent of all students were identified as disabled students, an increase of 300 percent since 1976.[13] The blind, deaf, incarcerated, mentally retarded, emotionally disturbed, physically handicapped—these are some of the categories of students who are entitled to special education services. Obviously, what counts as progress varies within and between these categories. Furthermore, inasmuch as the objectives are established individually, it is practically impossible to evaluate the "value added" or the criteria applicable to all of the students receiving special education services. In fact, whether a student rightfully belongs in one of these categories is itself a much litigated issue, as is virtually everything else about the legislation and its implementation. Recognizing these concerns, in its 2002 report, the President's Commission on Excellence in Special Education recommended that IDEA "focus on [educational] results—not on process."[14]

Understandably, nobody knows what, if anything, has been achieved by our huge expenditures for special education; nor is anyone likely to know as long as the main features of the legislation remain in place. Whom do dissatisfied parents or taxpayers hold "accountable?" The teachers of special education? Their principals? Superintendents? Board members? State education officials? Members of Congress who continue to support the program? Staff members of the U.S. Department of Education? The sponsors of the legislation? Media personnel who ignore the subject? All of the above? What can be said is (1) accountability requires parties with the power to discipline the actors; and (2) as long as collective action by parents or taxpayers or the citizenry is required for accountability, the absence of it in public education will continue.

Would there be accountability in a competitive education industry? Parents need not get involved in collective action to effectuate their displeasure; they can transfer their children wherever they wish to do so. Accountability would be achieved through the actions of parents individually, as they transferred their children to more parent-friendly schools. Of course, the need for more accurate information on costs will not be the motivating factor in a change to more private-sector provision of education. The change, if it materializes, will be the result of other considerations.[15] Nevertheless, it is somewhat surprising that the lack of accountability in public education has received so little attention from supporters of competitive markets instead of government schools; the lack of accountability in public education is one of its major weaknesses.

## THE IMPACT OF ACTUAL COSTS ON TAXES FOR PUBLIC EDUCATION

Undoubtedly data on the real costs of public education would render raising taxes for it more difficult. This will happen even though the real costs of private schooling are also systematically underestimated. Parents absorb a much higher percentage of the costs of private schooling; hence an emphasis on private schooling serves the interests of most taxpayers as taxpayers. It should be noted, however, that in many private schools, the utilization of unpaid parental time is a reason why the real costs of private schooling are underestimated. Of course, the fact that a much higher percentage of the private school costs is absorbed voluntarily may lead to support for private schooling as a desirable public policy option.

Two points must be kept in mind in efforts to compare costs in a competitive education industry with costs under public education. First, the fact that taxpayers would pay less in a competitive education system, if such turns out to be the case, does not necessarily mean that students would receive less in services. The critical issue is whether the same dollar amount would have the same consequences in both systems, and it is unlikely that this would be the case.

Second, it is important to avoid the mistake of treating the initial costs in a competitive education industry as the permanent costs. Competitive industries show constant improvement in achieving better outcomes at lower costs. The issue is whether there is any reason to expect different results in a competitive education industry.

## HIGHER EDUCATION

Information about the real costs is likely to influence institutions of higher education to drop or curtail remedial education programs. This trend is already under way, but its main component appears to be that low-cost institutions of higher education, especially community colleges, are absorbing most of the students who need remedial programs.

It would be desirable for the field of education finance to devote more attention to the real costs of education, but this may not happen; few academics are likely to pay much attention to the real costs of public education unless they are forced to do so by external forces. Furthermore, their de facto clients are the public school community, and this community does not welcome a real-cost approach. Nevertheless, we can expect significant improvement as GASB Statement Nos. 14 and 34 are implemented, and others are considered. As this happens, we can expect more pressure by taxpayer organizations and organizations supportive of school choice to emphasize the cost advantages of private schooling. Heretofore, these groups have not emphasized cost issues very much in their efforts to promote a larger role for private schools. Companies that sell services in education markets could also benefit from a real-cost approach, and therefore, may promote it in the future.

## SCHOOL BOARD POLICY AND PRACTICE

The most important immediate effect of a real-cost approach at the school board level may be a much more sophisticated approach to contracting out. Public employee unions trying to prevent school boards from contracting services are quick to point out the uncounted costs of contracting out the services. Meanwhile the companies are pointing out the uncounted costs of utilizing district employees to provide the services. Consequently, a great deal of information on the subject is readily available, but most of it relates only to the conventional cost categories of local school districts. School boards are likely to choose the option that minimizes their costs, not the option that minimizes the total costs of a service. State legislators could require school boards to adopt a more comprehensive accounting of taxpayer costs, but there does not appear to be any political movement supportive of this change.

## IMPLICATION FOR SCHOOL CHOICE

School choice raises a large number of issues that are not considered in this study.[16] Although several school choice issues are discussed, this study has not discussed several important issues that should be considered in decisions about system change. Nonetheless, this study has several implications for the desirability of a competitive education system as public policy. For one thing, such a system would reveal the actual costs of schooling, thus helping parents, taxpayers, and policymakers evaluate the cost/benefit issues in choosing schools. This is virtually impossible to do in a system in which costs are as diffuse and difficult to assess as they are in public education. The fact that school choice would resolve many issues that are legislated or litigated or reached through political action in public education should play a more prominent role in the school choice controversies.

In education, it is frequently impossible to conduct a realistic cost/benefit analysis because neither the costs nor the benefits can be assessed. Multiple sources of funding add another complication. Assume that the cost of a program to enhance reading ability is divided 48, 44, and 8 percent among state, local, and federal sources. Suppose further that the local school board undertakes a cost/benefit analysis to assess whether the program is worthwhile, and finds that the total contribution does not achieve benefits worth the money spent. Will the school board withdraw from the program? Not necessarily. Withdrawal from the program would result in the local school district's losing the federal and state contributions. Even if the benefits of the total contribution are not worth the total expenditure, they may be worth more to the local district than its contribution to the cost. The same outcome is likely, or at least possible, from the local and federal perspectives.

The upshot is that although the contributors jointly do not achieve benefits worth the total contribution, each contributor may receive more in benefits by participation instead of by withdrawal from the program. Undoubtedly, this often happens whenever two or more governments share the costs of a program that is indefensible in toto but nevertheless a good deal for each participating government considered individually.

## THE COSTS OF EDUCATION IN A VOUCHER SYSTEM

As the cost of public education escalates, the pressure to analyze its costs will increase. As this happens, the allocation of costs between government and private sources, such as parents, will also receive more attention. Hopefully, more consideration will be given to the dynamics of expenditures in school choice systems in which for-profit schools are allowed to compete.

Inasmuch as school choice plans vary on almost every imaginable issue, it is impossible to estimate who will pay how much in the absence of the details applicable to specific plans. For present purposes, however, let us assume a universal voucher that provides $4,000 for education at parent-selected schools. How would such vouchers affect the amounts paid for education by various demographic and socioeconomic groups?

Although many factors would affect the answer to the question, it is likely that a voucher plan as suggested would lead to greater amounts being spent for education in toto, especially by parents. The reason is that a voucher system would render it more feasible to tap into personal income for schooling.

Currently, the burden of paying for private schooling falls largely on parents. Except for scholarships, parents who cannot pay the private school charges cannot enroll their children in private schools. Now consider parents who can afford to spend $3,000 but not $4,000 for private schooling. An increase in personal income of $1,000 or more will enable these parents to enroll their children in a private school. Meanwhile, public schools and parents have no feasible way to tap into increases in personal income promptly.

These possibilities must be considered in the context of how our economy functions. Parents, like everyone else, are bombarded with advertising to buy an enormous range of products and services. Private school advertisements tend to be limited to publications that reach parents who can pay the full cost of private education—that is, affluent parents and parents of children in heavily subsidized denominational schools, or in charter schools. Consider the parents who would like to enroll their children in private schools that charge $4,000 per year but can afford only $1,000 from personal resources for this purpose. Before the availability of vouchers, these parents were unable to enroll their children in private schools; with the availability of vouchers providing at least $3,000, they could afford to do so.

The counter-argument is that private schools would raise their tuition by the amount of the voucher, thus forestalling any increase in private schooling as a result of the introduction of vouchers. This is likely to happen to some extent, especially among private schools that pay teachers the least in salaries and benefits. However, except for vouchers in small amounts (arbitrarily, under $1,000), it is unlikely that many private schools would charge the full amount of the voucher plus the full amount of the pre-voucher parental contribution. Moreover, this argument assumes that there would not be any new producers who would appeal to parents at or near the pre-voucher level. In the absence of unreasonable restrictions on entry, a sizable number of new producers offering education at different price levels is likely to emerge.

The extent to which private schools would raise their prices if and when vouchers materialize would depend on several factors. If vouchers were means-tested, there might be very little increase, if any, in tuition. Because teacher compensation in private schools lags far behind compensation in public schools, some private schools would raise their tuition in order to survive, but many other scenarios would come into play. Most would lead to more private spending for education and some might result in more spending in toto for K–12 education than is the case under the existing system. Furthermore, the more that parents spend for education, the more that information on the cost and quality of educational services will become available.

## REAL COSTS AND STATE INITIATIVES

One of the most harmful features of our political system is the fact that costs are typically ignored when legislators take credit for enacting benefits.

Clearly, the lack of attention to costs in legislative affairs is exacerbated (if not created) by the widespread legislative practice of promoting benefits while ignoring the costs of providing them. Thus in the 2002 election, Florida voters approved a constitutional amendment to limit class size to 20 in the first three grades. The costs were not included in the initiative; even the Democratic candidate for governor, who supported the initiative, was unable to provide a coherent estimate of its costs, a failure that was a significant factor in his defeat even though the initiative passed by a narrow margin.

States could require an estimate of the costs to be included in initiatives with space for an opposition statement. We do not assume that voters are going to read and deliberate upon these statements in their voting booths, but their dissemination 30 to 60 days before an election would promote a more balanced discussion of initiative issues.

## COOKING THE GOVERNMENT BOOKS

In 2002, accurate financial reporting became an important political issue. News reports of corporation executives who pocketed hundreds of millions while submitting financial reports that misled investors and wiped out employee retirement funds were a staple in the media during the entire year, and are likely to continue. A plausible case can be made, however, that inaccurate data on government costs is or can be a more important problem than accurate data on private-sector costs. Public education illustrates this point.

Of course, no one publicly disputes the importance of accurate financial data in either the public or the private sector. If the issue is raised, the educational interest groups concede its theoretical importance, but as a practical matter, their resources are devoted to more appropriations for education. If government expenditures must be reduced, their position is that the reductions must be made in other government programs. Unfortunately, the advocates of other government programs adopt the same attitude toward education; hence the political influence of the various interest groups dominates the outcome.

In all of these controversies, however, reasonably accurate data on the costs of government programs are essential for sound public policy. Unless we know the costs within a reasonable margin of error, we cannot decide whether the benefits of government programs are worth the costs. What are the costs of public education? We simply do not know the answer to this question for several reasons, technical and political. Although GASB Statement No. 34, if widely implemented, will remedy some of these reasons, it will be several years before estimates based on the corrections become available. Even then, the government estimates of the costs of public education will be substantially less than the real costs.

Greater accuracy on the costs of public education would have far-reaching implications for the future of America's largest industry, but achieving this objective faces at least two major interrelated problems. First, most of the technical problems are not likely to be resolved in the near future. In many cases, the ability to estimate costs within a broad range is the only improvement that can be expected in the near future.

The most important problem is the lack of political will to achieve more accurate estimates of the real costs of government services. As previously noted, the GASB reforms now in progress resulted from private, not public, initiatives. "The lack of political will" is largely due to the fact that the public education lobby benefits from the status quo. The interests that would benefit from more accurate estimates of the costs of public education, which include most taxpayers, are unaware of the political benefits of pressing the issue; lack of awareness generates lack of interest, and lack of interest generates lack of awareness. Nevertheless, the amounts are so large that even some of the allies of the public education lobby, such as other public employee unions, may become interested in pursuing the cost-of-education issues.

Clarity, and hence more accountability regarding the costs, could be achieved through a competitive system of education that would link the costs with the prices for educational services; however, this remedy is not likely to materialize in the near future. In the short run, the new GASB reporting requirements for governmental entities present the best opportunity to achieve more realistic reporting of the costs of public education, but political activism will be essential to capitalize on this opportunity.

## NOTES

1. The National Taxpayers Union (NTU) is the largest and most effective taxpayer organization, but it is obviously impossible for an organization of only 17 employees, including secretarial/clerical staff, to monitor the expenditures by the federal government.

2. U.S. Department of Education, "Why No Child Left Behind Is Important to America," 1. At http://www.nochildleftbehind.gov/next/stats/index.html [accessed November 12, 2002]. See also Nina Shokraii Rees, "A Close Look

at Title I, the Federal Program to Aid Poor Children," *The Heritage Foundation Backgrounder* 1271 (April 13, 1999).

3. U.S. Department of Education, *No Child Left Behind*, 1.

4. From the Congressional Research Service in response to author's inquiry of October 25, 2002.

5. See Terry M. Moe, *Schools, Vouchers, and the American Public* (Washington, DC: Brookings Institution, 2001), 142–167.

6. For an argument that public education saves parents the time and trouble of identifying good schools and avoids the probability of poor choices by parents, see Michael Krashinsky, "Why Educational Vouchers May Be Bad Economics," *Teachers College Record* 88 (Winter 1986): 139–151; response by Edwin G. West and rejoinder by Krashinsky.

7. This paragraph was written verbatim prior to Myron Lieberman's recent experience with CNN's Money Line. He was called from New York City on a Wednesday to participate in a program on teacher shortages being taped the next day. The taping took place in CNN's Washington studio, with a host from Atlanta. Eight seconds of the tape were used when the program on teacher shortages (two minutes and forty seconds in duration) was shown one week later—an impressive display of technological capability utilized to trivialize public policy issues.

8. End notes 13 and 14 in chapter 1 provide strong confirmation of the neglect of cost issues among advocates of educational reform.

9. An example is James T. Bennett and Thomas J. DiLorenzo, *Official Lies: How Washington Misleads Us* (Alexandria, VA: Groom Books, 1992).

10. Patricia Cayo Sexton, *Education and Income* (New York: Viking Press, Compass Books Edition, 1964).

11. United States Department of Education press release, "Back-to-School Address by U.S. Secretary of Education Rod Paige to the National Press Club," September 4, 2001.

12. Krista Kafar, "Special Education 101," *The Heritage Foundation Web Memo #169,"* November 5, 2002. At http://www.heritage.org/Research/Education/index.cfm [accessed November 12, 2002].

13. Ibid.

14. U.S. Department of Education Office of Special Education and Rehabilitative Services, *A New Era: Revitalizing Special Education for Children and Their Families* (Washington, DC: U.S. Department of Education, 2002).

15. See Myron Lieberman, *Public Education: An Autopsy* (Cambridge, MA: Harvard University Press, 1993); and Andrew Coulson: *Market Education* (New Brunswick, NJ: Social Philosophy and Policy Center and Transaction, 1999).

16. For a more comprehensive account of these issues, see John D. Merrifield, *The School Choice Wars* (Lanham, MD: Scarecrow Press, 2001); Terry M. Moe, *Schools, Vouchers, and the American Public* (Washington, DC: Brookings Institution, 2001); and Myron Lieberman, *Public Education: An Autopsy* (Cambridge, MA: Harvard University Press, 1993).

# *Appendix*
## Unmet Infrastructure Needs by State in 2000

**Estimated Cost per Pupil over Five- and Ten-year Periods for Unmet Infrastructure Needs by State in 2000**

| | | *Duration of Cost Per Pupil* | |
|---|---|---|---|
| *State* | *Total Need in $* | *$/5 years* | *$/10 years* |
| Alabama | 1,519,210,061 | 398 | 221 |
| Alaska | 727,014,291 | 1,074 | 588 |
| Arizona | 4,748,568,494 | 983 | 536 |
| Arkansas | 1,761,701,495 | 758 | 422 |
| California | 22,000,000,000 | 704 | 386 |
| Colorado | 3,805,239,627 | 1,045 | 575 |
| Connecticut | 5,000,000,000 | 1,828 | 1,033 |
| Delaware | 1,046,354,648 | 1,836 | 1,022 |
| Florida | 3,300,000,000 | 271 | 151 |
| Georgia | 7,061,967,931 | 942 | 517 |
| Hawaii | 752,533,936 | 713 | 386 |
| Idaho | 699,469,537 | 517 | 278 |
| Illinois | 9,213,000,000 | 824 | 458 |
| Indiana | 2,477,797,613 | 486 | 269 |
| Iowa | 3,359,129,953 | 1,386 | 776 |
| Kansas | 1,793,241,845 | 744 | 430 |
| Kentucky | 2,441,607,196 | 749 | 418 |
| Louisiana | 3,104,098,619 | 812 | 454 |
| Maine | 452,064,540 | 448 | 253 |
| Maryland | 3,891,926,876 | 905 | 504 |
| Massachusetts | 8,919,014,500 | 1,822 | 1,025 |
| Michigan | 8,071,127,040 | 963 | 541 |
| Minnesota | 4,517,232,516 | 1,068 | 597 |
| Mississippi | 1,038,890,864 | 406 | 226 |
| Missouri | 3,475,160,989 | 759 | 423 |
| Montana | 901,492,663 | 1,101 | 607 |
| Nebraska | 1,608,849,896 | 1,119 | 622 |
| Nevada | 5,256,000,000 | 2,888 | 1,568 |

*(Continued)*

**Estimated Cost per Pupil over Five- and Ten-year Periods for Unmet Infrastructure Needs by State in 2000 *(Continued)***

| | | *Duration of Cost Per Pupil* | |
|---|---|---|---|
| *State* | *Total Need in $* | *$/5 years* | *$/10 years* |
| New Hampshire | 409,511,478 | 403 | 226 |
| New Jersey | 20,709,650,065 | 3,247 | 1,810 |
| New Mexico | 1,410,624,747 | 778 | 422 |
| New York | 47,640,000,000 | 3,214 | 1,802 |
| North Carolina | 6,210,938,727 | 902 | 502 |
| North Dakota | 420,000,000 | 749 | 420 |
| Ohio | 20,900,000,000 | 2,302 | 1,291 |
| Oklahoma | 2,204,070,041 | 732 | 410 |
| Oregon | 2,407,425,974 | 859 | 475 |
| Pennsylvania | 8,465,134,387 | 927 | 521 |
| Rhode Island | 1,420,952,603 | 1,882 | 1,060 |
| South Carolina | 2,574,018,400 | 803 | 451 |
| South Dakota | 498,604,766 | 706 | 390 |
| Tennessee | 2,273,702,904 | 466 | 257 |
| Texas | 9,467,620,774 | 453 | 248 |
| Utah | 8,490,336,757 | 3,385 | 1,841 |
| Vermont | 220,090,007 | 425 | 239 |
| Virginia | 5,701,313,528 | 986 | 548 |
| Washington | 5,478,902,777 | 1,067 | 589 |
| West Virginia | 1,000,000,000 | 686 | 384 |
| Wisconsin | 4,762,337,059 | 1,087 | 608 |
| Wyoming | 530,888,665 | 1,125 | 614 |
| Total: | $266,138,818,788 | | |

Note: The states' unmet infrastructure funding need exceeded $266 billion in 2000. The infrastructure includes deferred maintenance, new construction, renovation, retrofitting, additions to existing facilities, and major improvements to grounds, landscaping, and pavement. The $266 billion also includes $53.7 billion for technology (hardware and software) and other technology costs, such as wiring and adapting facilities to accept emerging technologies.

Source: Faith E. Crampton, David C. Thompson, and Janis M. Hagey, "Creating and Sustaining School Capacity in the Twenty-First Century: Funding a Physical Environment Conducive to Student Learning." A paper presented to the University Council for Educational Administration. Albuquerque, NM (2000), published in *Money & Schools*, 2nd edition (Larchmont, NY: Eye on Education, 2001), 261–262.

# Index

# *About the Authors*

**Myron Lieberman** received bachelor's degrees in law and education from the University of Minnesota and earned his M.A. and Ph.D. in education at the University of Illinois. In addition to teaching two years at high schools in Minnesota and Illinois, he has taught or served as an administrator at several universities, including the University of Illinois, Rhode Island College, City University of New York, University of Southern California, Ohio University, and University of Pennsylvania. From 1962 to 1969, Dr. Lieberman served as a consultant and expert witness for the NAACP Legal Defense and Education fund in critical desegregation cases. Since 1993, he has served as senior research scholar with the Social Philosophy and Policy Center at Bowling Green State University, Bowling Green, Ohio. His publications include seventeen books and scores of articles in *The Public Interest*, *National Review*, *Harper's*, *Nation*, *Harvard Educational Review*, *Phi Delta Kappan*, *Teachers College Record*, and other leading lay and professional journals.

As president of the Education Policy Institute, **Charlene K. Haar** is an educational policy analyst specializing in teacher/parent relations and local, state, and federal education policy. She is also research associate with the Social Philosophy and Policy Center at Bowling Green State University, Bowling Green, Ohio. Prior to her work with EPI and SPPC, Ms. Haar taught French, English, and American government for eleven years, most recently at Madison High School in Madison, South Dakota. She attended public schools in South Dakota, graduated from the University of South Dakota with a B.A. in French, and later received an M.A. in gifted education from Augustana College in Sioux Falls, South Dakota. In 1992, after twenty years of local and state political involvement, Ms. Haar was the Republican candidate for U.S. Senator from South Dakota. As a teacher and a candidate for office, she also had extensive first-hand experience with the political operations of teacher unions. In addition to numerous articles on parental involvement and teacher unions, Ms. Haar is coauthor of *The NEA and AFT: Teacher Unions in Power and Politics* and author of *The Politics of the PTA*.